IMAGES
of America

ZIEBACH COUNTY 1910–2010

I0806340

ON THE COVER: Touch the Cloud is seated at left in 1877 with other members of his delegation to Washington. Touch the Cloud, a Minnicoujou, was the cousin of Crazy Horse. When Crazy Horse was murdered on September 5, 1877, Touch the Cloud comforted his cousin until he died. Touch the Cloud settled at Cheyenne River in the Cherry Creek area next to Hump and Big Foot. In 1905, he died on September 5 like his cousin and is buried near Hump in Ziebach County. (Courtesy of Donovin Sprague.)

IMAGES
of America

ZIEBACH COUNTY 1910–2010

Donovin Sprague

ARCADIA
PUBLISHING

ISBN 978-0-7385-7783-8

Published by Arcadia Publishing
Charleston SC, Chicago IL, Portsmouth NH, San Francisco CA

Printed in the United States of America

Library of Congress Control Number: 2009943893

For all general information contact Arcadia Publishing at:
Telephone 843-853-2070
Fax 843-853-0044
E-mail sales@arcadiapublishing.com
For customer service and orders:
Toll-Free 1-888-313-2665

Visit us on the Internet at www.arcadiapublishing.com

Dedicated to Darrel and Velda Sprague and all the people of Ziebach County and Dylan, Rhiana, Ella, and Ava

Contents

ACKNOWLEDGMENTS

Thanks to everyone in Ziebach County and to these people, past and present, who helped or shared inspiration, history, and fun along the way:

Brian Akipa, Kay Knife Allison, Bill and Geraldine Anderson, Evelyn Anderson, Paula Anderson and family, Leo Bakeberg and family, Lou Ann Barton, Gwen and Frank Baum, Russell and Cordelia Benoist, Mildred Benway, Wilbur and Cheryl Between Lodges, Jack Bickel, Lorenzo Black Lance, Cheryl Bogue, Doyle and Barbara Bramhall, Doyle Bramhall II, Cutter Brandenberg, Eddie Brigati, Clarence "Gatemouth" Brown, Bruce Brown Wolf, Oliver Brown Wolf, Eugenia Burgee and family, Steve Charging Eagle family, Marilyn Circle Eagle, Eddy Clearwater and Renee Greenman, Clown Tiwahe, Tom and Laurie Coleman, Freida Condon, Pat Condon and family, Arlie and Janie Davis, Bud Day, Jace DeCory, Wanda Dexheimer, Ephriam Dickson, Fred Dupris / Dupree and descendants, Ronnie Eagle Chasing, Bill and Trula Fields, Wilbur Flying By, Jim and Thelma Frame, Billy Gibbons, Ernie Gottschalk, Orville and Helen Graslie, Jerome Greene, Bill Groethe, Merle Haggard, Ted Harvey, Francis He Crow, Michael He Crow, Darlene Helper, Pete Helper Sr. and family, Bernard Hickenbotham, Codi High Elk, Paul and Clara High Elk, "History Channel," "History Detectives," Kandice Hoffman, Hollow Horn family, Johnny and Sharon Holloway, Hump Tiwahe, Ellen In The Woods, Frank Jeffries and family, Waylon Jennings and Jessi, Calvin Jones, Irean Jordan, Mick and Jane Jung, Sidney and Shirley Keith, Linda Keehner, B. B. King, Deb Knight, David Laudenschlager, Casimir LeBeau, Marcella Ryan LeBeau, Mary LeBeau, Bob Lee, David and Joanie Lindley, Amy Linn, Leonard Little Finger, Beau and Mary Little Sky, Bud Longbrake, Delbert Longbrake, Faye Longbrake, Jake Longbrake, Pete Longbrake, Ruby Marshall, Bill Matson, Frank McDaniel, Dondra Menzel and family, Fred and Shirley Menzel, Jodee Messina, Wilmer Mesteth, Berneita Miller and family, Jim and Kathy Nelson, Lana Nelson, Willie Nelson, Donna Rae Peterson, Donna Pooley, Pooley family, Prairie Edge-Rapid City, Carlos Red Legs, Donnie and Charlene Red Thunder, Faye Reeves, Irwin Richardson, Jimmy Rogers, Lavera Rose, Junior Rousseau, Neil Rousseau, Alvina "Lucille" Runs After, Charlene Schmidt, Monica Garreau Schmidt, Donald Schuchhardt and family, Twila Schuler, Dee Schumacher, Grover Scott, Doren Serfling, Robert and Kimberly Shannon, Tommy Shannon, Mark Shillingstad, Harold Shunk, Ruth Slaughter, Elsie Slides Off, Vance and Virginia Driving Hawk Sneve, Sprague family, Harry and Marian Stambach, Steve Thomas, Timber Lake and Area Historical Association, Ben Trent, Mike Trent, Edith Traversie, Tanya Tucker, Rev. Bob Two Bulls, Matt and Nellie Two Bulls, Jan Two Shields, Vance family, Jimmie Vaughan, Stevie Ray Vaughan, Odette Claymore Voss, Darla Vrooman, Doug War Eagle, Marilyn Wenlund, Jim White Feather, Francis White Lance, Philip Whiteman Sr. and Jr., Maurice Williams, Kim Wilson, Gordon and Carole Wince, Virginia Woodward, Gerald Yellow Hawk, Jim Yellow Hawk, and the Ziebach County Historical Association.

Introduction

Ziebach County is named for Frank M. Ziebach, who served in the territorial legislature and as commissioner of the U.S. Land Office. He also established the first newspaper in South Dakota at Yankton. Ziebach County, created by the Dakota Territorial legislature in 1877, consisted of what is now Pennington, east of the Cheyenne River. It existed only on paper until 1897, when Pennington was extended to its present boundaries. What became present-day Ziebach County in 1911 by the legislature was in 1875 part of Cheyenne that extended north and south of the Cheyenne River. In 1883, the county had been included in Schnasse, which extended to North Dakota, Pyatte to the south, Sterling, and Rush (later Dewey County). A part of it was also included in Armstrong in 1889. Armstrong was an unorganized county after Ziebach and Dewey Counties organized in 1911.

When the railroads built up a southern branch from Trail City to Faith, Dupree was the first community to spring up from this development. The town began with a few tents and rough lumber camps in late 1909. This original town site of Dupree was 2 miles east of the present location, just south of the junction of present Highway 212 and Highway 65. The town site was known for its muddy gumbo when it rained, so in June 1910, the town moved just west of where the railroad announced the new site would be. Following a lot sale in Aberdeen, Dupree moved a third time by late August to its present location just south of Bear Creek.

Along Bear Creek was the home of Edward Dupris, and this site is now the location of the Lawrence E. Woodward place on the northeast edge of present-day Dupree. Edward's mother, Mary Dupris, was a Minnicoujou Lakota from Cherry Creek known as Good Elk Woman. His father, Fred Dupris, was a wealthy Frenchman who had arrived at Fort Pierre by 1838 from Quebec, Canada. Fred died in 1898, and Good Elk Woman died in 1900. Edward Dupris donated land he had inherited from his parents for the town of Dupree to be built upon. The Dupris name was misspelled as "Dupree" and that name was accepted and never corrected by the U.S. Post Office. Family members today use both Dupris and Dupree for their names.

The first mail into Dupree came from Cherry Creek and later from Thunder Butte and Isabel when an Indian agency substation was established. The first school in Dupree was established in 1911, along with several churches. As the railroad was built west of Dupree, the construction crew established a camp at Red Elm, also known as Redelm, in the fall of 1910. The camp of Arrowhead started the same way as the railroad construction worked towards Faith. By 1911, all of the railroad towns along with Cherry Creek, Thunder Butte, Chase, and Red Scaffold were developing. In 1912, Dupree was named the permanent county seat in a close election, with Dupree selected by one vote over Redelm. Glad Valley had a general store, post office, a church, and a school by 1936. Chase had a post office, and Pleasant Valley had a church and a school. The two historically most important Indian agency substations were the communities of Cherry Creek and Thunder Butte. Cherry Creek is credited with being the oldest historical site in Ziebach County. Bridger is located in the southwest corner of the county and was established in 1891 at the request of some survivors of the Wounded Knee Massacre. The name of Bridger comes from the town being named after a homesteader, Carv Bridge.

The Cheyenne River Sioux Reservation was created for the four Lakota bands known as Minnicoujou, Itazipcola, Si Hasapa, and Oohenumpa. Ziebach County is the west half of the reservation and was originally comprised mainly of Minnicoujou and Itazipcola. The largest of the four bands is the Minnicoujou and many settled in the Ziebach County communities of Cherry Creek, Takini-Bridger, Red Scaffold, Thunder Butte, Iron Lightning, and Dupree.

Two well-known buttes in the county are Thunder Butte and Rattlesnake Butte, with Thunder Butte also being a community. In northern Ziebach County is the Moreau River. In the south is the Cheyenne River. These two rivers are joined by smaller tributaries, the best known of which are Cherry, Felix, Bull, Redelm, Bear, Flintrock, Thunder Butte, Beaver Trap, Sophia, Irish/Worthless, Red Earth, Pretty, Red Scaffold, Rattlesnake, Cottonwood, Dupris, Rudy, Sand, Snake, Stinking Bear, Abear, Ash, Red Coat, and Turtle Butte Creeks.

There are three Hump Flats named for Chief Hump and his campsites. They are near Iron Lightning, Red Scaffold, and east of Bridger. Famous Lakota leaders resided in Ziebach County while also living a nomadic life of travel in pursuit of the buffalo and trade. In addition to Hump, others were Black Buffalo, One Horn, Crazy Horse, Touch the Cloud, Si Tanka (Big Foot), Sitting Bull, Gall, Rain in the Face, One Bull, and White Bull. One Bull and White Bull, nephews of Sitting Bull, settled in Cherry Creek. Black Buffalo and family met Lewis and Clark at present Fort Pierre. Black Buffalo and One Horn (his son) were sketched by the artist George Catlin in 1832.

Later generations of people with ties to Ziebach County who became known outside the county include: Casey Tibbs, Bud Day, Billy Circle Eagle, Ralph Maynard, J. R. Knight, Bud Longbrake, Tom Reeves, T. C. Holloway, C. L. Johnson, Kody Woodward, Chelsey Kelly, Harold and Pauline Davis, Johnny Holloway, Pete Longbrake, Holloway Rodeos, Longbrake Rodeos, Dale Sprague, Jess Woodward, J. C. Woodward, Tony Murray, Walt Stocklin, and Vicki Parker Birkeland—all in the sport of rodeo. Many others have excelled and competed through the years. Several of the ladies have won powwow titles for appearance, dress, or competition, including Codi High Elk, who won the title of Miss Indian World; Jerilyn LeBeau, who won Miss Indian America; and Marina Allison, who won titles in the areas of competition and powwow. Actress Catherine Bach also spent time with family in the area of Ziebach County.

Today Ziebach County has a population of 2,519, based on the 2000 census. The county seat of Dupree has a population of 435. The area has rich grasslands, numerous buttes, rolling hills, and river breaks. It is abundant in wildlife and game, and the size of the county is 1,971 square miles. Alphabetically, the county is the last listed county in the United States. Most of Ziebach County is on the Cheyenne River Sioux Reservation or on the northern part of the Standing Rock Sioux Reservation, which extends into North Dakota.

Ziebach County is rich in its history and beauty of the natural environment. I am very pleased to have the opportunity to work with the Ziebach County Historical Society and enjoyed working with their members: Darla Vrooman (president), Robert Shannon (vice president), Twila Schuler (treasurer), Dondra Menzel (secretary), Evelyn Anderson, Kandice Hoffman, Amy Linn, and Kimberly Shannon (media). I encourage everyone to keep their histories alive and well, and contact this group for research and networking. The wonderful photographs of this group are credited as ZCHS.

—Donovin Sprague
2010

One

Early Ziebach County

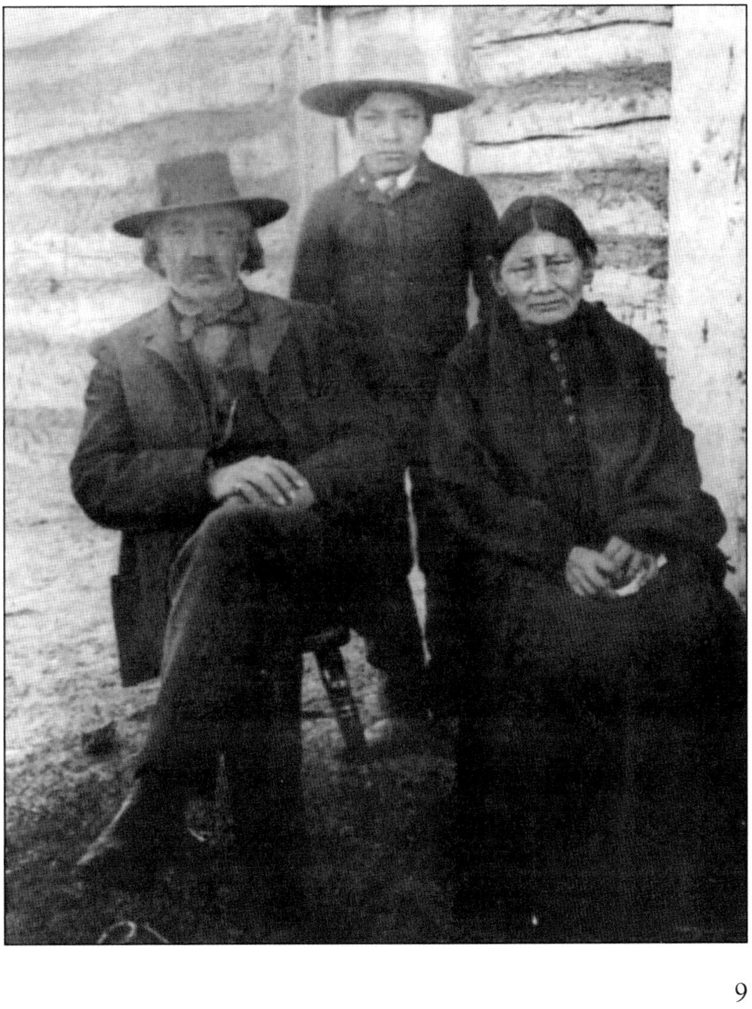

Pictured here are Fred Dupris Sr., his grandson Pete Dupris, and wife Good Elk Woman. Fred was French and arrived in the area for the fur trade. He married Good Elk Woman, a Minnicoujou from Cherry Creek. Fred was inducted into the South Dakota Hall of Fame and was the first inductee into the National Buffalo Association Hall of Fame for his role in saving the buffalo from extinction. Dupree, South Dakota, is named for Fred and his family. (Courtesy of Donovin Sprague.)

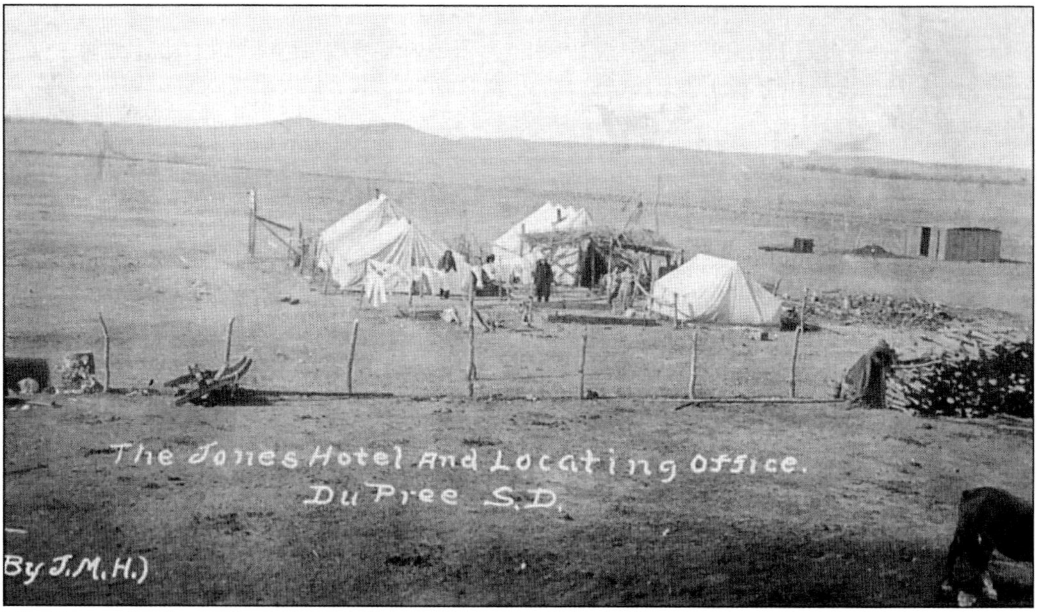

The Jones Hotel and Locating Office in Dupree assisted people who had new land claims. The owner was Eb Jones, and this view is looking west towards the camelback hills on the horizon. Jones settled on Little Bear Creek, east of Dupree, before Ziebach County was opened for settlement under the Homestead Act. Some settlers lived with Jones until he found them a place. The tents are in the approximate location of Main Street today. (Courtesy of ZCHS.)

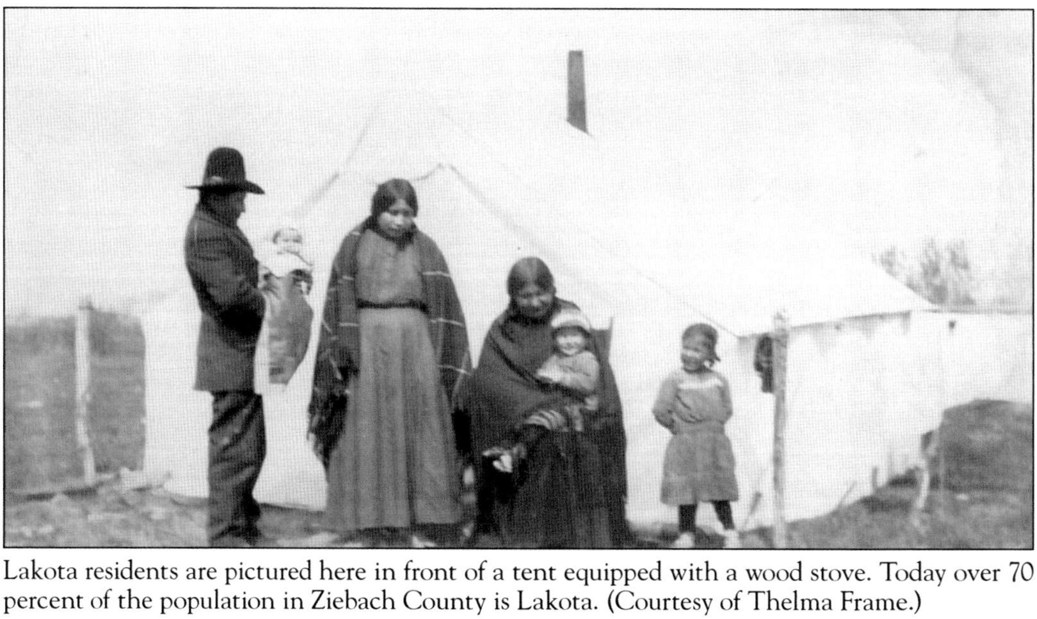

Lakota residents are pictured here in front of a tent equipped with a wood stove. Today over 70 percent of the population in Ziebach County is Lakota. (Courtesy of Thelma Frame.)

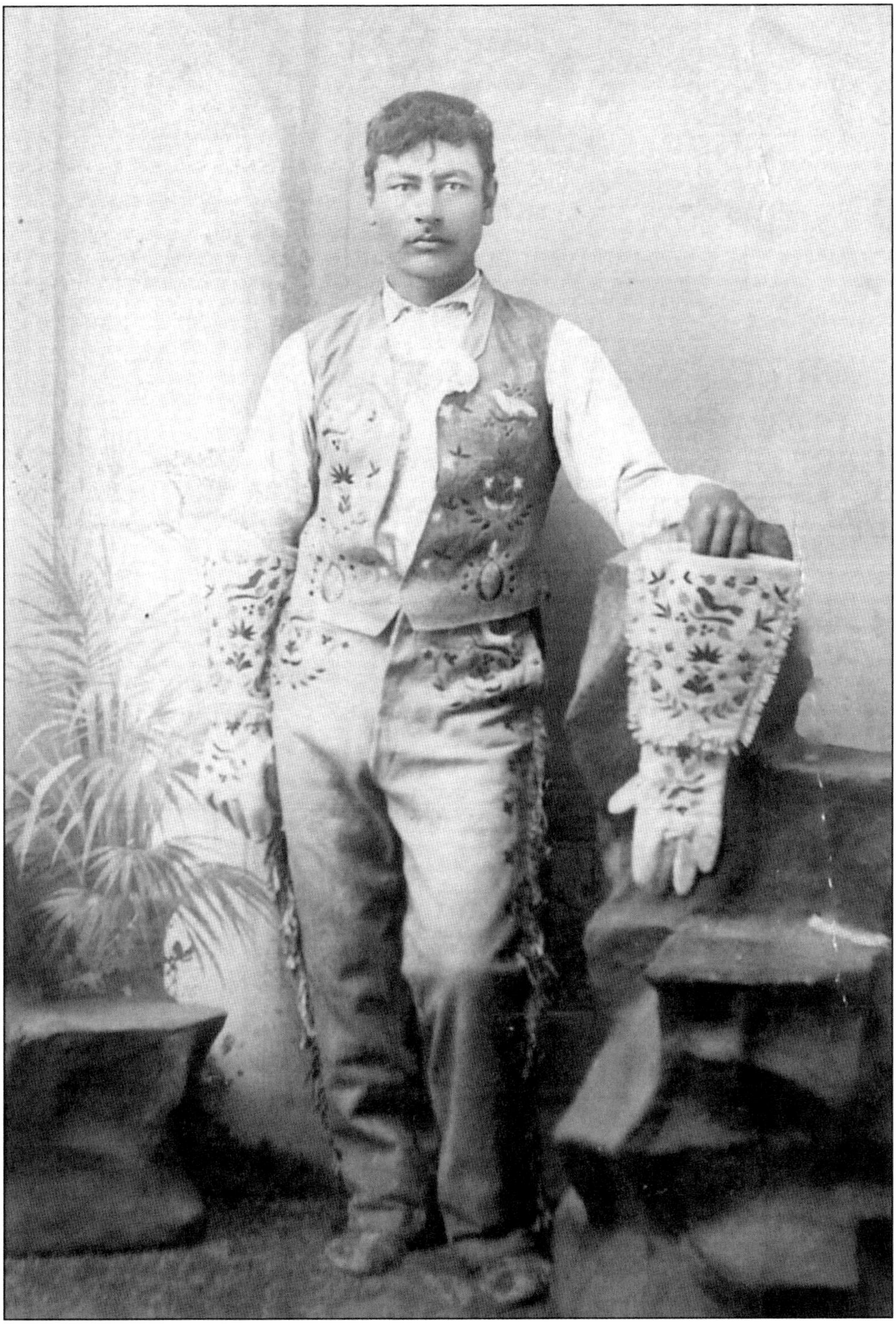

Fred Dupris Jr. is shown with a fine assortment of quillwork and beaded clothing and gloves. He was born in 1849 and married Emily Eagle Shield, who was born in 1867. Their children were Ed (who died at age two), Edna (Garreau), Susie (LaPoint), Mary/Molly (Annis), Johnny, Christine (Arpan-Swift-White Eyes), and Phillip. Fred's Lakota name was Cunkagipa, which means carpenter. (Courtesy of Eugenia Burgee.)

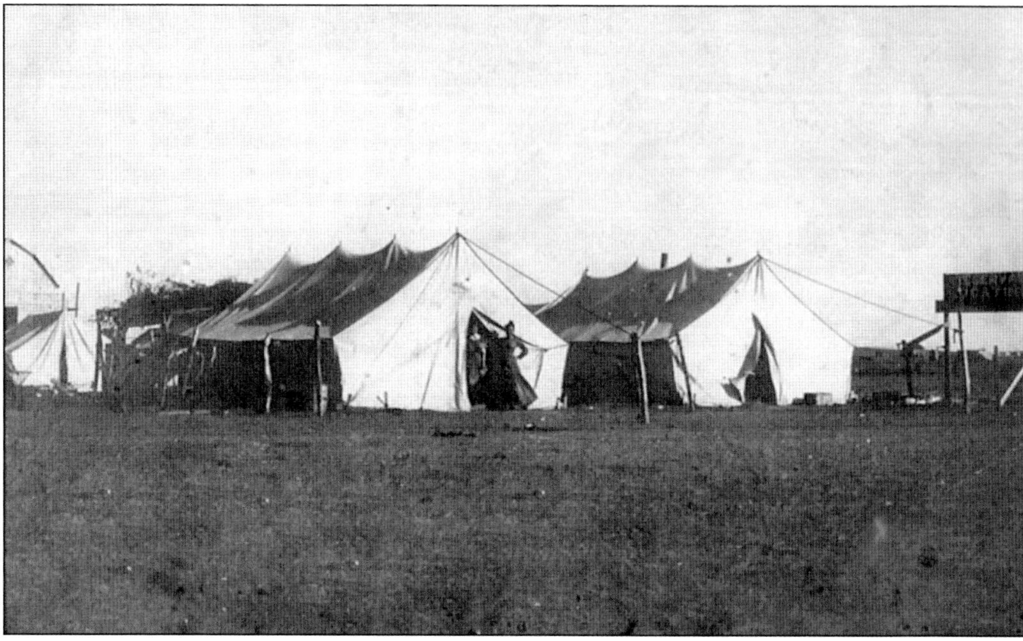

Jones Camp at Dupree probably refers to the land business of Elbert "Eb" Jones, who was born in Dakota Territory in 1866. He also worked for many cattle outfits and was a U.S. Army scout. In 1888, he married Julie Anne Langlois, and they moved to Cherry Creek in 1906. After Julie Ann died, he married Dessie Jamieson. They lived at Cherry Creek until moving to Whitewood, South Dakota, in 1936. (Courtesy of Irean Jordan.)

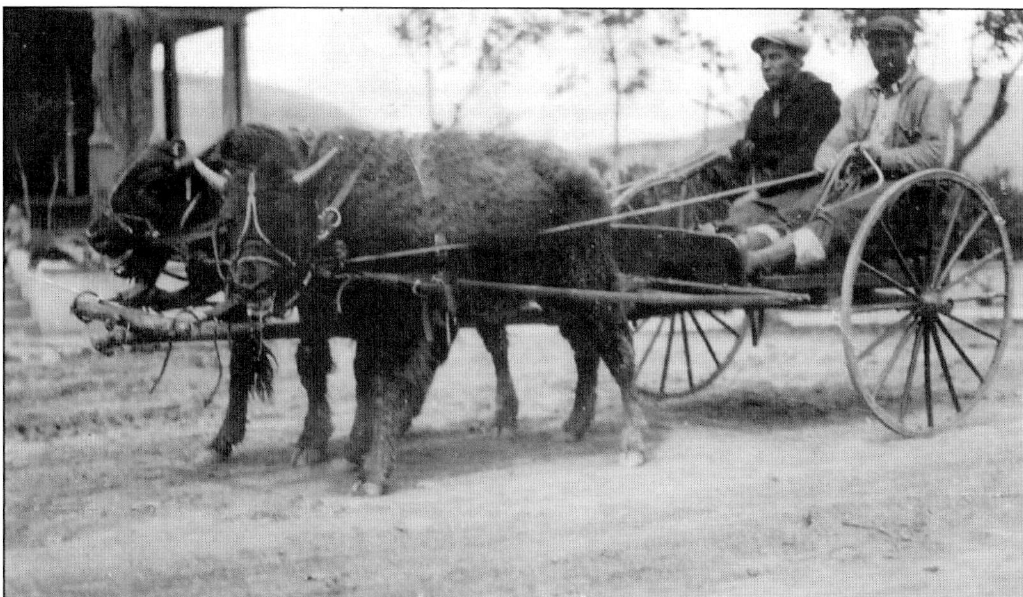

Following the deaths of Fred Dupris and Good Elk Woman, Scotty Philip purchased their buffalo herd and later sold buffalo to Custer Sate Park, which sold them to other areas in the country. Scotty Philip is often listed as the first buffalo rancher in South Dakota, but Fred and Good Elk Woman had the original herd and lived a generation before their friend, who died young. Pictured are Jess Powell, left, and Walter Carlin, right. (Courtesy of Donovin Sprague.)

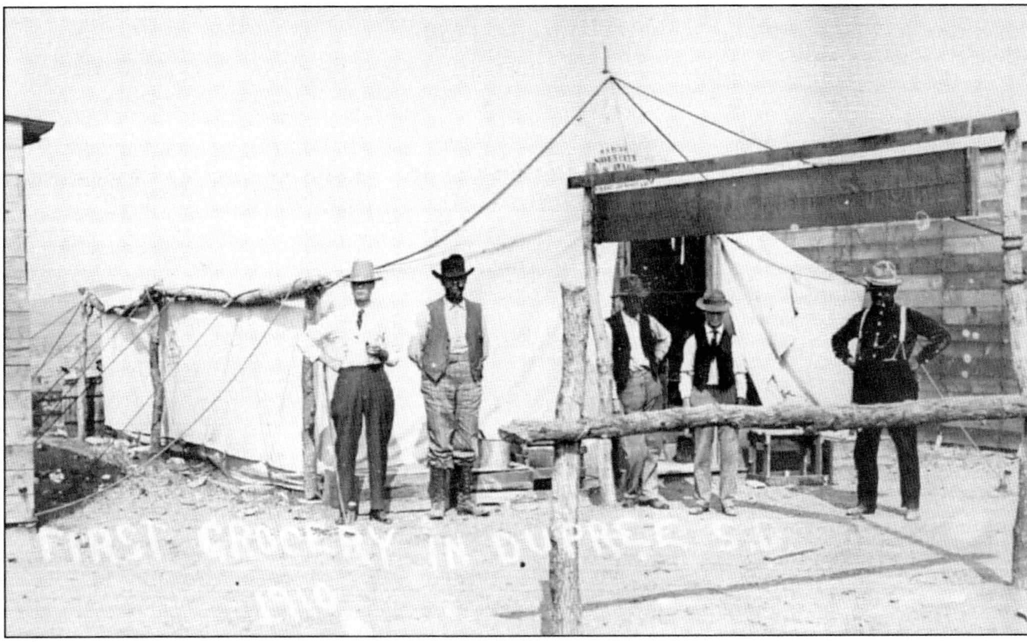

This photograph shows the first grocery store in Dupree in 1910, which was owned by Henry "Hank" Maupin, standing at far left. Art Lafferty, Jimmy Crorkin, and Bill Sculley may be the men to his left. The man on the far right is unidentified. In the background is half of camel's butte, just west of town. The first location of Dupree to the east also likely had groceries. (Courtesy of Irean Jordan)

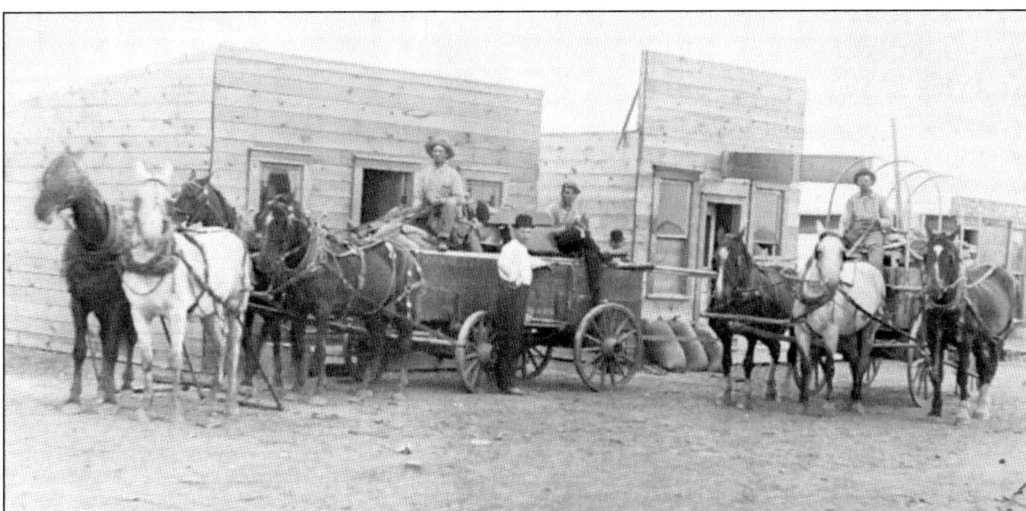

Freight arrives into Dupree by wagon in 1910, before the railroad existed, in the era of homesteads. (Courtesy of Irean Jordan.)

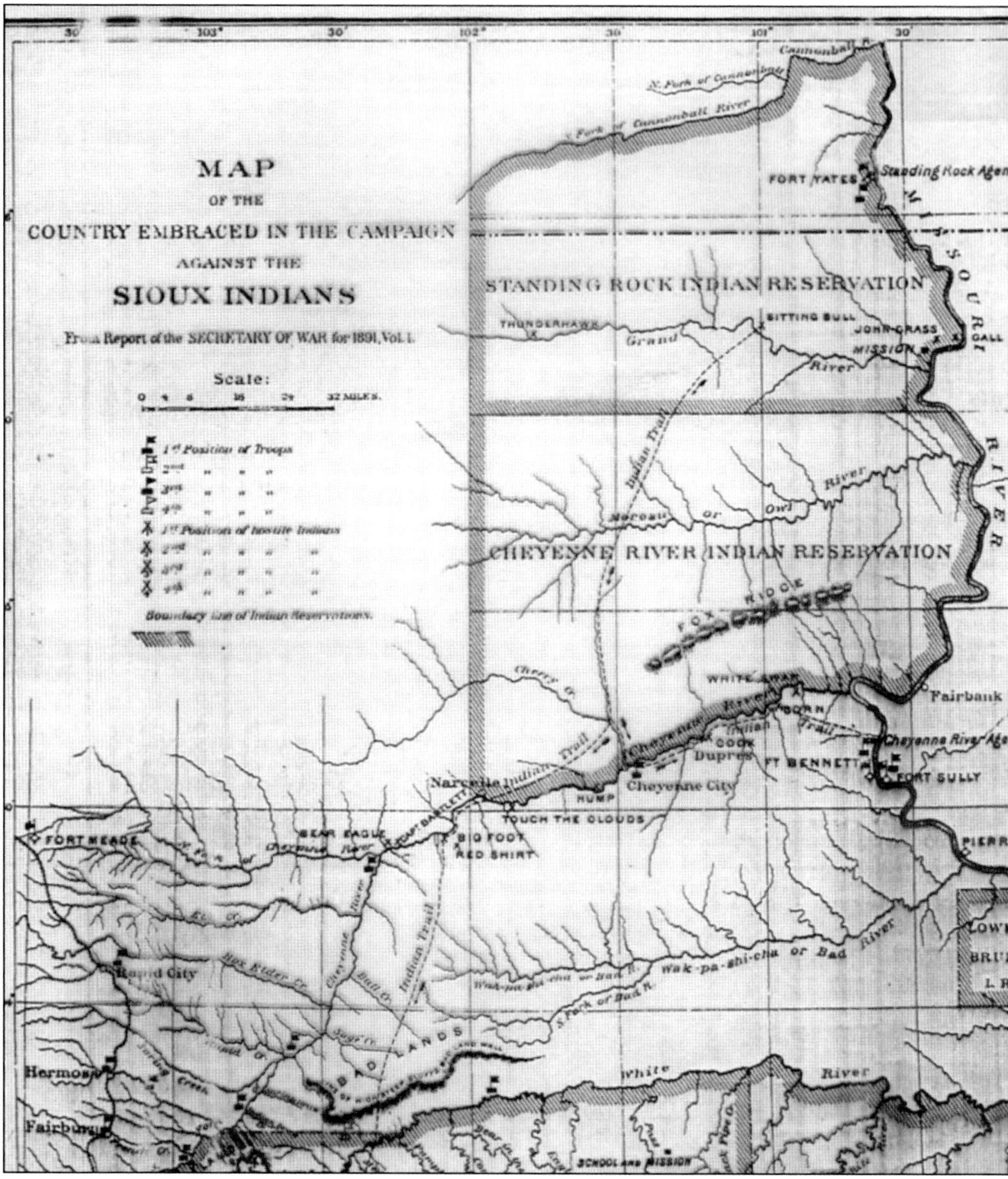

Here is an 1891 map of the Cheyenne River and Standing Rock Indian Reservations. The map shows the camp locations of Lakota headmen Hump, Touch the Cloud, Big Foot, and Red Shirt in the area that would become Ziebach County. The Dupree and Narcelle family camps are also shown, and farther east are the camps of Cook, Corn, and White Swan. (Courtesy of Donovin Sprague.)

Spotted Eagle was an Itazipco Lakota *itancan* (leader) who led his warriors at the Battle of the Rosebud and the Battle of the Little Bighorn in 1876. He went to Canada and later returned to the United States. He was sent to Fort Bennett and then settled at Bear Creek, where he had a large following of Christian Lakotas. Many attended Riggs Oahe School and were lay readers. He died at age 65 in 1898 at Bear Creek. This photograph was taken in 1880. (Courtesy of Donovin Sprague.)

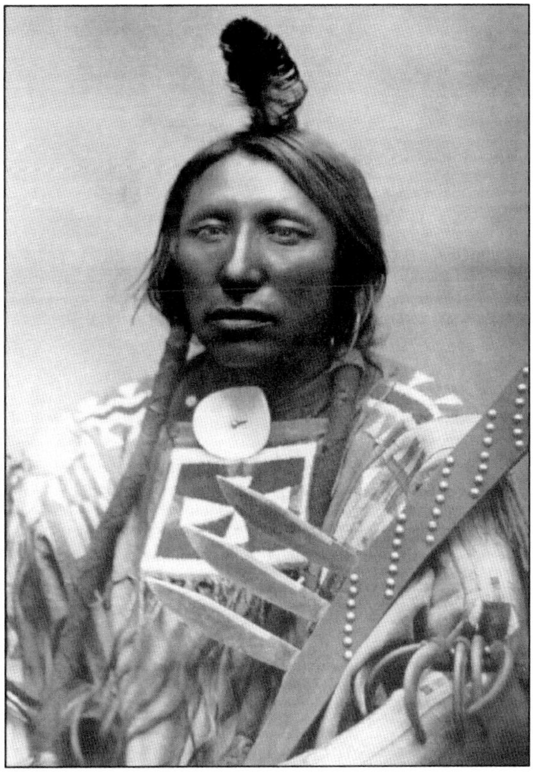

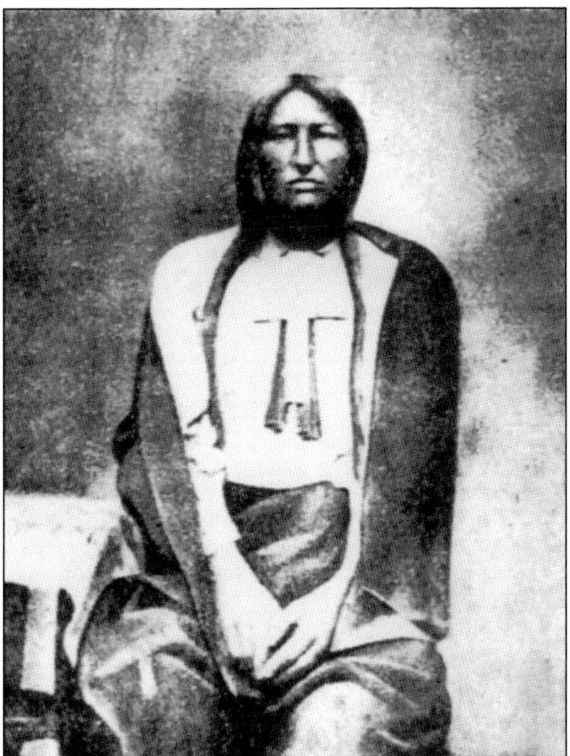

Si Tanka (Big Foot) was a Minnicoujou leader and brother of Touch the Cloud. Upon the creation of the Cheyenne River Reservation, his main camps were along the Cheyenne River near Cherry Creek, Bridger, and the Pedro area. On December 29, 1890, he died at the Wounded Knee Massacre along with about 300 people of his band. (Courtesy of Donovin Sprague.)

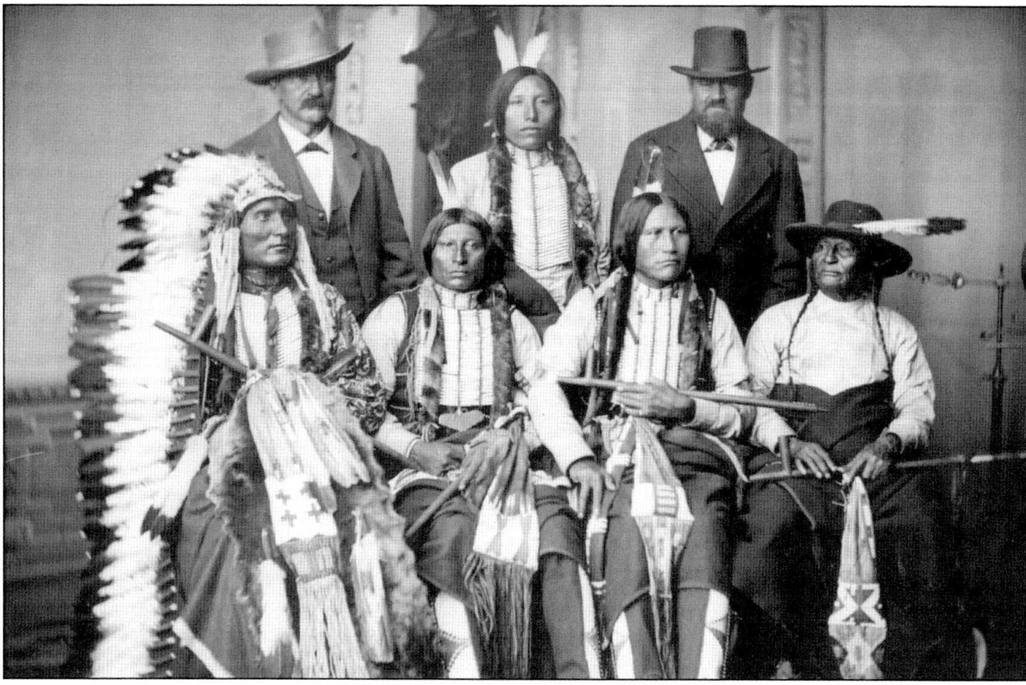

Pictured are, from left to right, (first row) Touch the Cloud, Sharp Nose, Black Coal, and Dangler; (second row) Antoine Janis, Young Spotted Tail, and Joe Merrivale. Touch the Cloud, from Cheyenne River, was described as 7 feet tall but may have been closer to 6 feet, 8 inches. The photograph was taken in 1877 and included an Arapaho delegation, seated next to Touch the Cloud. (Courtesy of Donovin Sprague.)

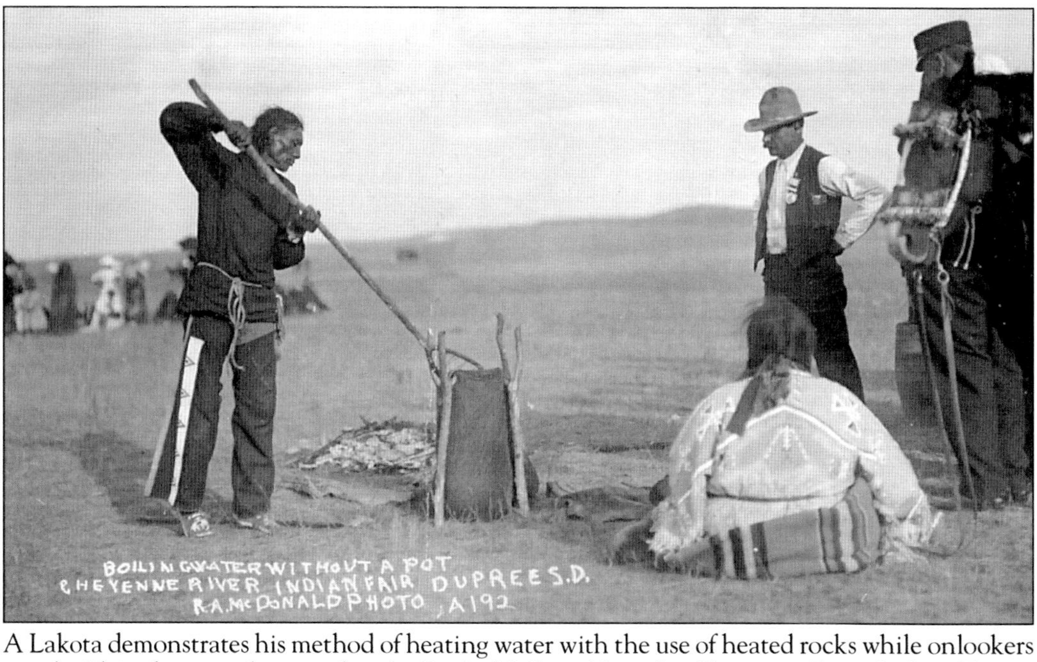

A Lakota demonstrates his method of heating water with the use of heated rocks while onlookers watch. This photograph was taken by R. A. McDonald at the Cheyenne River Indian Fair in Dupree, South Dakota. (Courtesy of Thelma Frame.)

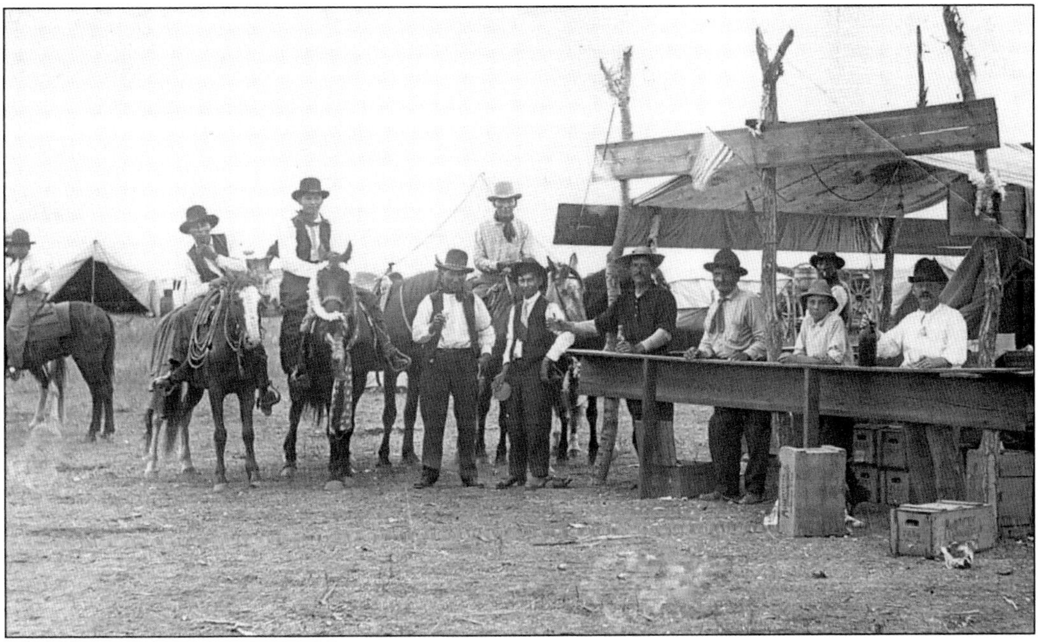

A small American flag hangs above a concession stand at the 1912 Cheyenne River Indian Fair held in Dupree, South Dakota. Wooden boxes have the word "Mobridge" written on them, and they are part of the concession goods. (Courtesy of ZCHS/Virginia Woodward.)

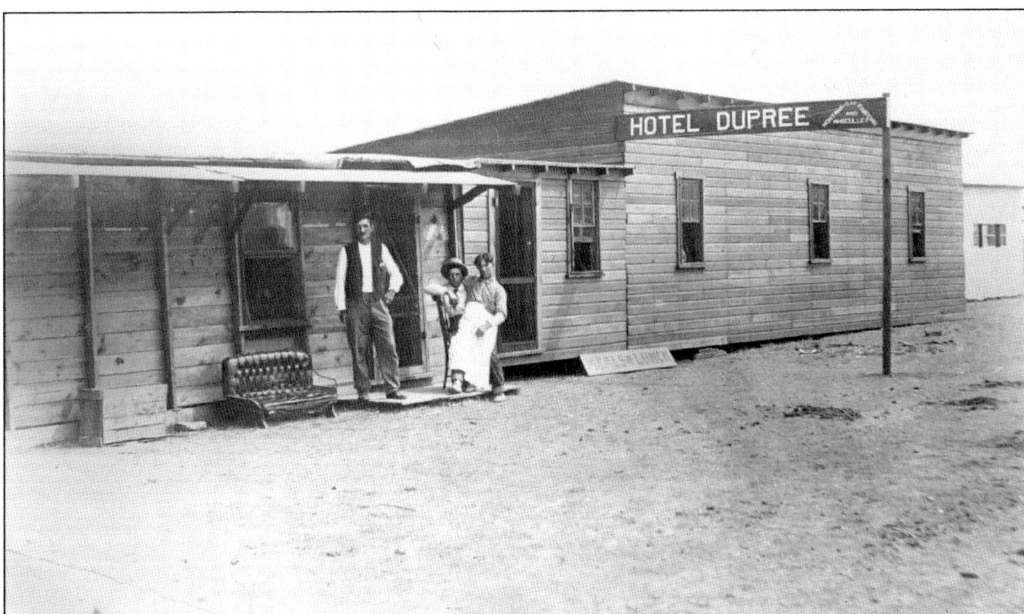

James A. Shelton bought a plot of land from the U.S. Land Office, where he built the Shelton Hotel. This photograph is undated, but it is known that in 1931, Matt Stephenson changed the name to Hotel Dupree, which served meals to its guests. The Hotel Dupree sign boasts the names of its proprietors: Montana, F. A. Brown, and H. H. Sculley. (Courtesy of ZCHS/ Virginia Woodward.)

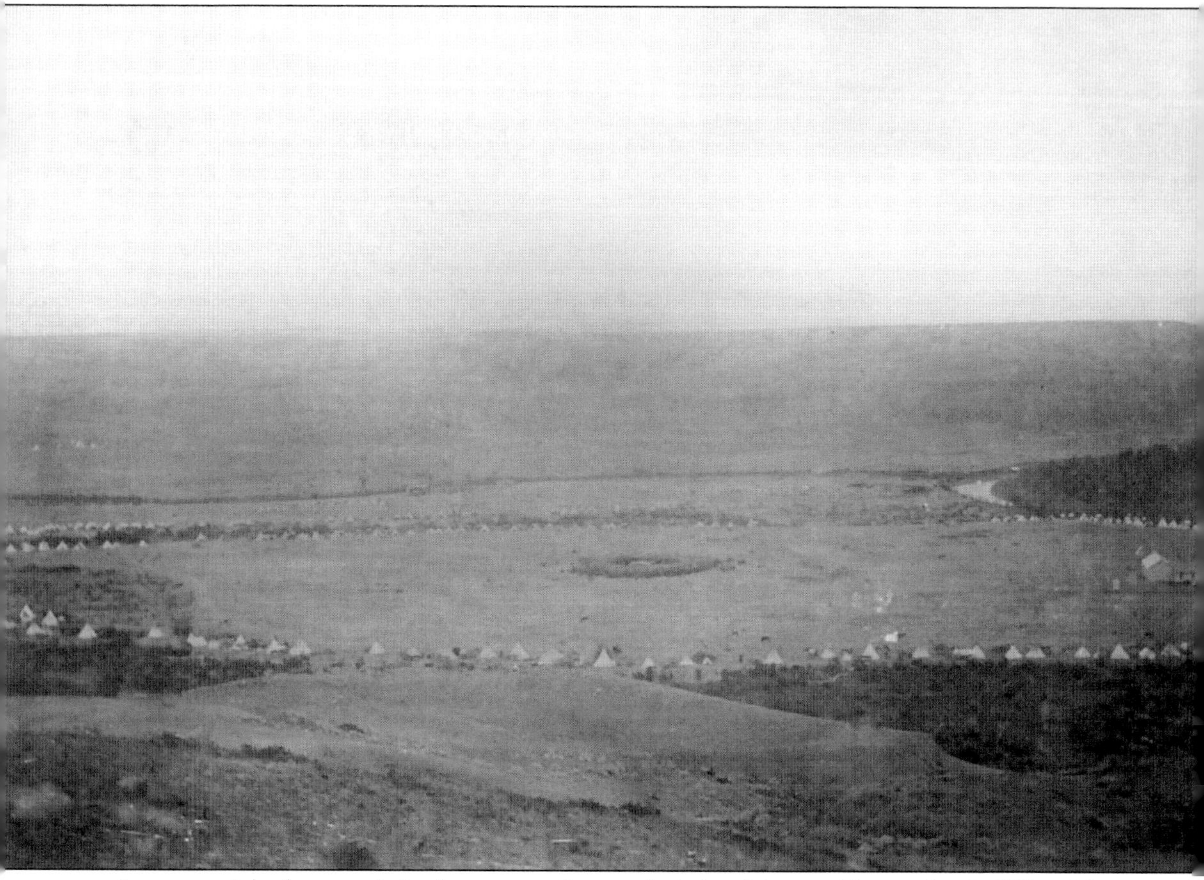

A ceremonial arbor stands in the center of a grand circle of tipis at Cherry Creek. When Hump made his second surrender from Canada, he was taken to Fort Keogh, Fort Yates, and then to Fort Bennett, which was the Cheyenne River Agency. He settled at the west end of the reservation, in camps near Iron Lightning, Red Scaffold, Bridger, and Cherry Creek. He had the largest band on Cheyenne River. (Courtesy of Eugenia Burgee and Donovin Sprague.)

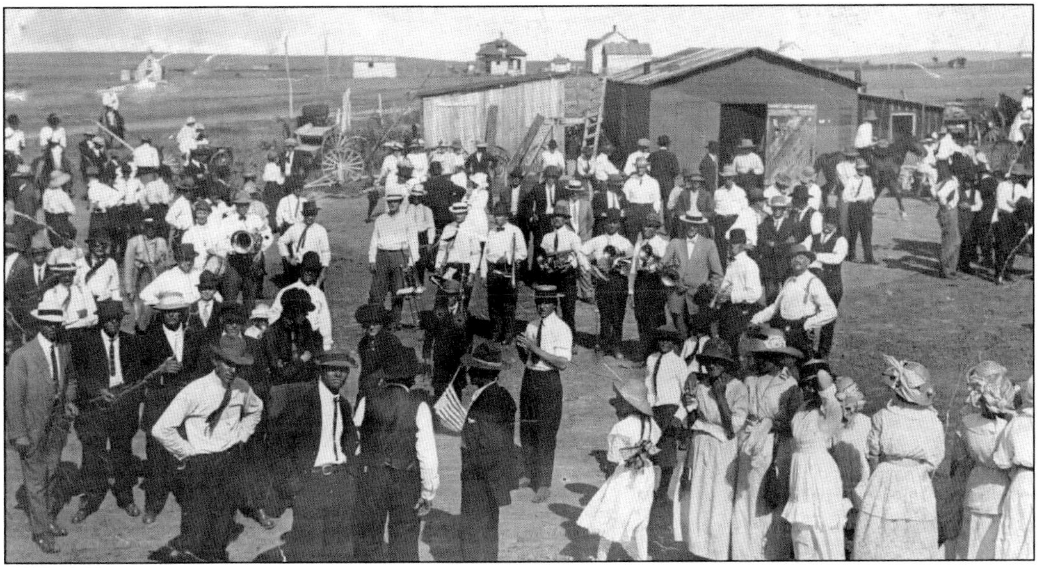

This photograph, taken around July 4, 1914, shows men dressed up in suits, ties, and hats, and women wearing their fine dresses and hats. The band features brass horns, and this is labeled as the first band. A youngster holds a tilted American flag in front of the band, at center. (Courtesy of ZCHS/Virginia Woodward.)

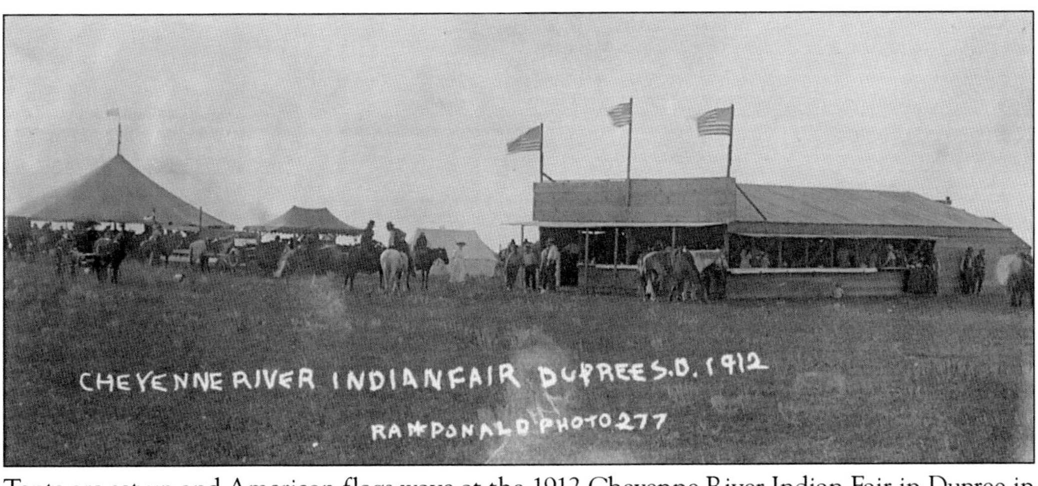

Tents are set up and American flags wave at the 1912 Cheyenne River Indian Fair in Dupree in this photograph taken by R. A. McDonald. (Courtesy of ZCHS.)

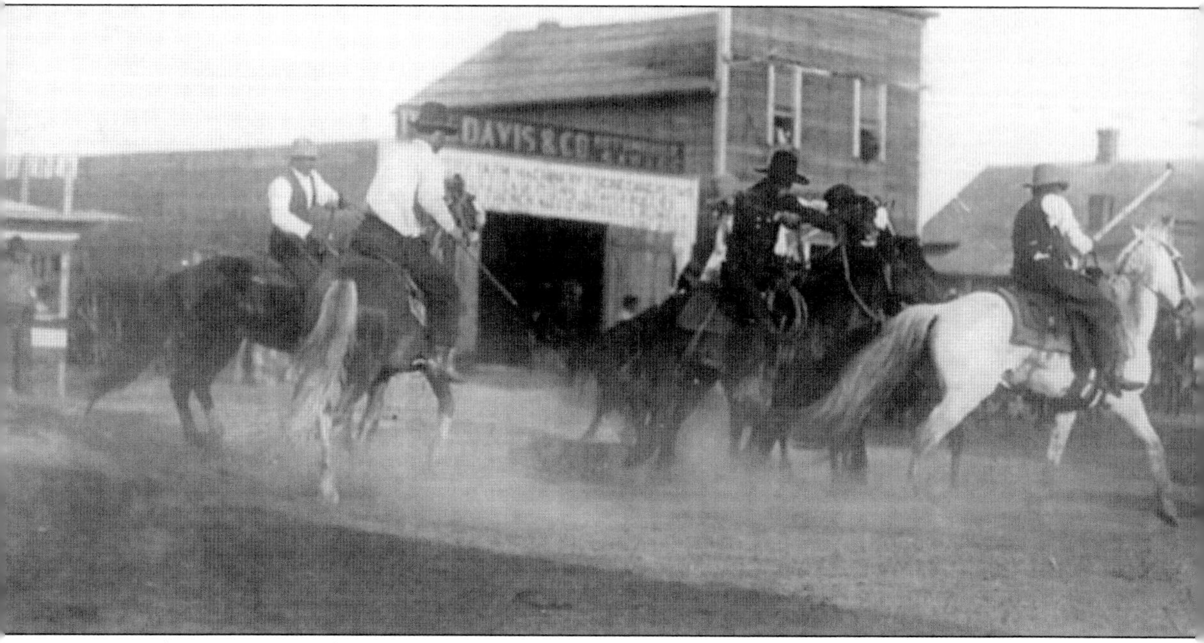

Cowboys are engaged in a game of polo on Main Street in Dupree. In the background is the store of Phil Davis and Company. (Courtesy of Virginia Woodward)

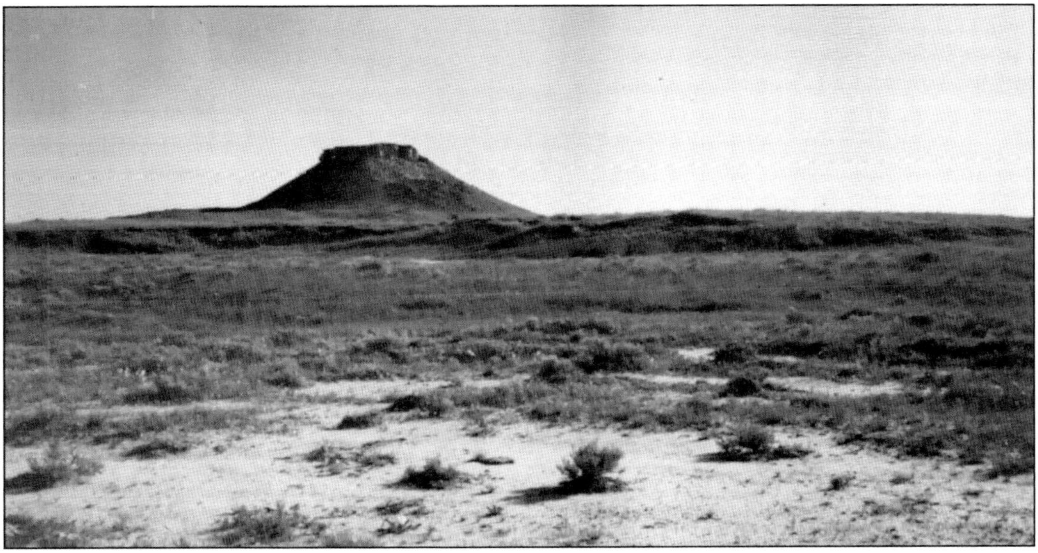

Thunder Butte is located in northern Ziebach County. The Lakota name for it is Wakanganhotan, meaning "place of holy thunder," and was so named because during storms the sound of thunder seemed to come from the butte. The thunder was thought by the Lakota to be the Great Spirit's voice and was sometimes heard on a clear day. Lakota came for miles to this site to undertake a vision quest known as *hanbleciyapi*. (Courtesy of ZCHS.)

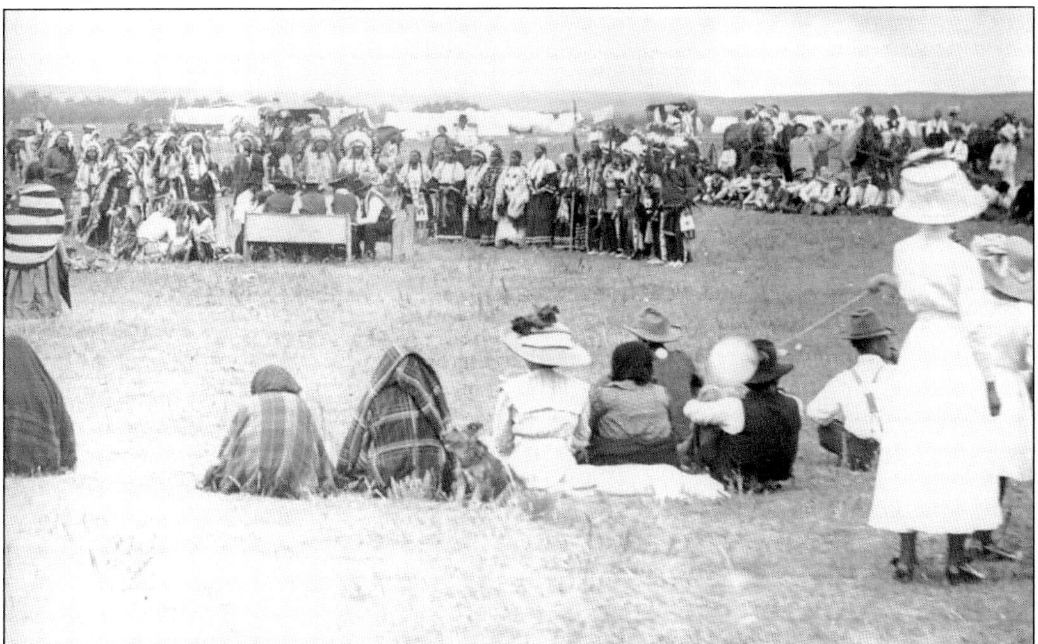

Pictured here is a Lakota celebration at Thunder Butte, South Dakota, in 1919. By 1907, the first buildings constructed at Thunder Butte included a warehouse, a farmer's cottage, and a school. Materials used in the construction were hauled overland from Evarts, South Dakota, south of Mobridge. Cottonwood lumber came from the old Cheyenne Agency, which had a sawmill. Evarts and the Cheyenne Agency are now flooded, beneath the Missouri River. (Courtesy of ZCHS/ Virginia Woodward.)

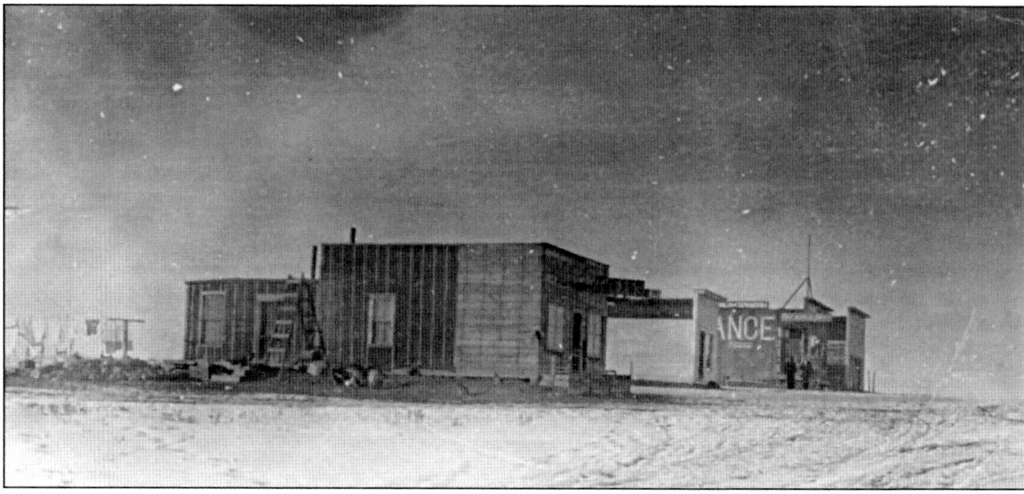

The store of Earl Vance is partially in view. Smith and Vance were partners. Earl Vance taught school in Bridger, South Dakota, and his wife was Ruby Harmon Vance. Some of the early teachers in Redelm (also known as Red Elm) were Earl Vance, Edna Walker Drummond, Mabel Reynolds Ross, Everett Reynolds, Lucille Eddy, Grace Stevens, Leona Callen, Mrs. L. W. Eaton, Esther Andersen Orbeck, Betty Johnson Tibke, and Lillian Birkeland. (Courtesy of ZCHS.)

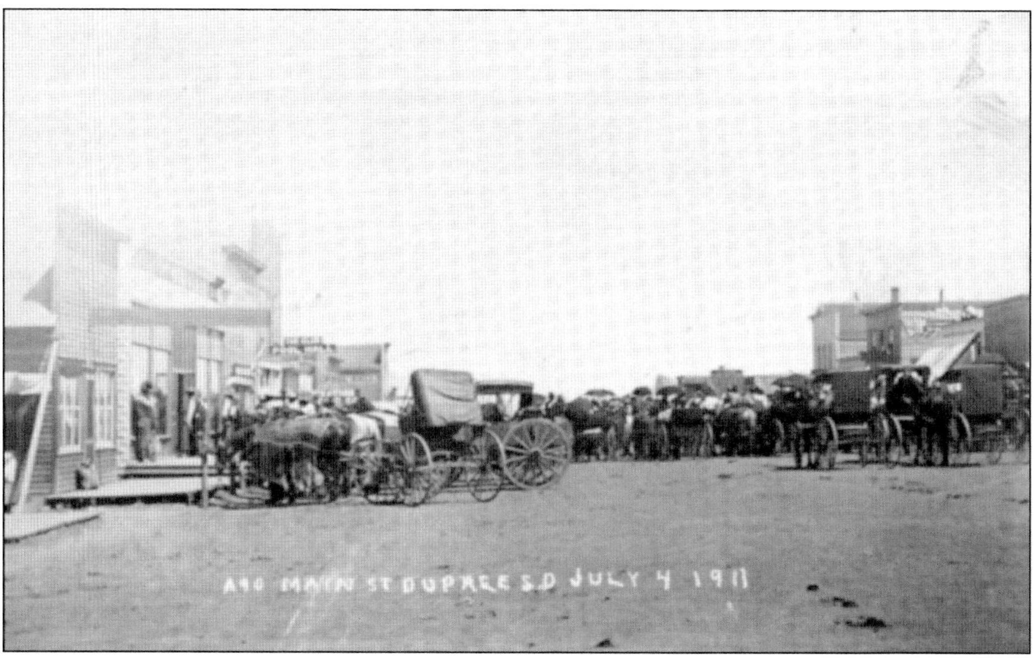

A large crowd with buggies lines Main Street for this celebration on July 4, 1911. The Club Pool Hall is shown on the left side of the photograph, with possibly another pool hall sign in the background. (Courtesy of ZCHS.)

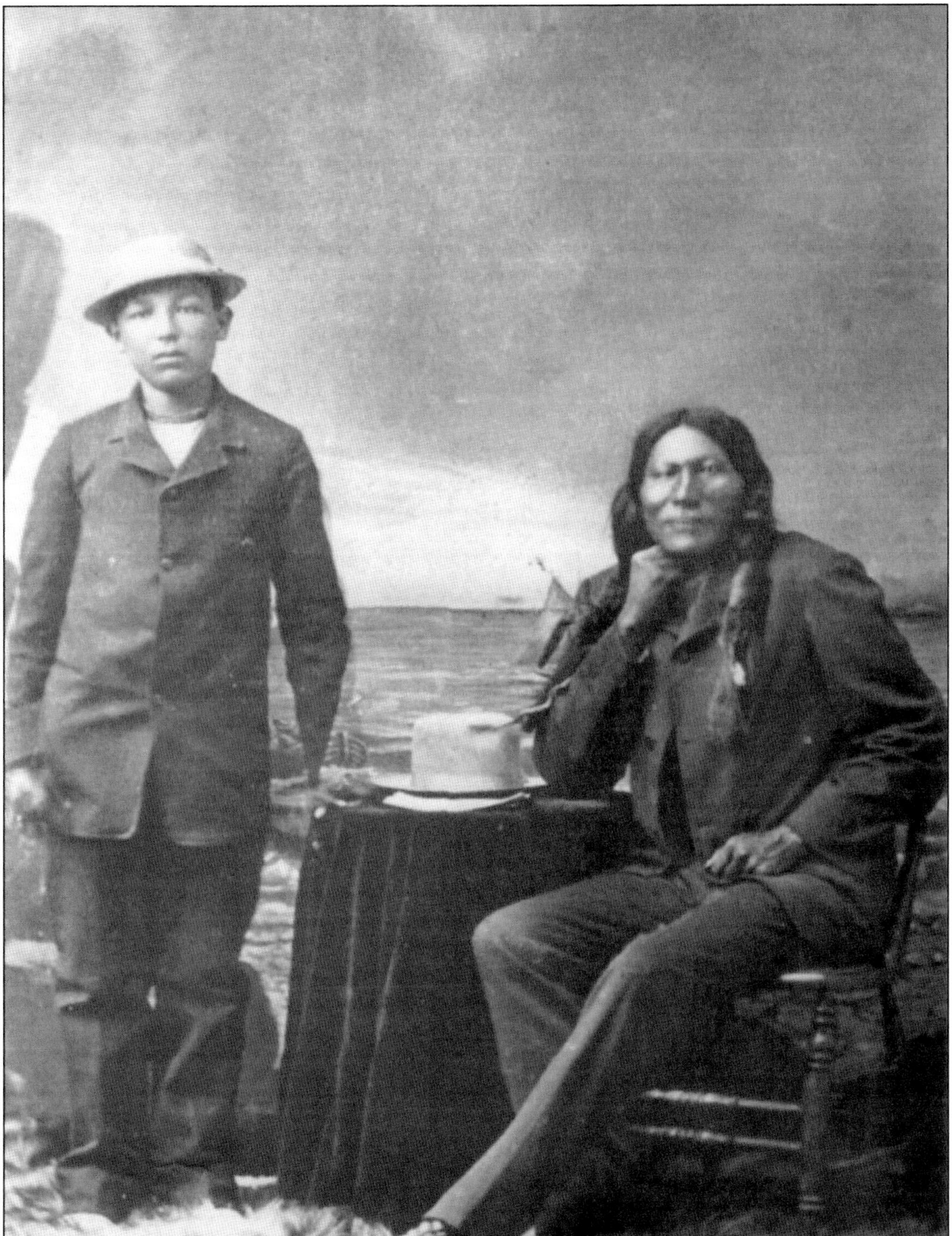

Chief Hump is pictured with his interpreter Andrew Traversie, who attended Hampton Institute and interpreted for Hump in Washington, D.C. After taking part in the Battle of the Little Bighorn in 1876, Hump surrendered to General Miles in 1877 and was a U.S. Indian scout under Miles briefly. He then took his band to Canada and joined Sitting Bull there. Upon a second surrender from Canada, he became a ghost dancer at Cherry Creek. (Courtesy of Donovin Sprague.)

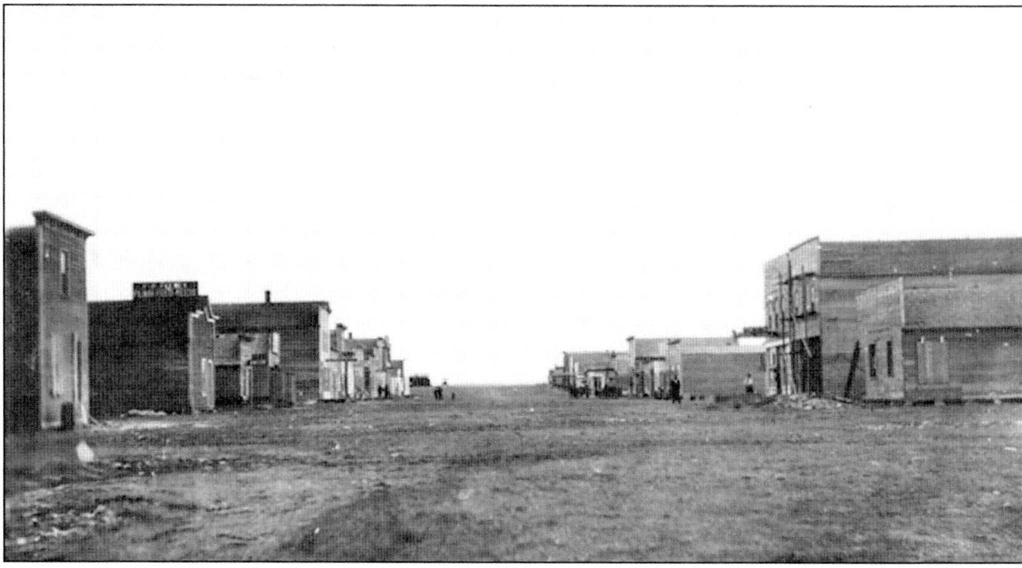

This is an early photograph of Dupree's Main Street, looking to the south. The Land of the Sioux Museum in Mobridge took or printed this photograph. (Courtesy of ZCHS.)

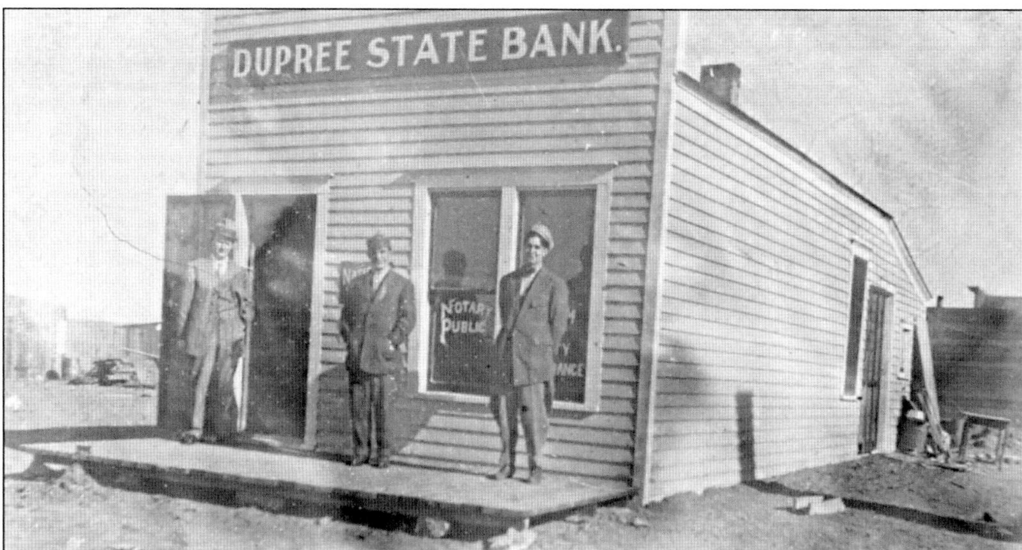

A. A. Karley built this bank in August 1910. He was the cashier and managing officer of the Dupree State Bank and came from Presho, South Dakota. The Farmers State Bank was incorporated in 1909 by Michael Dunn, Gilbert A. McGarraugh, and Patterson F. McClure. The first 20-year charter was issued in 1910, with Michael Dunn as president, McGarraugh as cashier and managing officer, and McClure as vice president. It became Farmers State Bank. (Courtesy of ZCHS.)

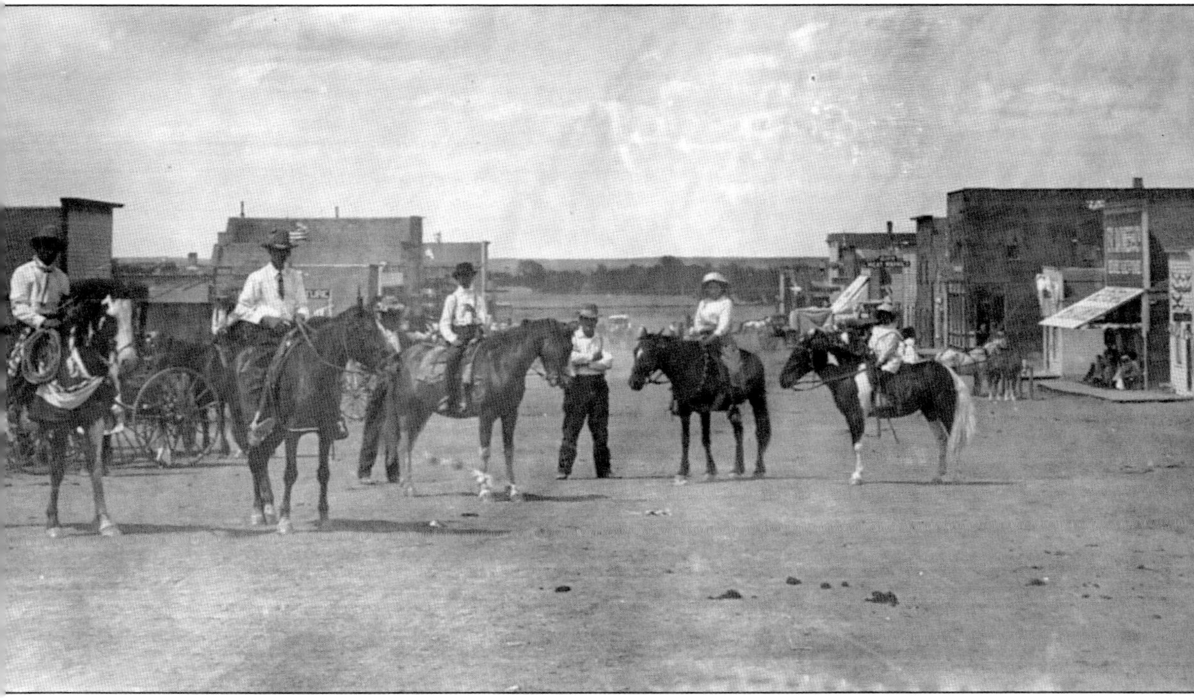

A scene from Main Street in Dupree reveals a meat market on the right side. The buildings behind the people are the north end of Main Street. (Courtesy of ZCHS/Virginia Woodward.)

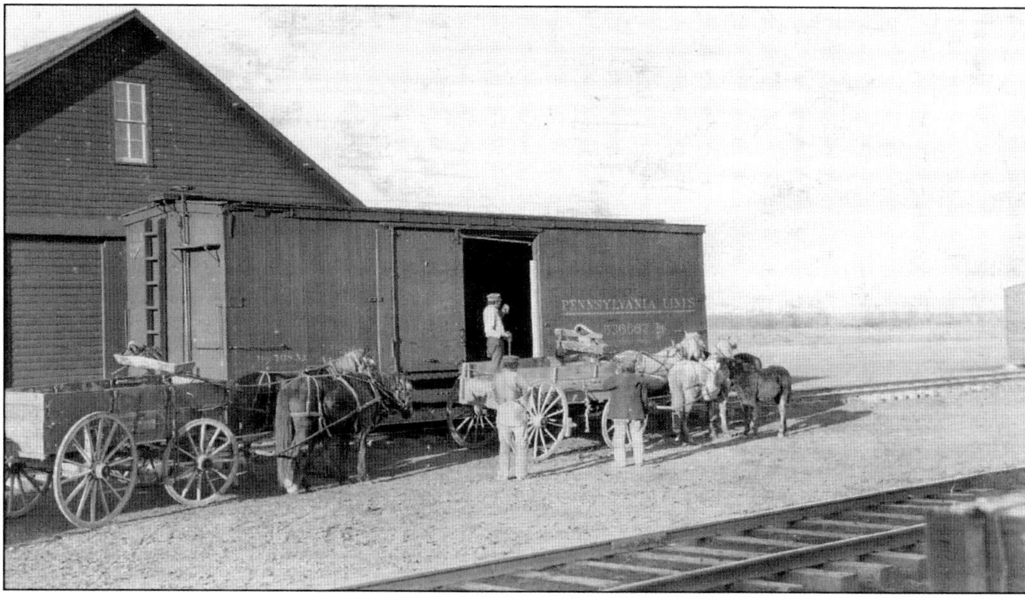

Men line up with their teams and wagons to wait for freight to be unloaded from a Pennsylvania Lines boxcar. This location is by the first Bagley Elevator in Dupree. (Courtesy of ZCHS/ Virginia Woodward.)

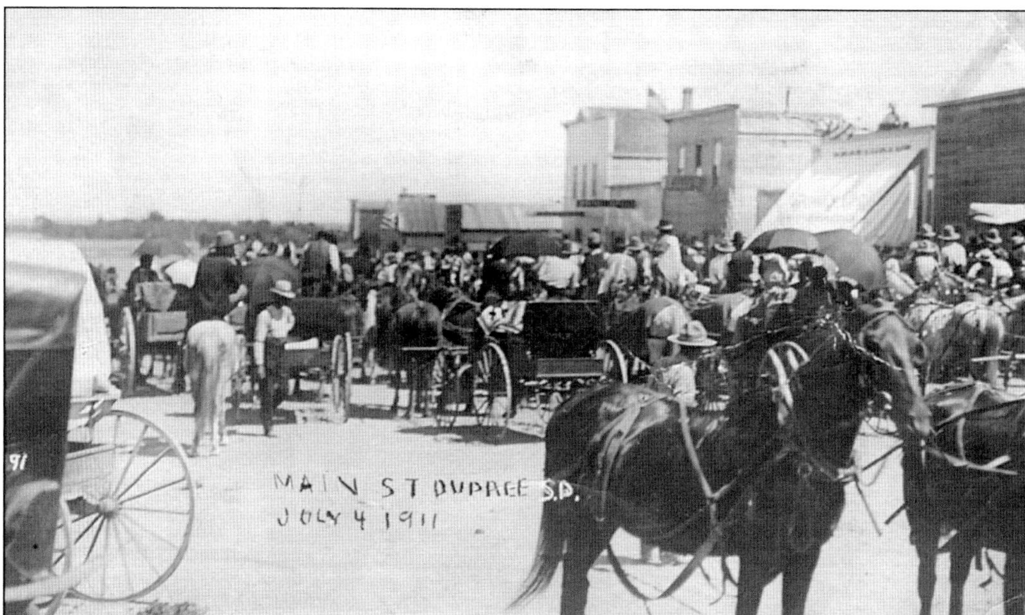

Large crowds of people in heavy traffic are pictured here for the July 4, 1911, celebration. They are looking northward. (Courtesy of Thelma Frame.)

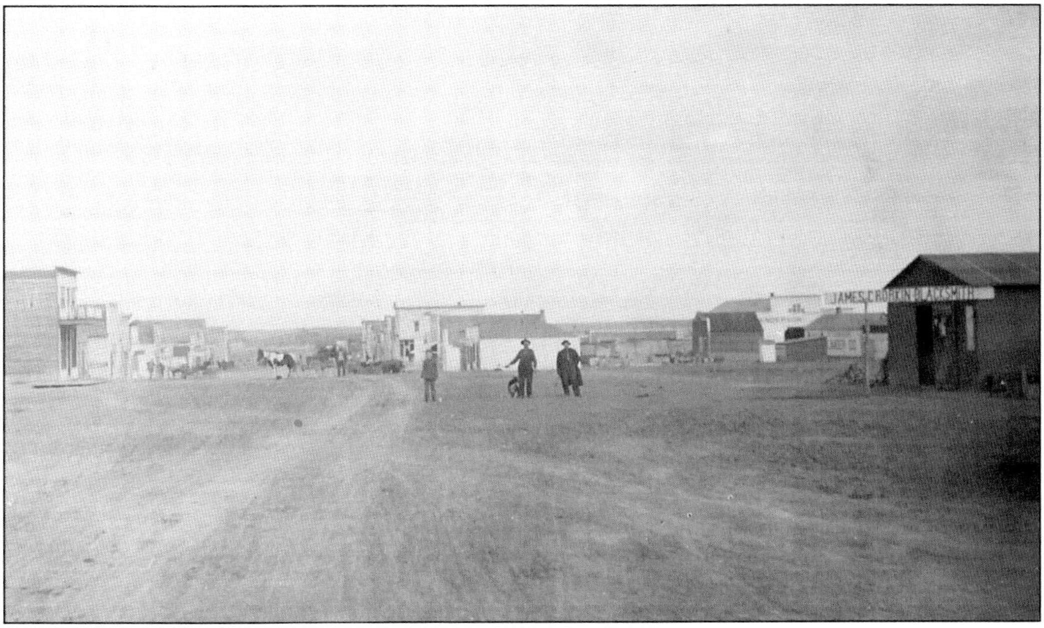

Pictured here is Main Street in Dupree with James Crorkin Blacksmith at right. The Anderson Lumber Company is in view in the background behind Crorkin Blacksmith and is in the same location today. (Courtesy of ZCHS/Harold and Joan Ross.)

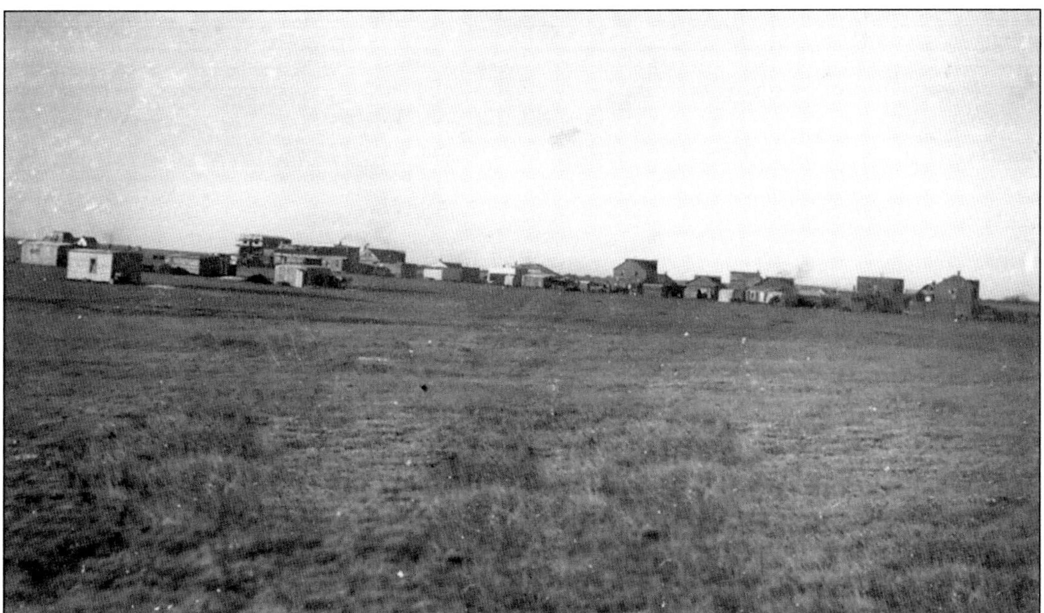

This is Dupree around December 15, 1910. There is no snow, but it must have been cold, as no one is out and the fires are burning. This would have been just days after the railroad came to town. (Courtesy of ZCHS/Virginia Woodward.)

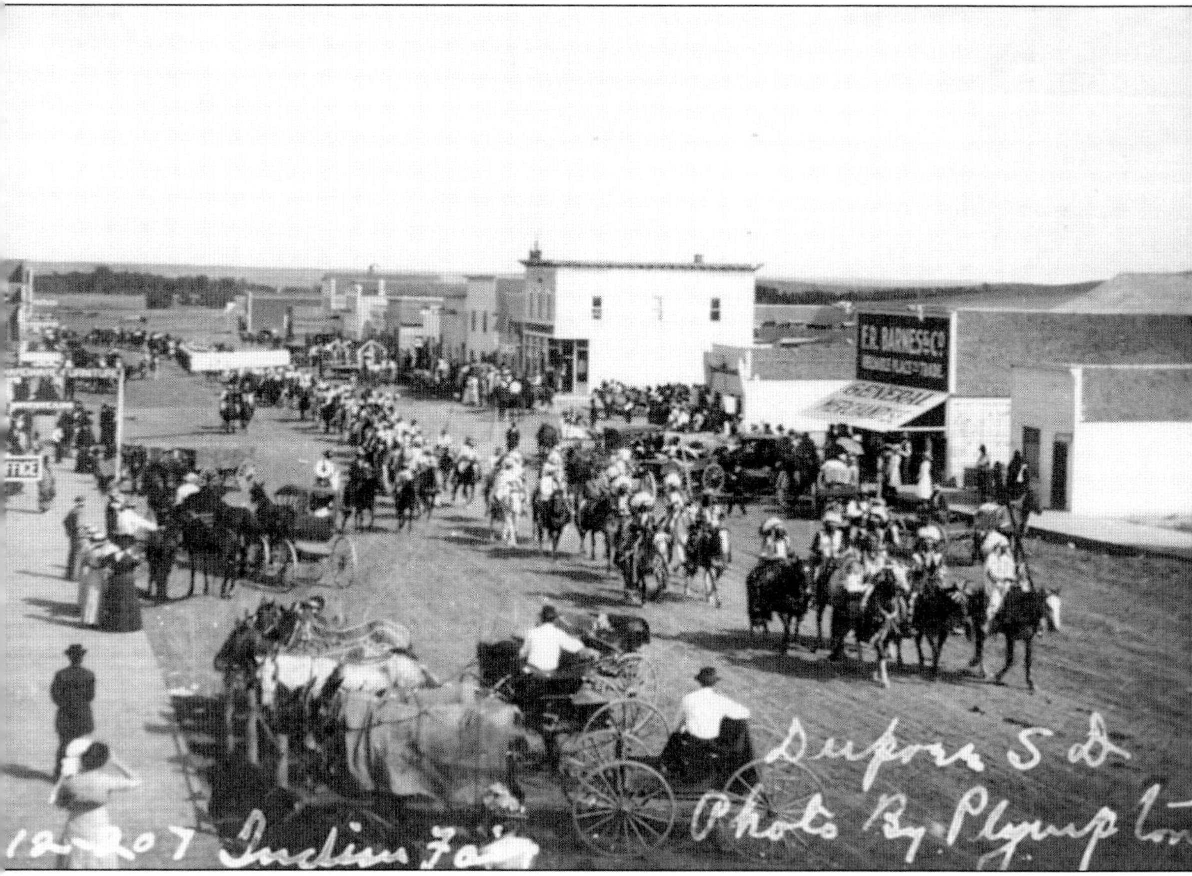

In 1912, the Cheyenne River Indian Fair celebration was held in Dupree with a parade on Main Street. The store at the center of the photograph on the east side of Main Street was built by Martin J. Sletten. (Courtesy of ZCHS/Virginia Woodward.)

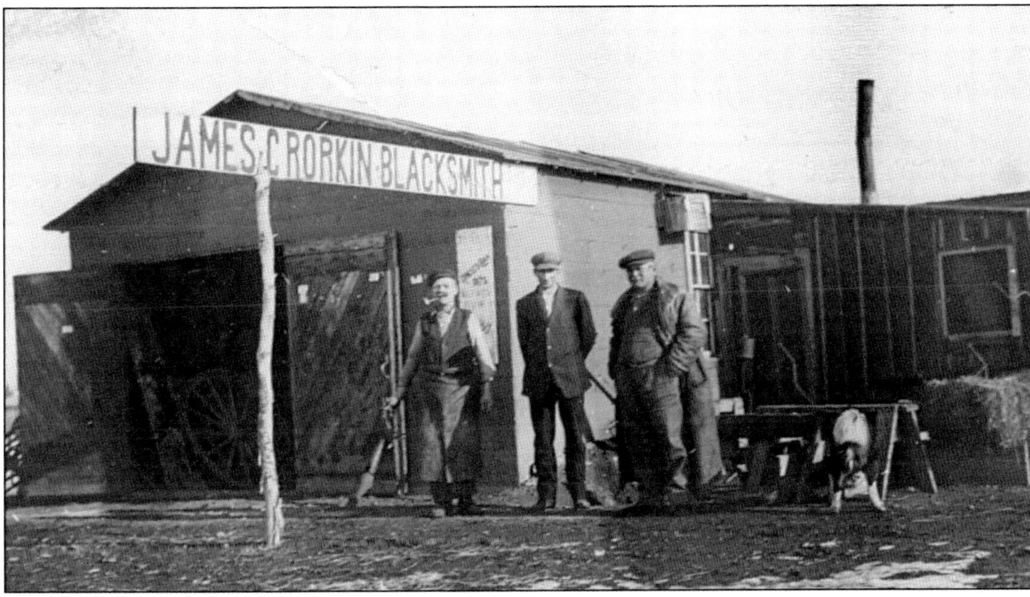

Three unidentified men are pictured in front of James Crorkin Blacksmith. Crorkin arrived in Dupree as part of the railroad construction crew. The Masonic Hall was later built on this same lot and is now the Dupree Senior Center. (Courtesy of ZCHS/Virginia Woodward.)

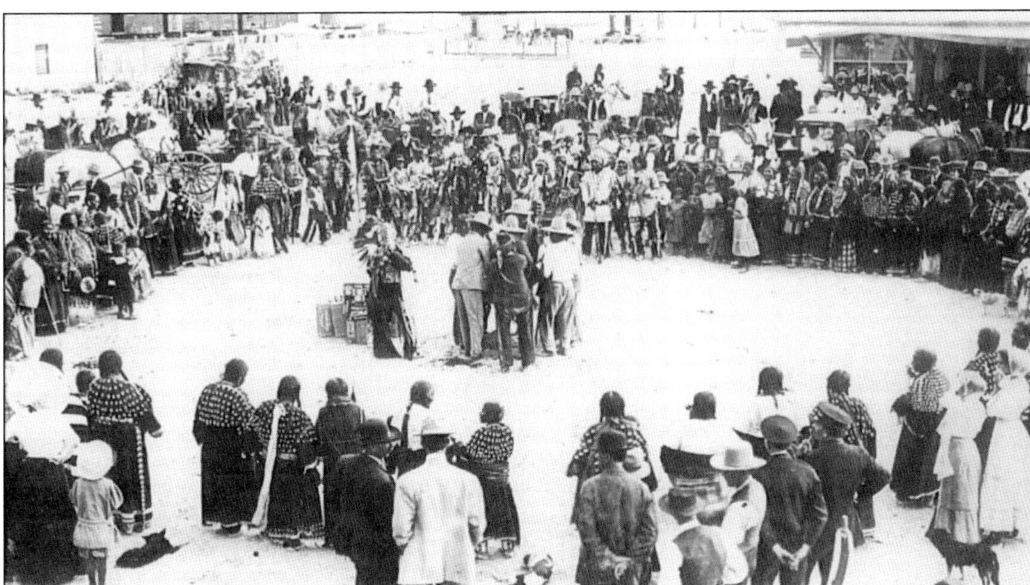

A large crowd has gathered near the railroad to listen to Lakota singers at the center of this photograph of a Lakota celebration. An honoring with a giveaway is also a part of this gathering. (Courtesy of Irean Jordan.)

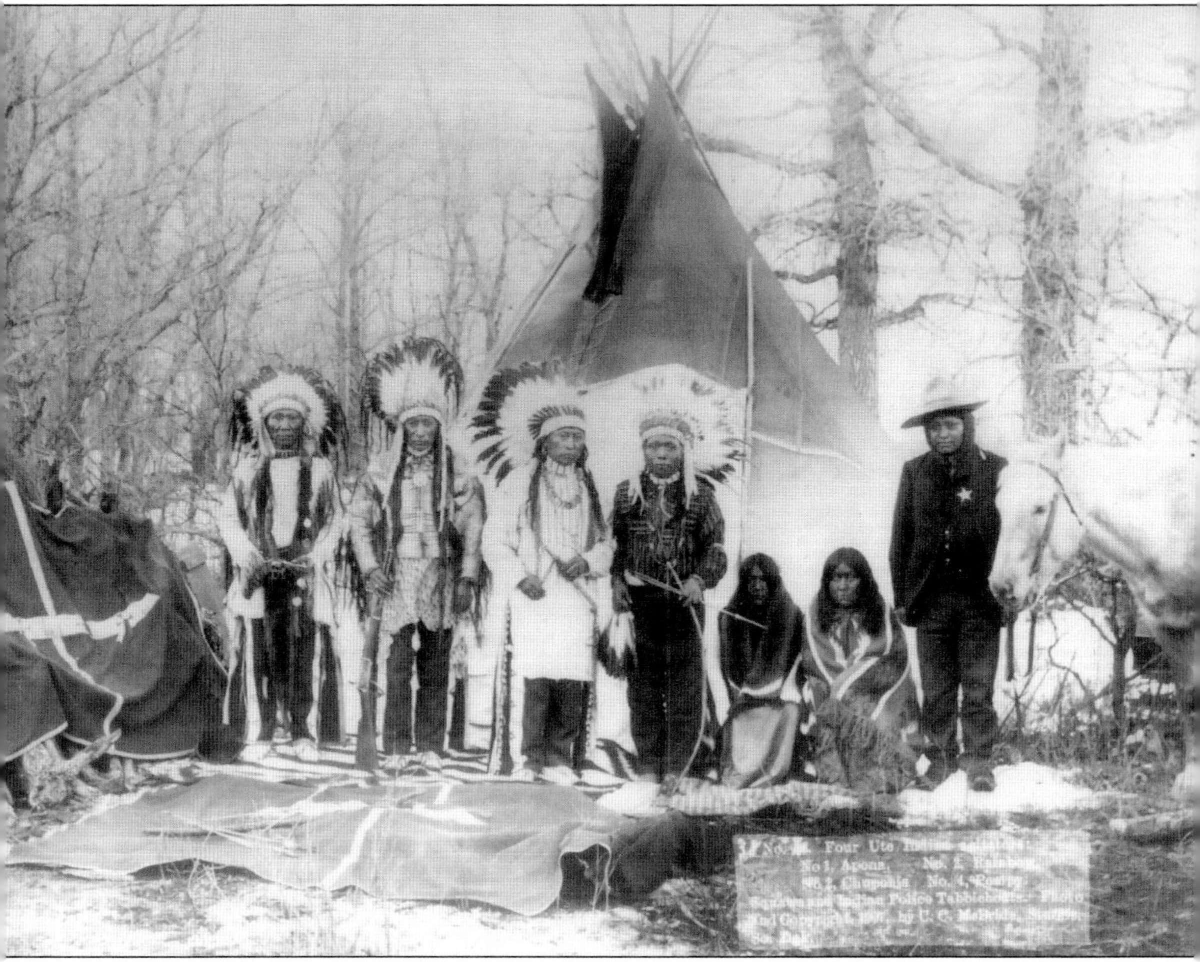

This picture of Ute Indians was taken near Fort Meade by C. C McBride in 1907. Pictured at left (standing) are Apona, Chuponis, Rainbow, and Pompy. The Indian policeman Tabbichoats is at far right. In 1906–1907, the Ute Indians left Utah, dissatisfied with U.S. Indian policy. When they arrived in South Dakota, they camped on Alkali Creek near Fort Meade and later, in 1907, requested a transfer to Thunder Butte, where they lived. (Courtesy of Donovin Sprague.)

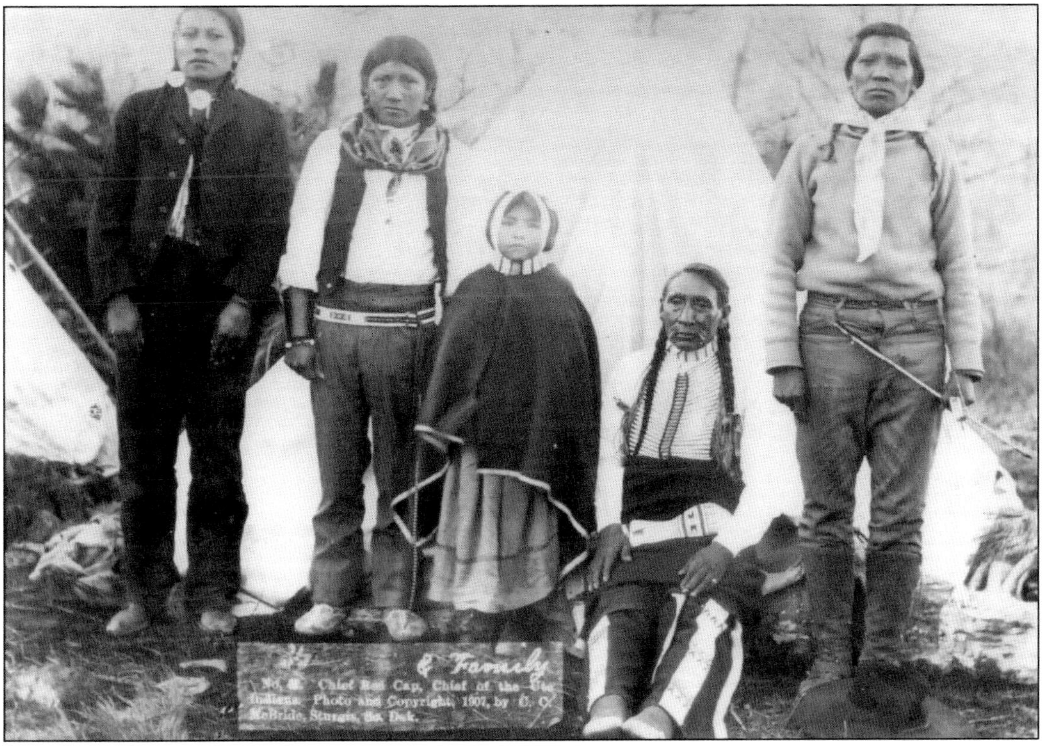

This photograph of Chief Red Cap (seated) and his family was taken near Fort Meade prior to them relocating to Thunder Butte. The author provided a sacred tour to Ute descendants in April 2007 and introduced the Utes to the community of Thunder Butte. The community came out for this historical meeting on the 100th anniversary of this event. The 2007 Ute visitors were descendants of the 1907 tribal members. (Courtesy of Donovin Sprague.)

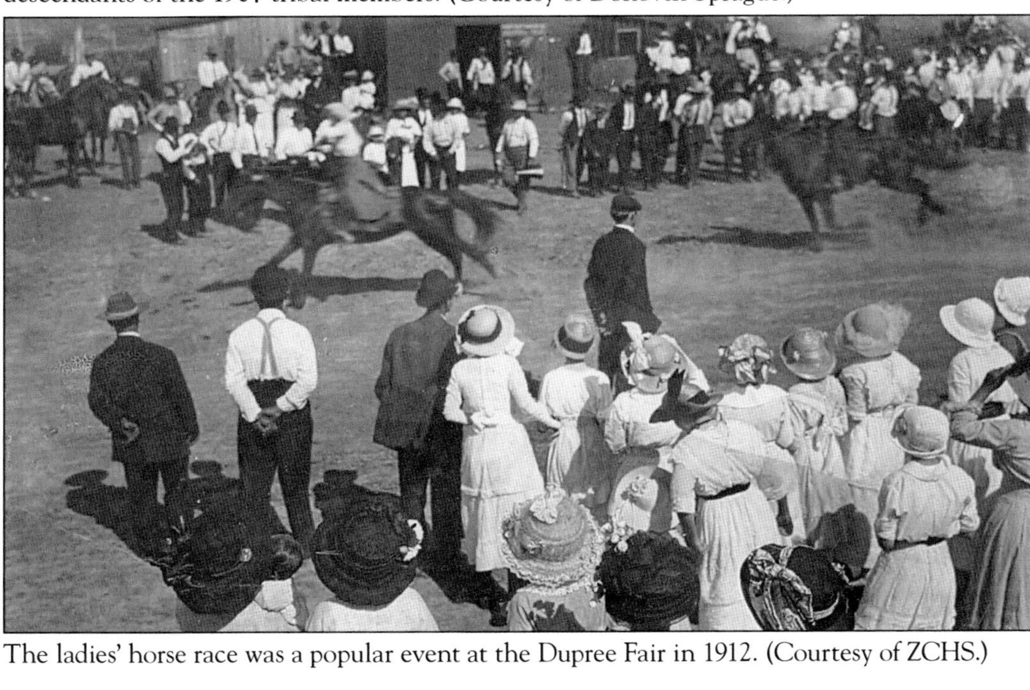

The ladies' horse race was a popular event at the Dupree Fair in 1912. (Courtesy of ZCHS.)

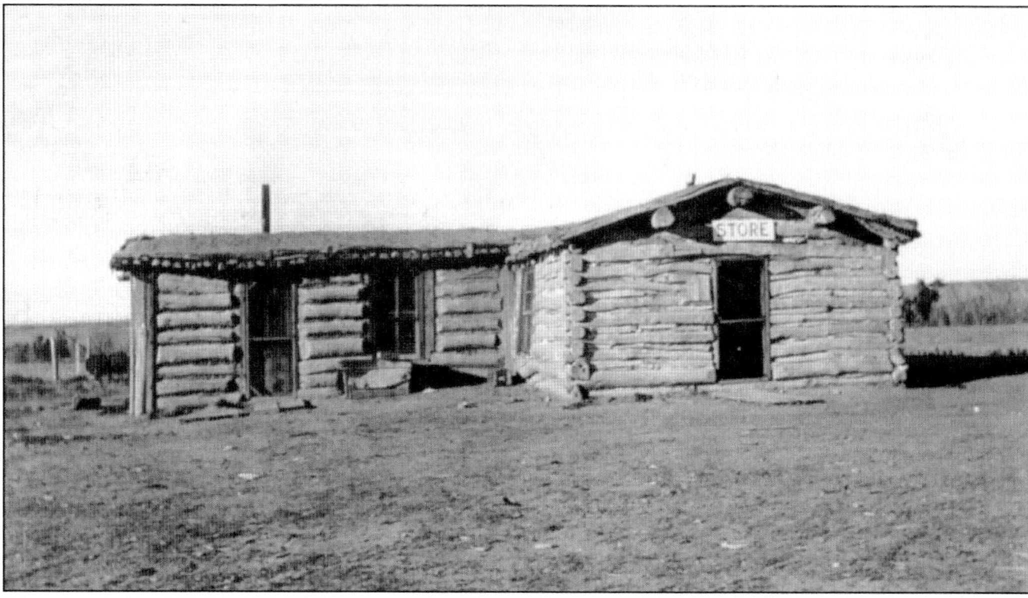

This log cabin store, opened by George J. Unterseher in 1916, is believed to have been north of Thunder Butte Station on the south side of the river. His daughter Freida was the main clerk and had mastered the Lakota language in 1922. (Courtesy of Calvin Unterseher.)

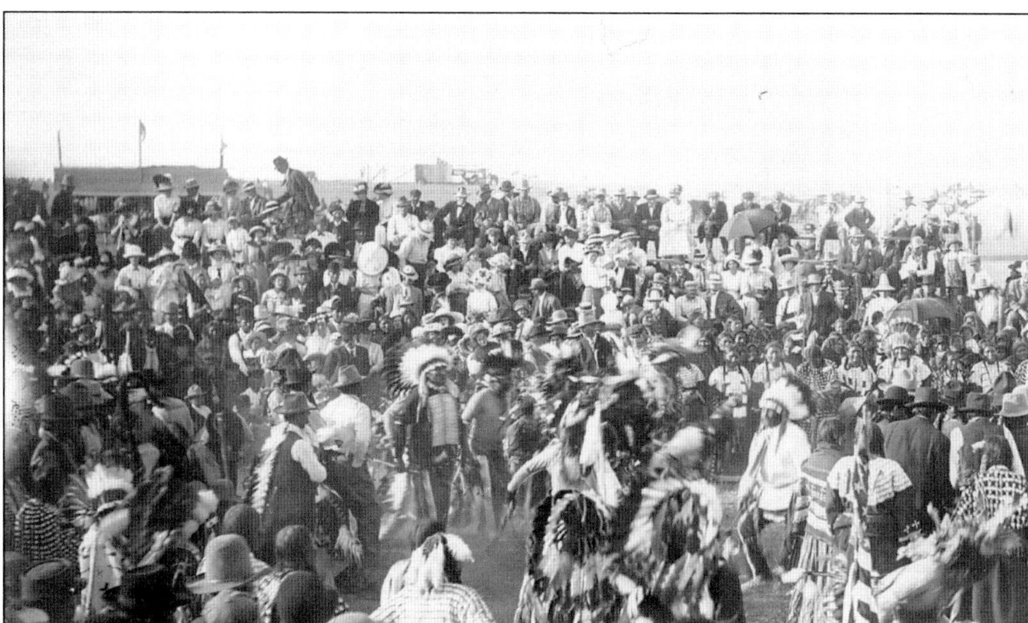

A large number of spectators and Lakota dancers are in attendance at the Cheyenne River Indian Fair in Dupree. (Courtesy of ZCHS/Virginia Woodward.)

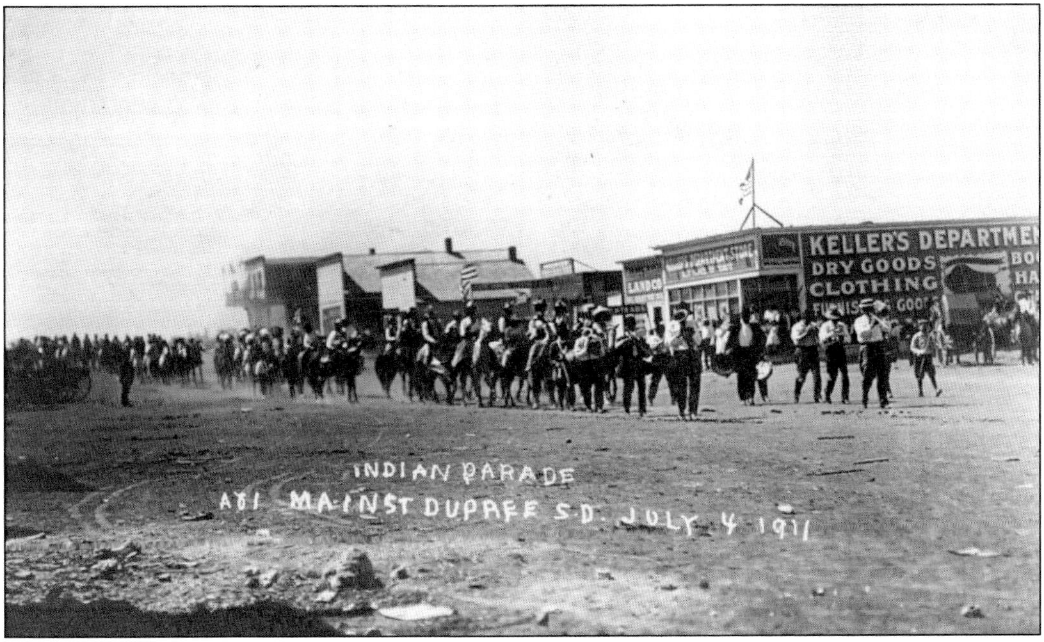

A large parade has been assembled for the July 4, 1911, celebration. A marching band, followed by cowboys and Lakotas, heads down Main Street in Dupree. (Courtesy of ZCHS.)

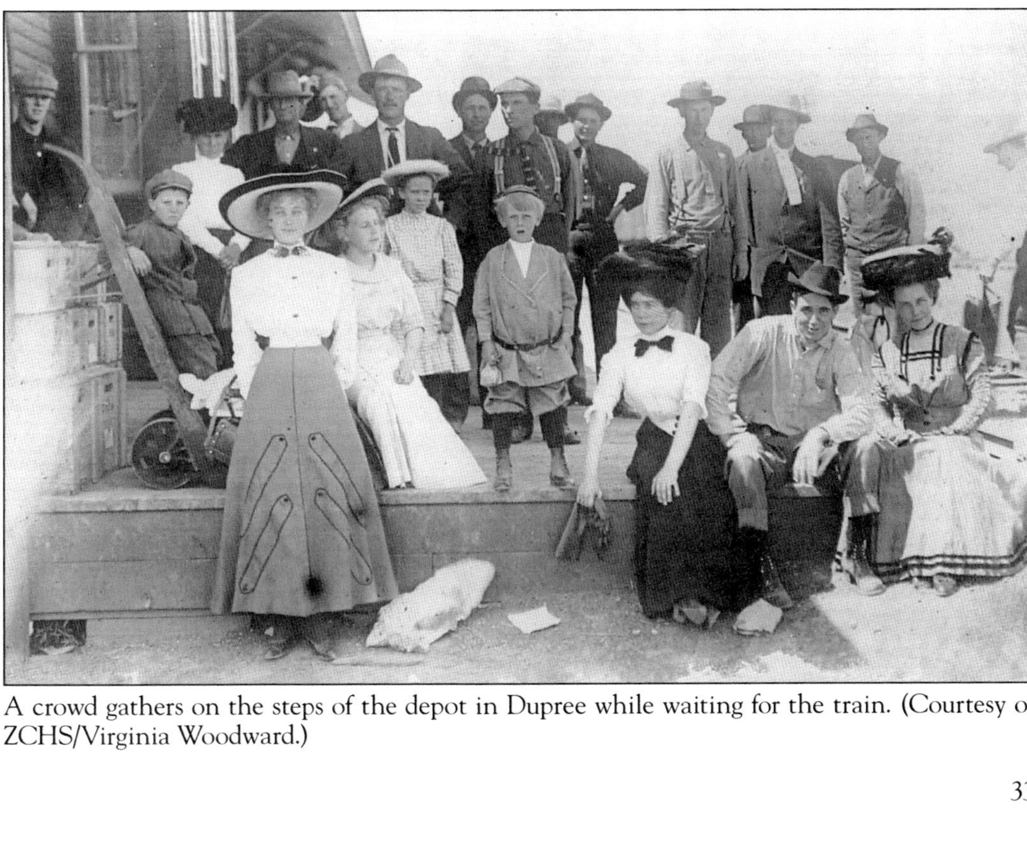

A crowd gathers on the steps of the depot in Dupree while waiting for the train. (Courtesy of ZCHS/Virginia Woodward.)

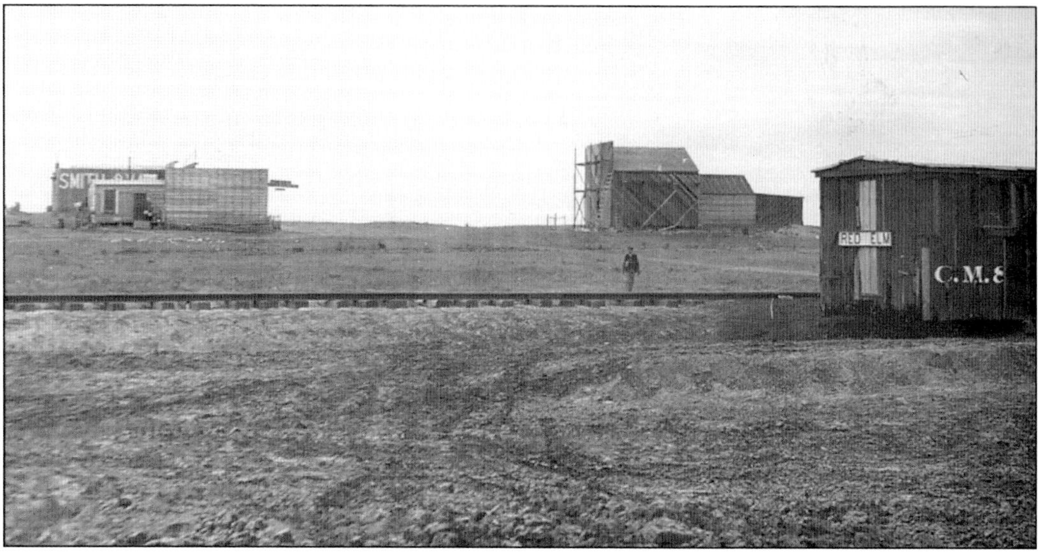

This is Red Elm, South Dakota. When the railroad reached this point, it was decided to build a town at this location. In partial view at left is the Smith Store, which became Smith and Vance. In 1912, Burt Smith's store and post office burned down, and L. O. Adams took over the post office until 1927, when he sold it and went into ranching. (Courtesy of ZCHS/Virginia Woodward.)

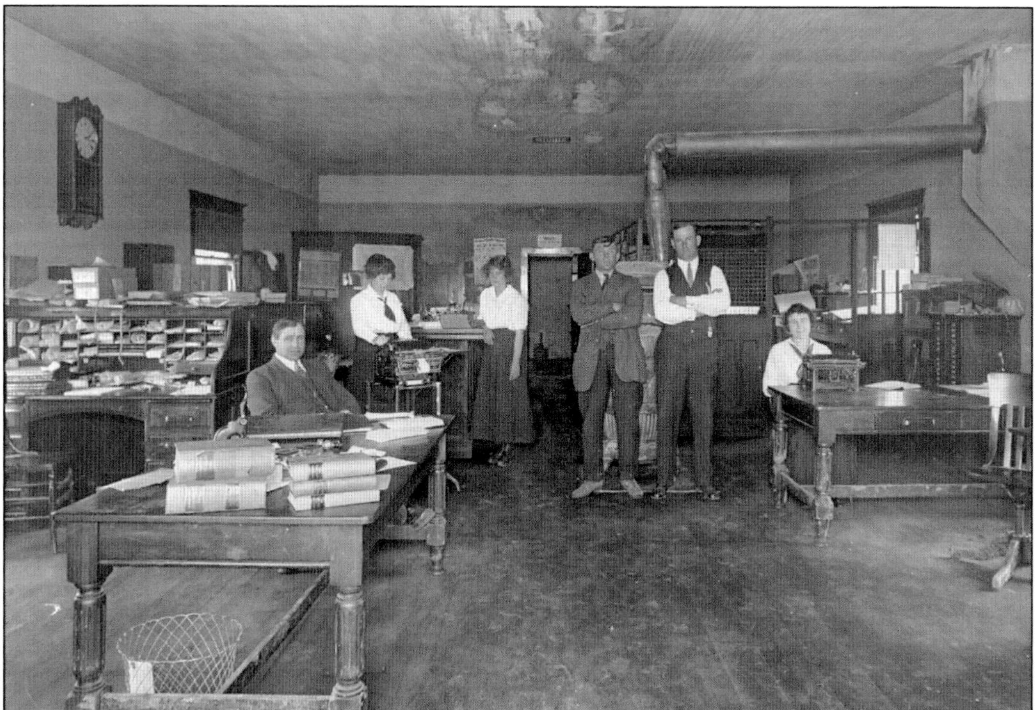

From left to right, Frank W. Ortmayer, Willina Van ?, Alice Birkeland, Louis Speker, Frank Fuller, and Ruth (Dunn) Riley are pictured in the Ziebach County Court House around 1915. Frank and Mattie Ella Ortmayer settled on a quarter section of land northeast of Dupree in 1911, which later became Calvin Anderson's farm. Alice Birkeland married Omar Vance, who was a barber. (Courtesy of ZCHS/Bakeberg family.)

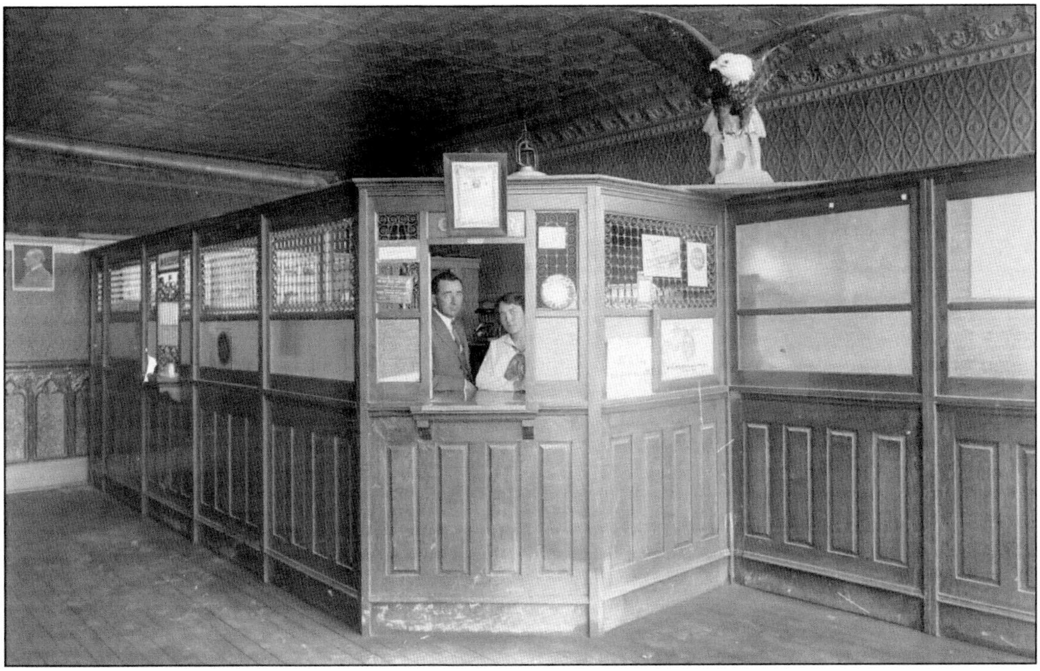

Ruth Doud Dunn Riley and Wilbur Scott are pictured at the Dupree Bank around 1915 or 1916. (Courtesy of ZCHS/Virginia Woodward.)

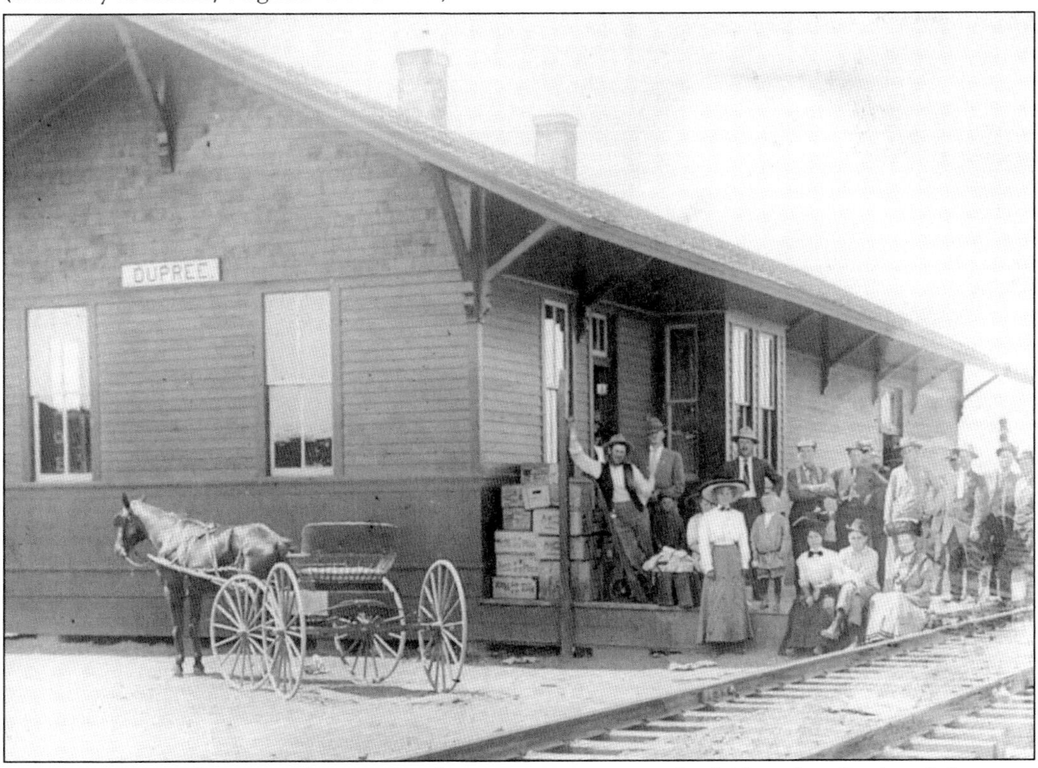

Family and friends anxiously wait for the train to arrive at the Milwaukee Railroad depot in Dupree. (Courtesy of ZCHS/Virginia Woodward.)

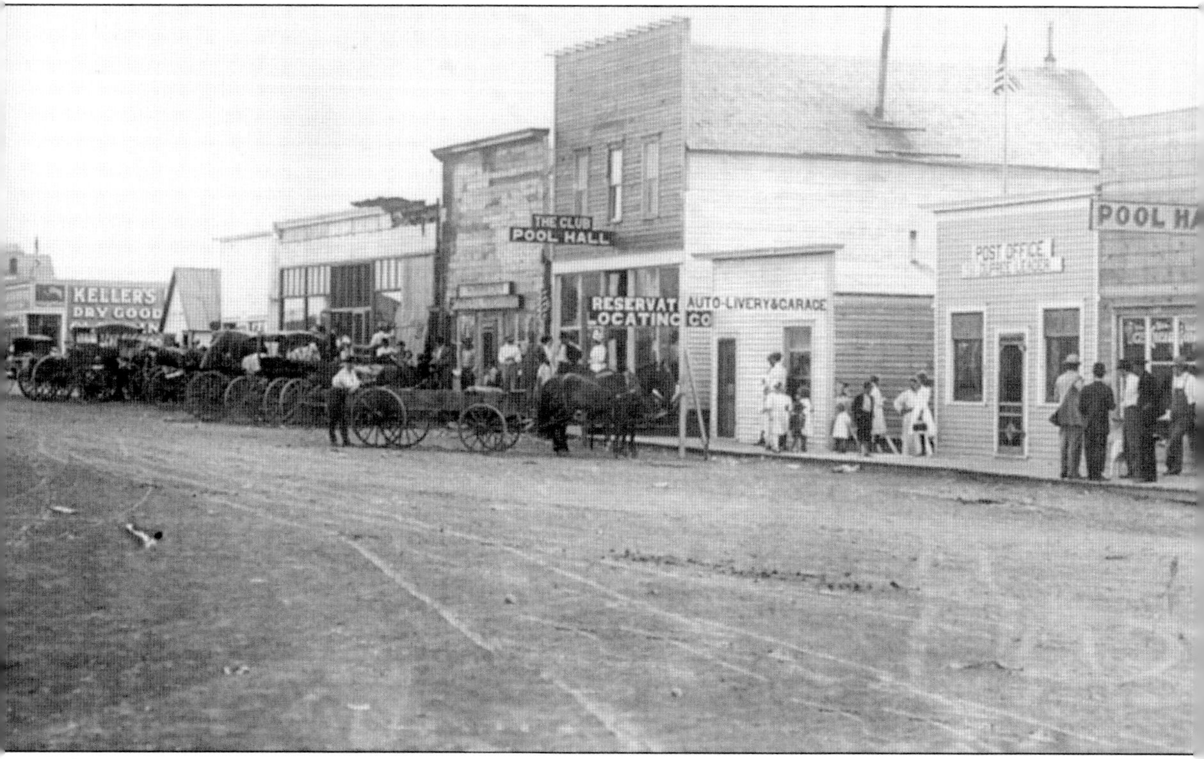

The west side of Dupree's Main Street is pictured sometime before 1916. Several buggies have gathered in town for a social occasion. Several of these buildings later burned in the worst fire Dupree has ever known. The fire began in the basement of the Club Pool Hall during a blizzard, and an entire city block was razed, burning seven businesses to the ground in less than two hours. (Courtesy of ZCHS/Virginia Woodward.)

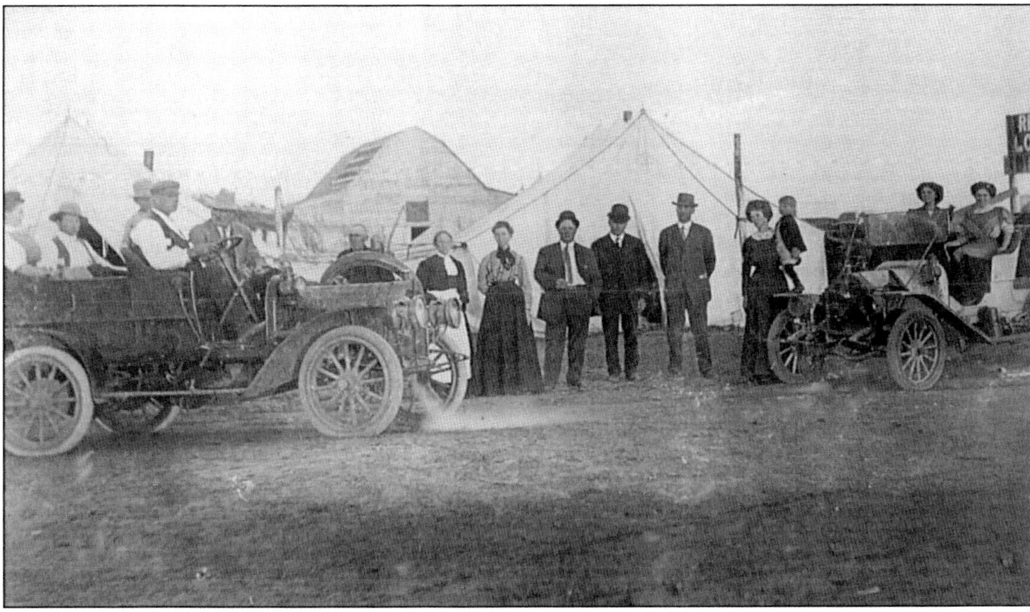

The reservation land locating office is just in view at right in this early picture of Dupree. (Courtesy of Irean Jordan.)

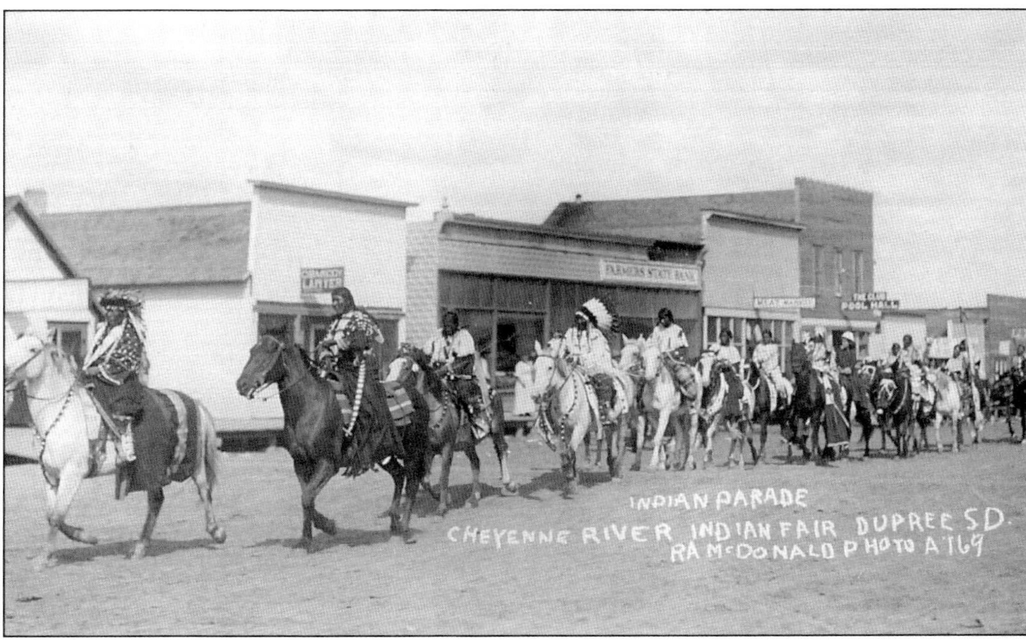

The Cheyenne River Indian Fair parade in Dupree is seen in this photograph by R. A. McDonald. The Main Street buildings in this photograph include, from left to right, a tailor shop, C. B. McCoy's law office, Farmers State Bank, a meat market, the Club Pool Hall, and another pool hall. (Courtesy of Thelma Frame.)

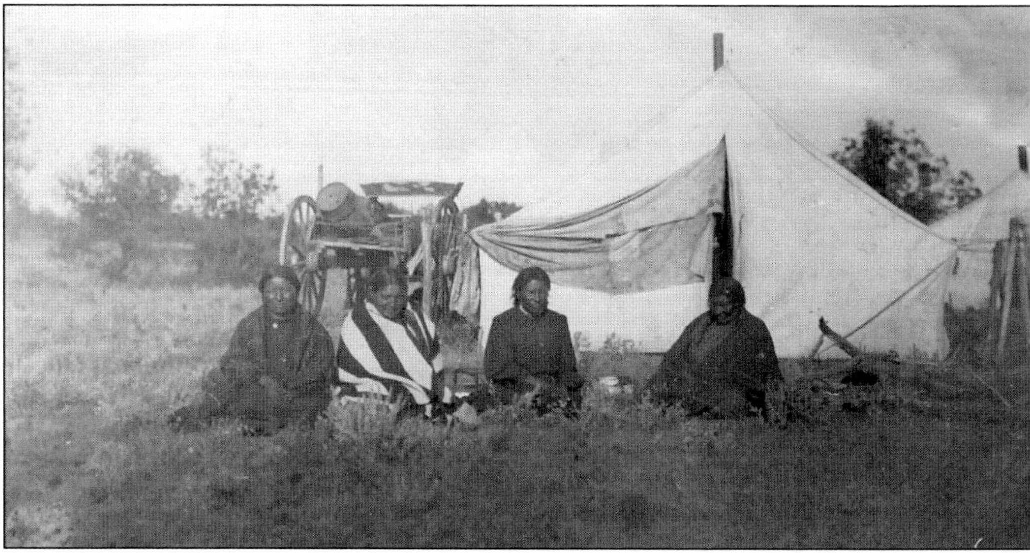

Unidentified Lakotas are seated in front of a tent with a wagon in the background. (Courtesy of ZCHS/Harold and Joan Ross.)

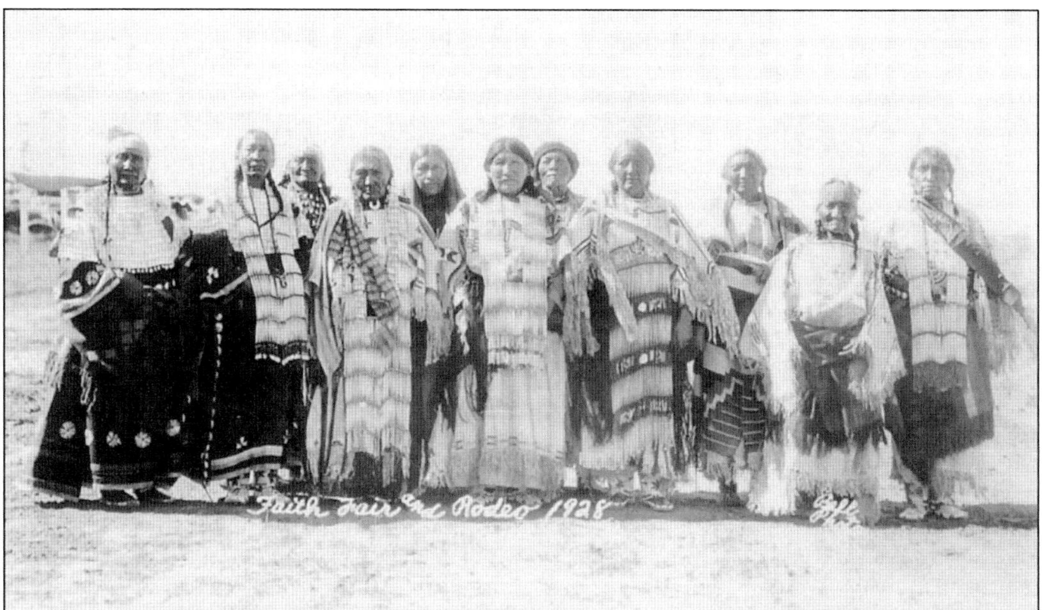

Lakota *winyan* (women) are gathered in 1928 at the fair and rodeo in Faith, South Dakota. From left to right are Mrs. Jessie Iron Hawk, Emily Hunter, Horse Looking, Mrs. Puts on His Shoes, Susie Blue Shield, Mrs. Corn, unidentified, Mrs. Jack Bull Eagle, Mrs. White Bull, Mrs. Buffalo, and Mrs. Shoots Off. (Courtesy of Donovin Sprague and Irean Jordan.)

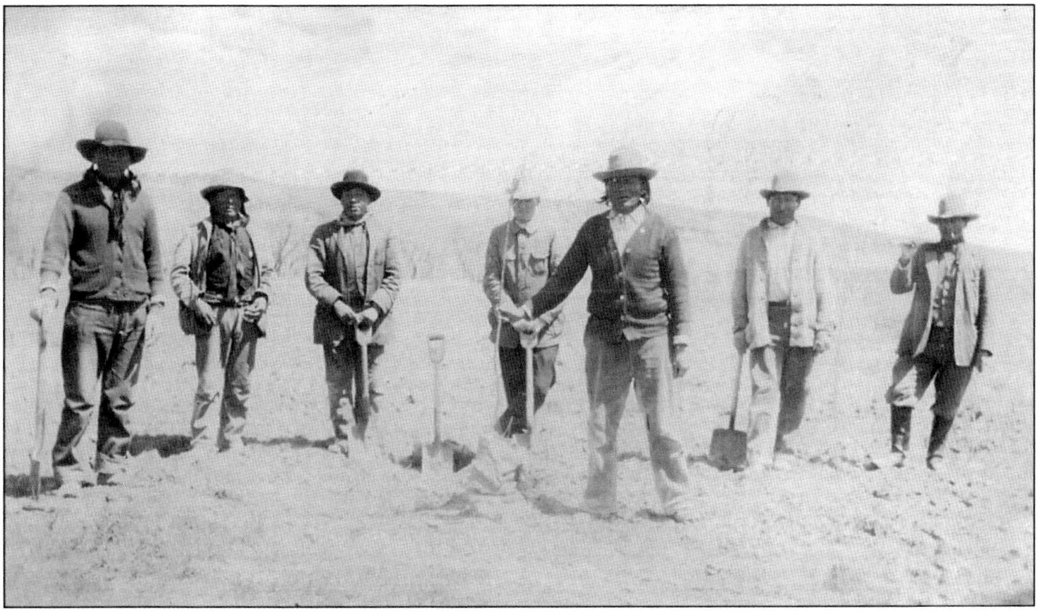

This shows Lakota men with shovels, possibly preparing for a ground breaking. The man with the white hat at center may be a non-Indian agency employee. There is a creek in the background. (Courtesy of ZCHS/Harold and Joan Ross.)

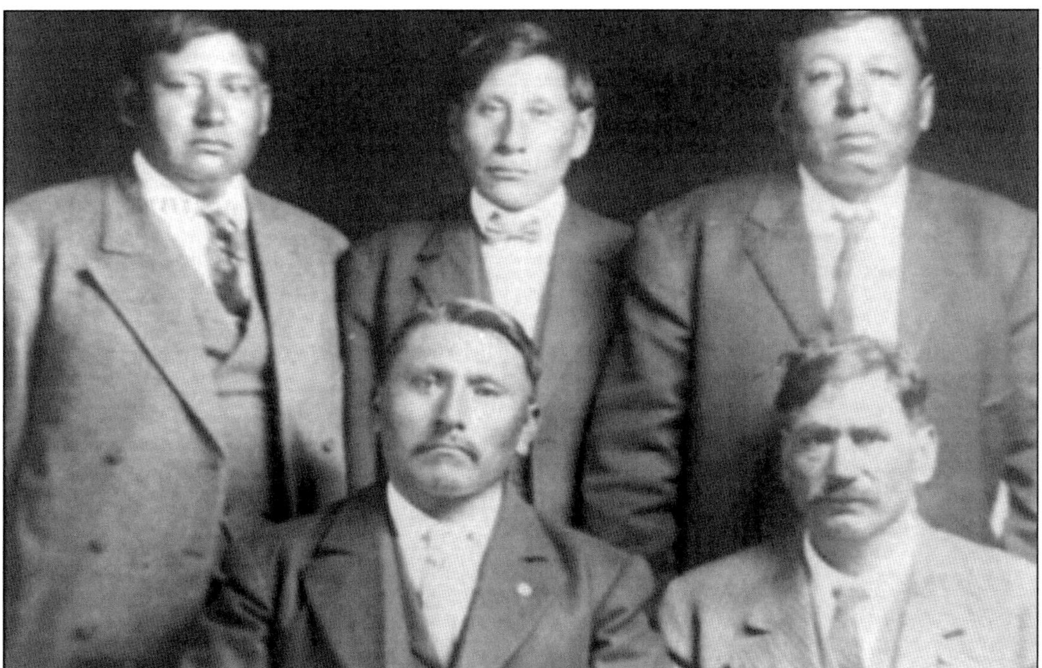

Pictured here are members of a 1912 Cheyenne River Agency delegation to Washington, D.C. From left to right are (first row) Straighthead and Bazille Claymore Jr.; (second row) Jim Swan, Black Eagle, and Ed Swan. (Courtesy of Donovin Sprague.)

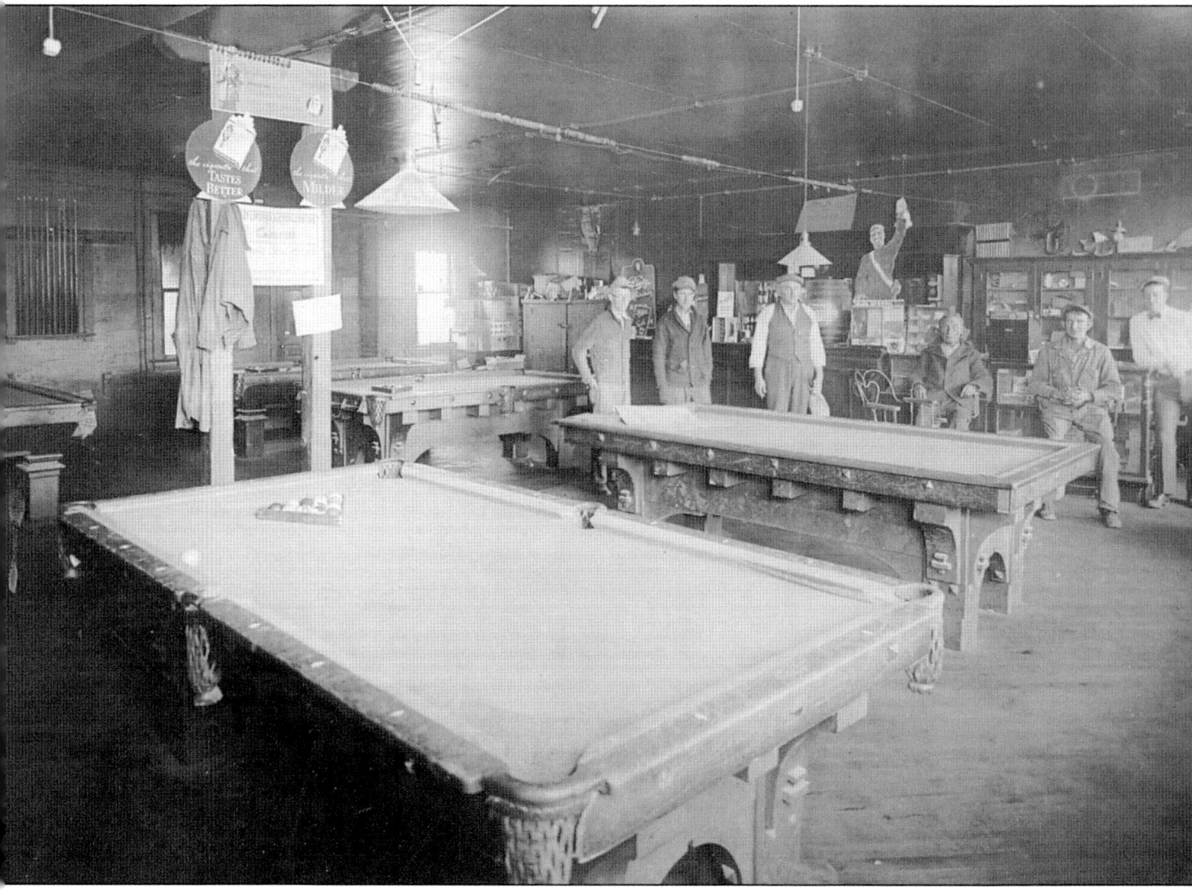

August Bakeburg is pictured in his Dupree pool hall in this photograph taken between 1918 and 1920. He is the third person from the left, wearing a white shirt and dark vest and holding a bank bag. The building was known as the Club Café and Pool Hall. (Courtesy of Bakeberg family.)

A Lakota *winyan* relaxes in a chair while enjoying a smoke with her pipe. (Courtesy of Thelma Frame.)

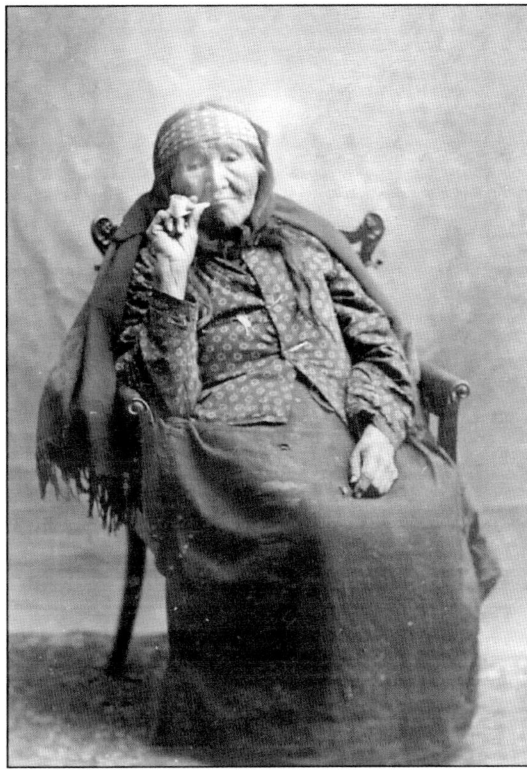

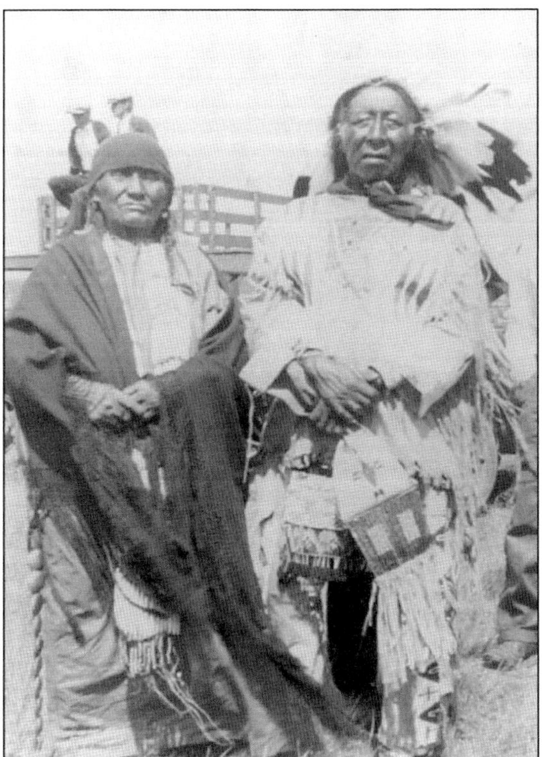

Paul Red Bird and Isabel Her Door, husband and wife, are seen here after providing a demonstration on how to boil meat using a cow stomach and heated rocks. Their family consisted of Moses, William, Mollie, Pretty Buffalo, Charlie, and Richard. Paul's father was (James) Fights the Thunder (1828–1916), who married Pazala/Thin Out/Rail/Rotation. Paul's brother and sister were Amos Clown and (Lucy) Grows in a Day, also known as Mrs. Poor Buffalo. (Courtesy of Carlos Red Legs.)

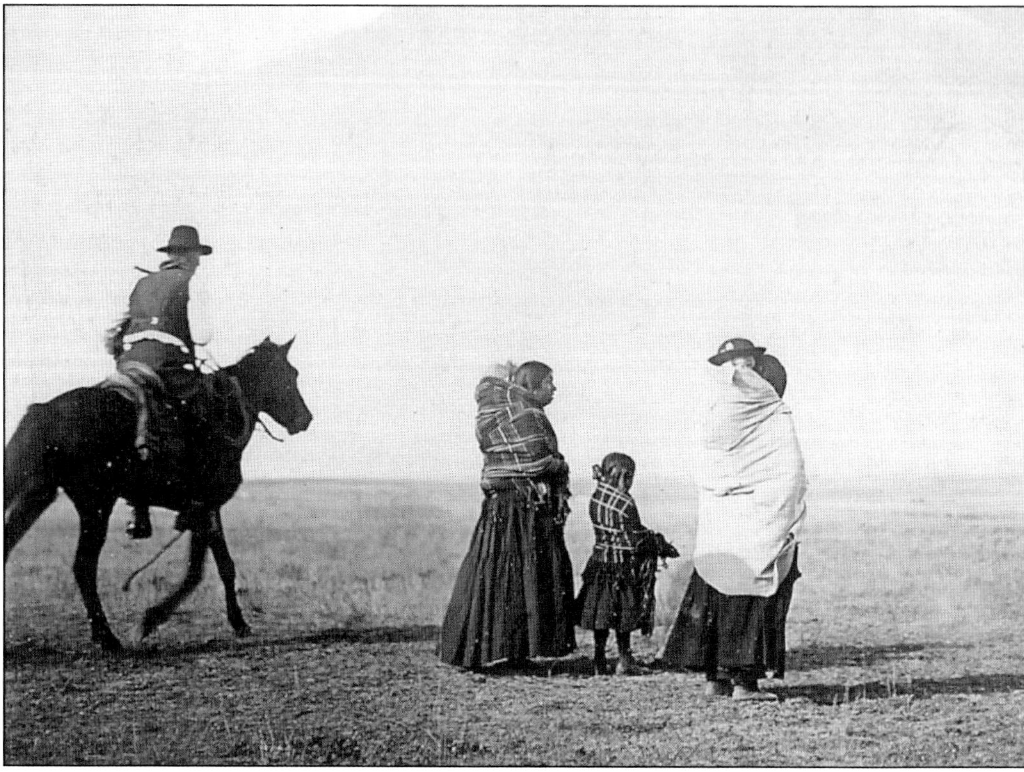

An unidentified Lakota family is pictured here. The women have babies on their back. (Courtesy of ZCHS/Harold and Joan Ross.)

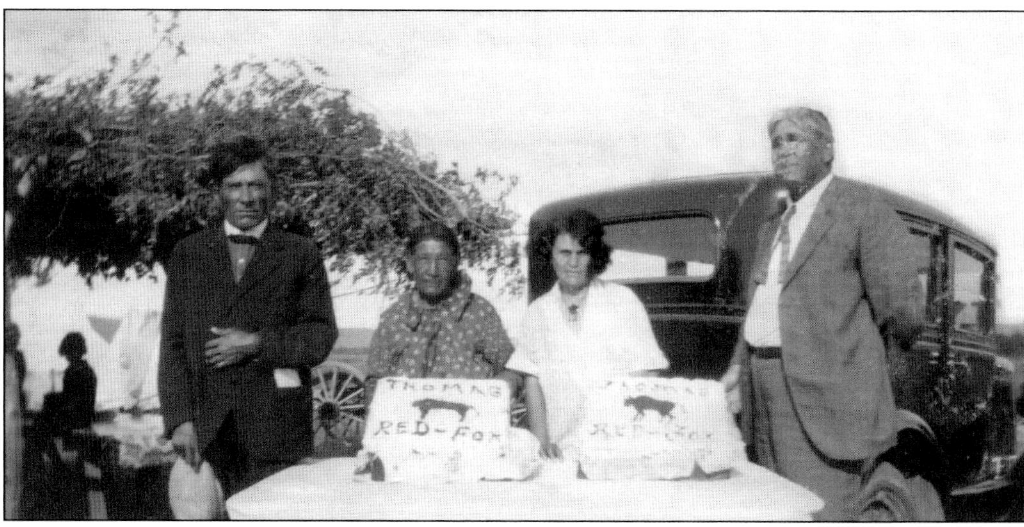

From left to right are Thomas Blue Eyes, Armene Blue Eyes, Lillian Carlin Briggs, and Reverend at a celebration being held for "Thomas Red Fox," another name for Thomas Blue Eyes. (Courtesy of Donovin Sprague.)

Two

The Railroad and Transportation

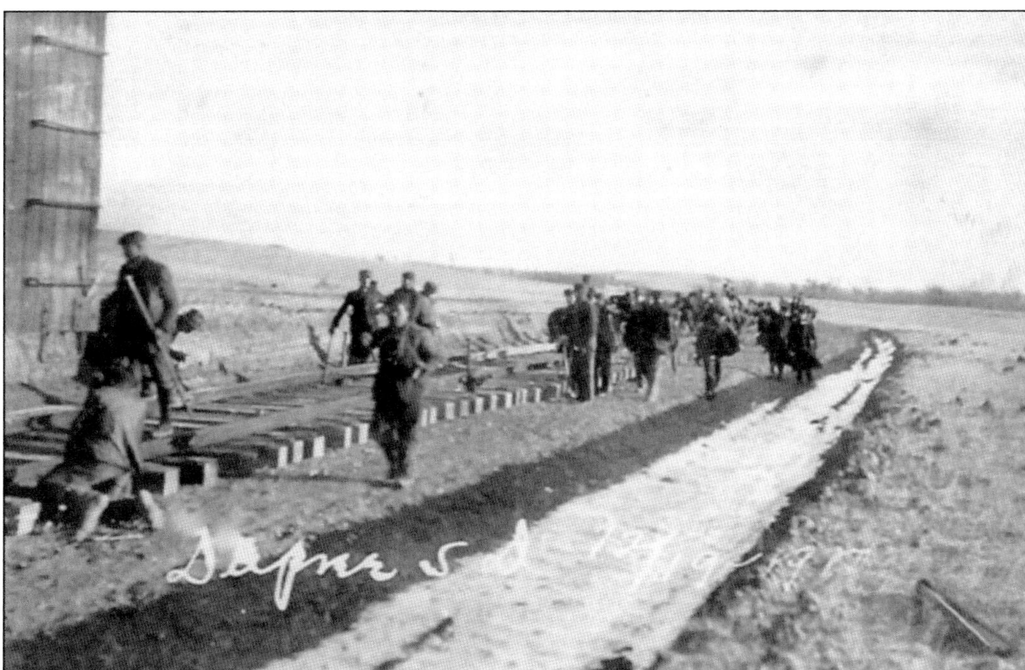

This photograph was taken on December 19, 1910, on a momentous day for Dupree. On that date, the track-laying crew completed the railroad into Dupree and the first train arrived. Prior to this, freight came overland by wagon teams from Evarts, LeBeau, Isabel, and Eagle Butte. Missing from this photograph is the snow so typical of South Dakota in December. (Courtesy of Irean Jordan.)

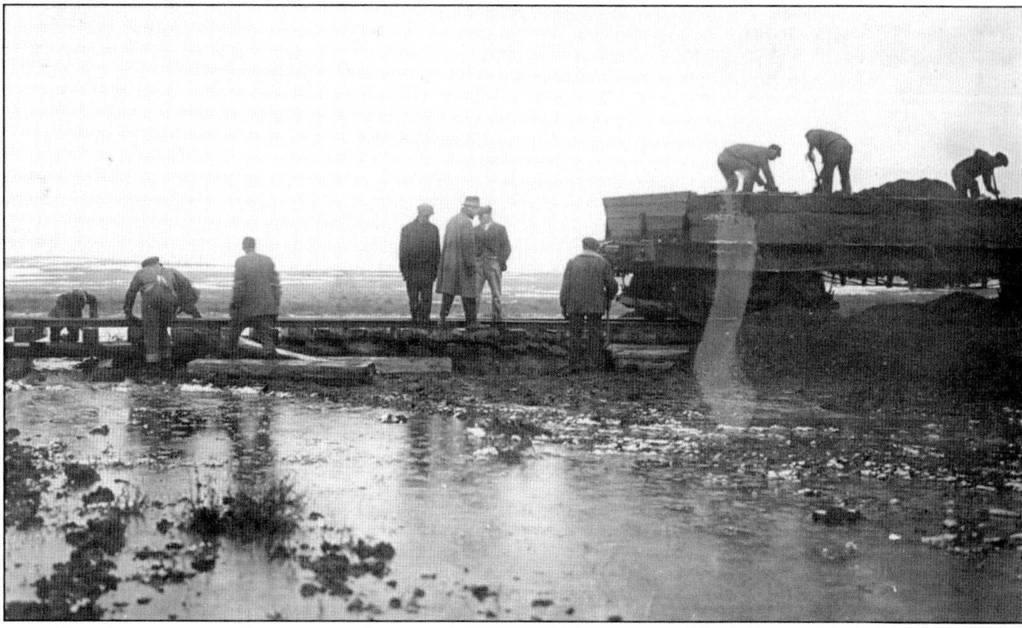

A railroad crew near Dupree works on a section of the railroad track. There appears to be an abundance of water from a rainstorm or melting of snow. (Courtesy of Irean Jordan.)

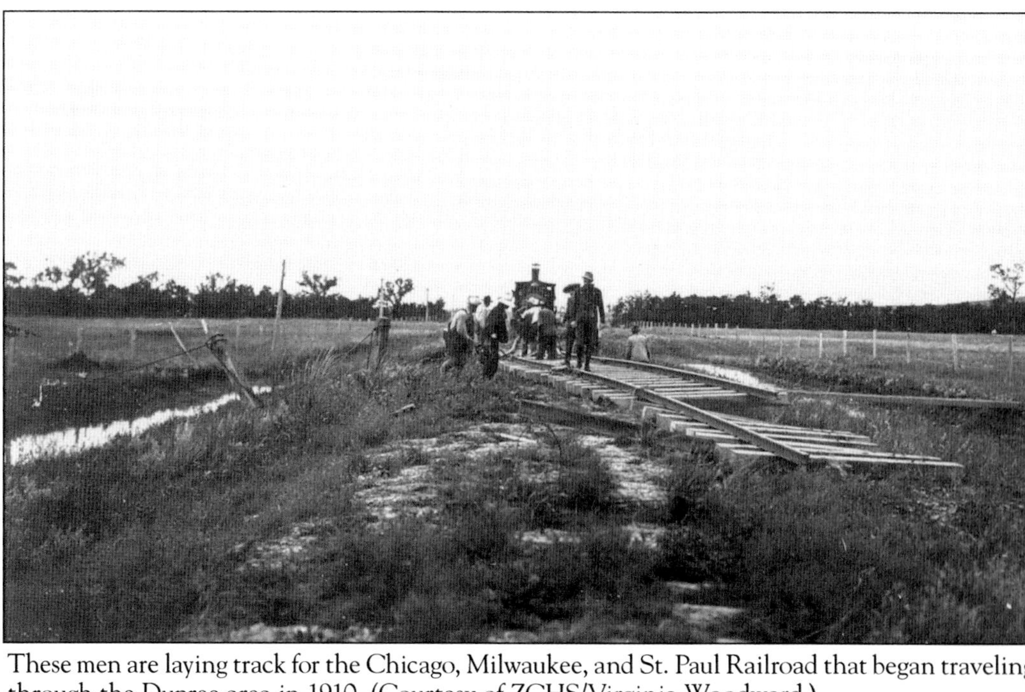

These men are laying track for the Chicago, Milwaukee, and St. Paul Railroad that began traveling through the Dupree area in 1910. (Courtesy of ZCHS/Virginia Woodward.)

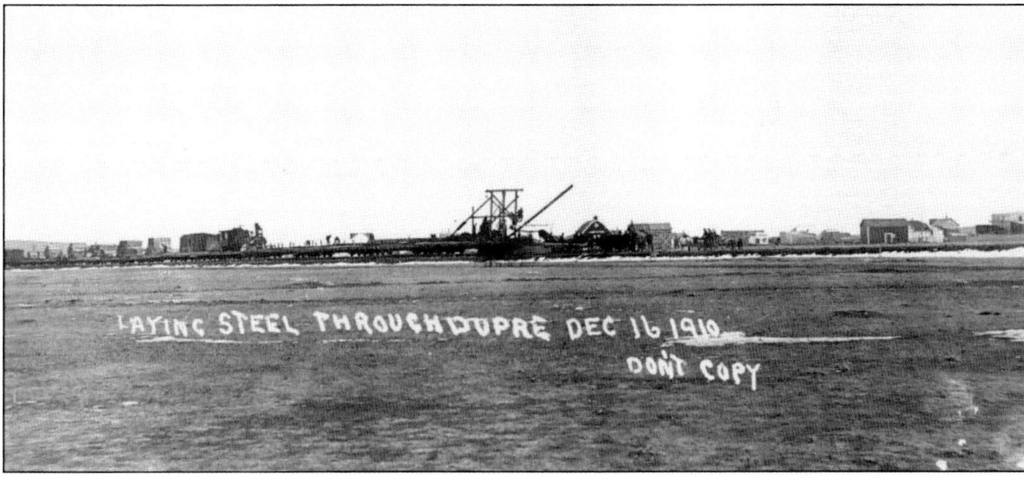

The railroad crew is laying steel through Dupree on December 16, 1910, shortly before completing the railway. (Courtesy of ZCHS/Virginia Woodward.)

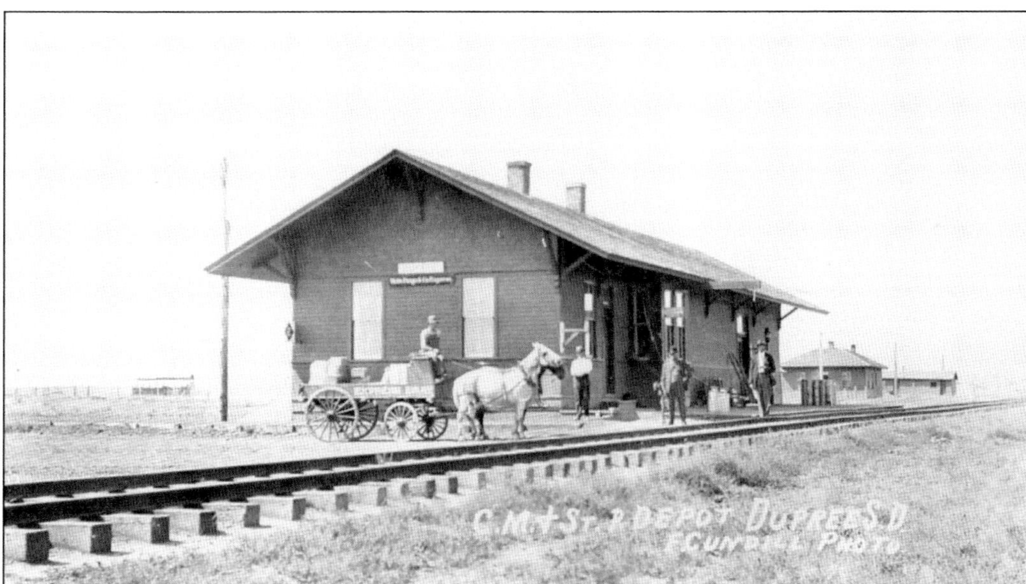

The Chicago, Milwaukee, and St. Paul Railroad depot in Dupree, seen in this photograph by Frank Cundill, was commonly called the Milwaukee Railroad depot. Wagons were used to deliver the freight. (Courtesy of ZCHS/Virginia Woodward.)

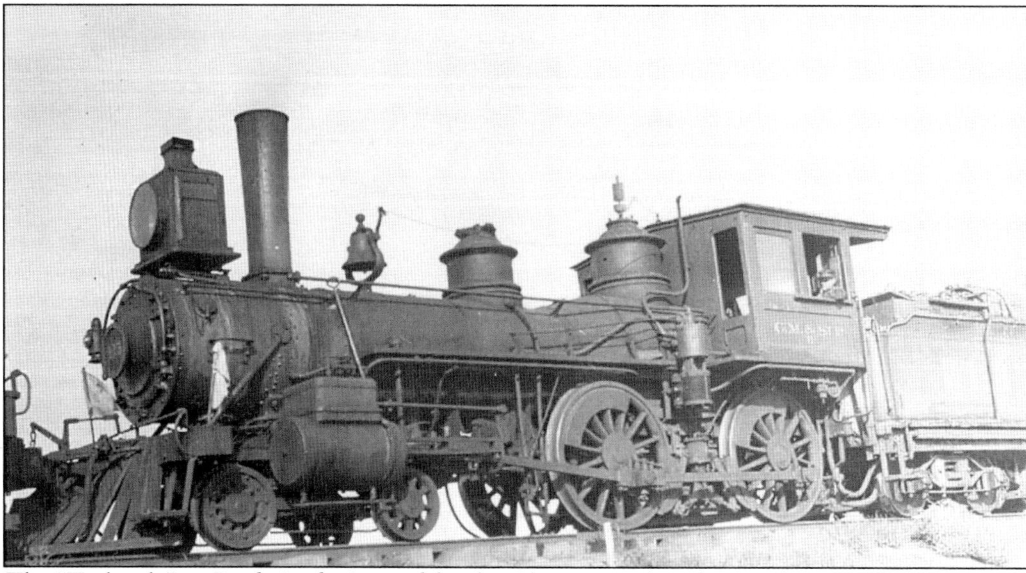

The "Teakettle" or *Rattle Snake Limited* for the Chicago, Milwaukee, and St. Paul Railroad is on the tracks. (Courtesy of ZCHS/Virginia Woodward.)

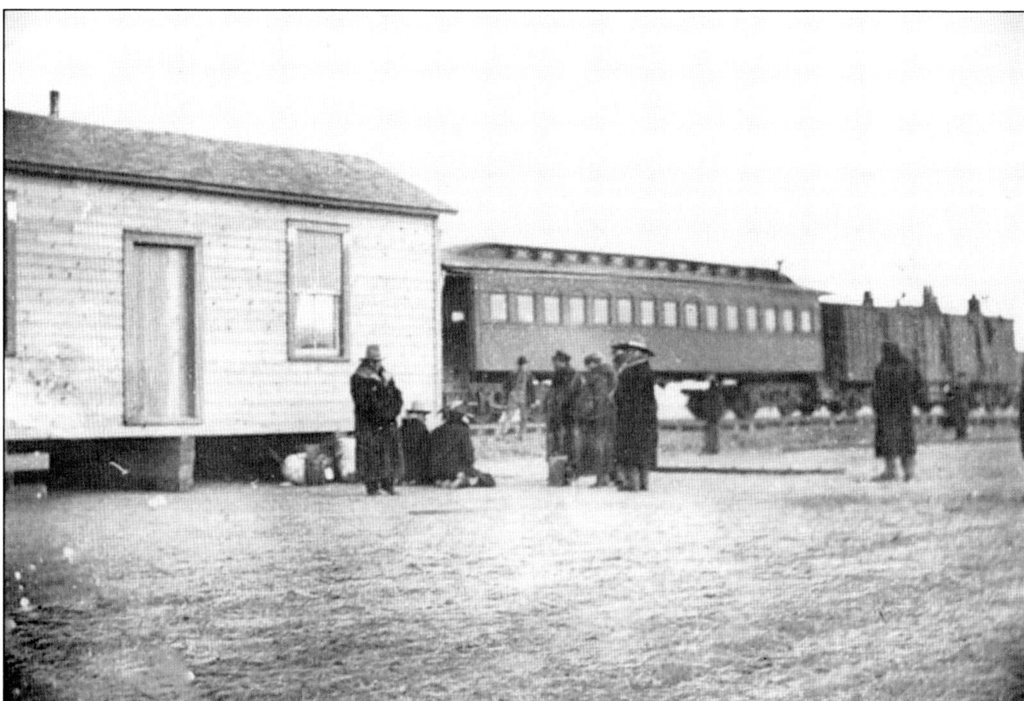

The first depot in Dupree was a busy place when the settlers gathered to meet the train. They were attired in their Sunday best and enjoyed visiting with each other while waiting. (Courtesy of ZCHS/Virginia Woodward.)

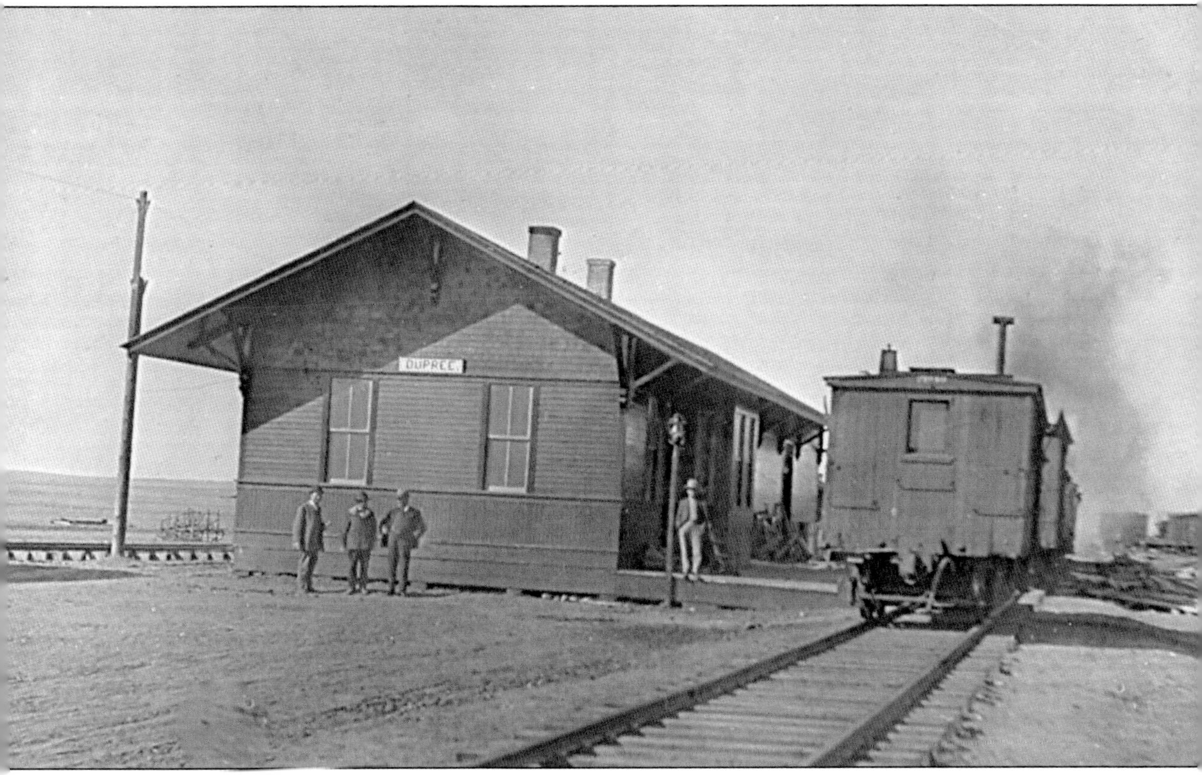

A train arrives at the Milwaukee Railroad depot in Dupree in 1910. (Courtesy of ZCHS/ Virginia Woodward.)

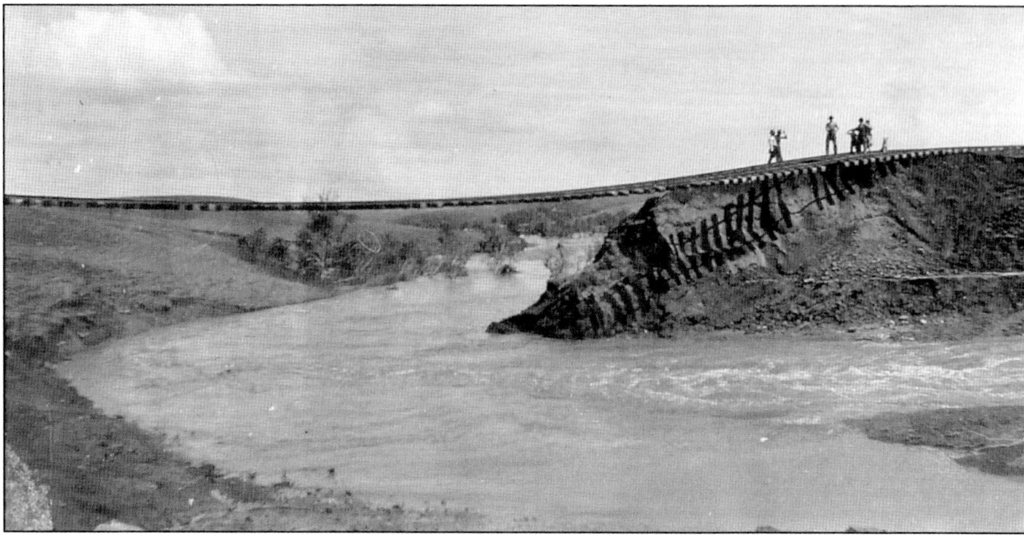

The railroad tracks are about to be laid across this waterway. No bridge or supporting posts have been built yet. (Courtesy of ZCHS/Harold and Joan Ross.)

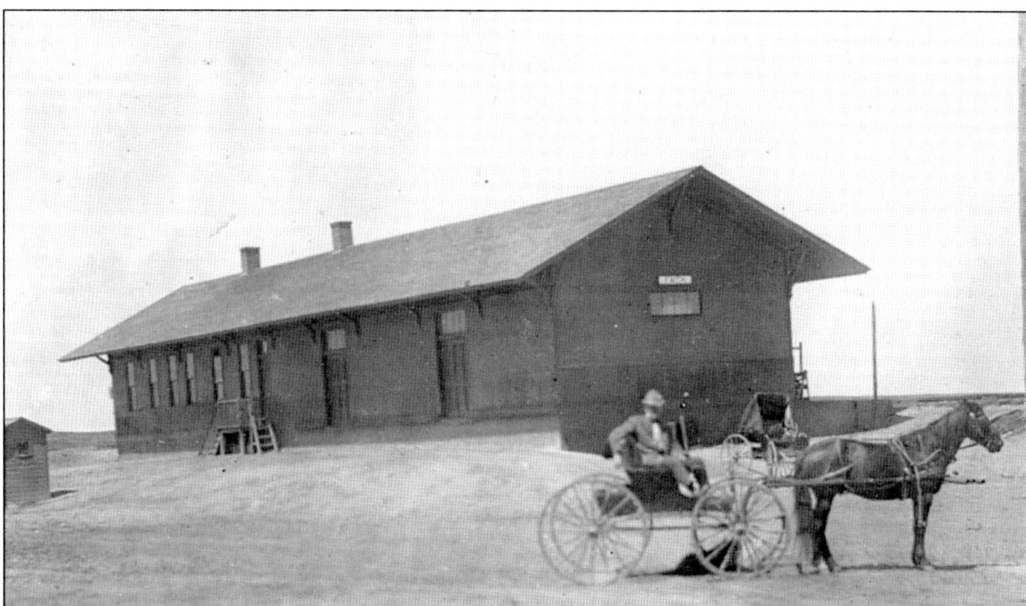

This man waits with his horse and buggy at the railroad depot. Perhaps they are waiting for a lovely lady! (Courtesy of ZCHS/Virginia Woodward.)

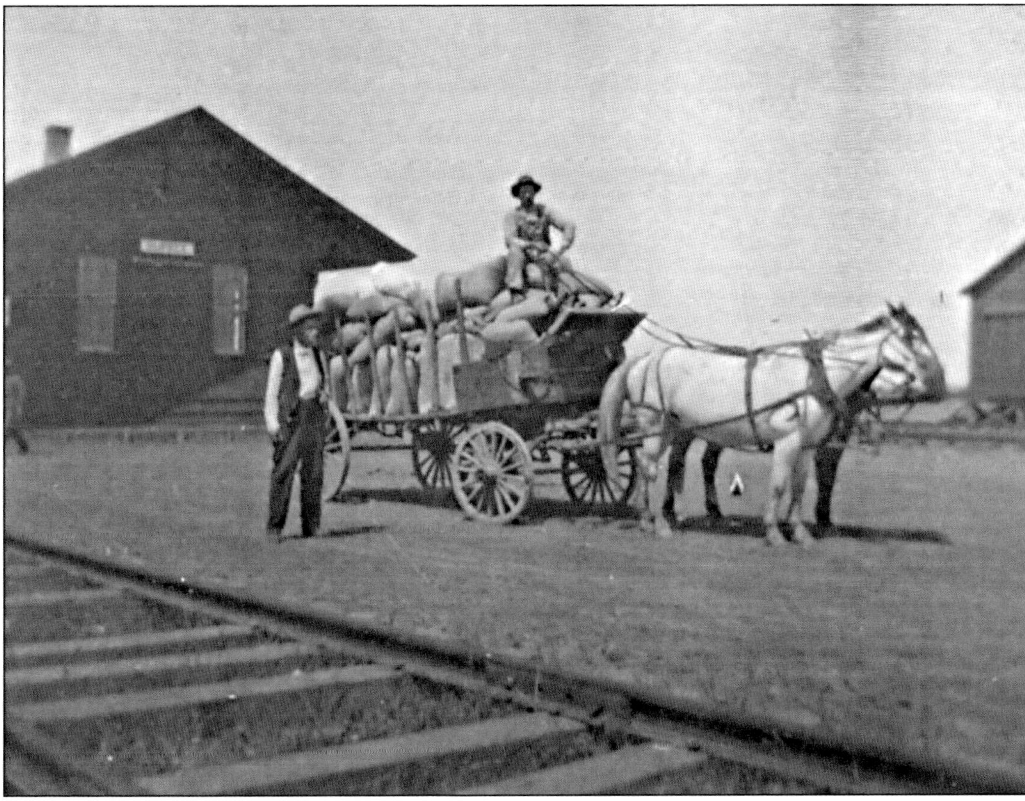

This wagon driver has his day's work cut out for him with such a huge load of freight to be delivered. (Courtesy of ZCHS/Virginia Woodward.)

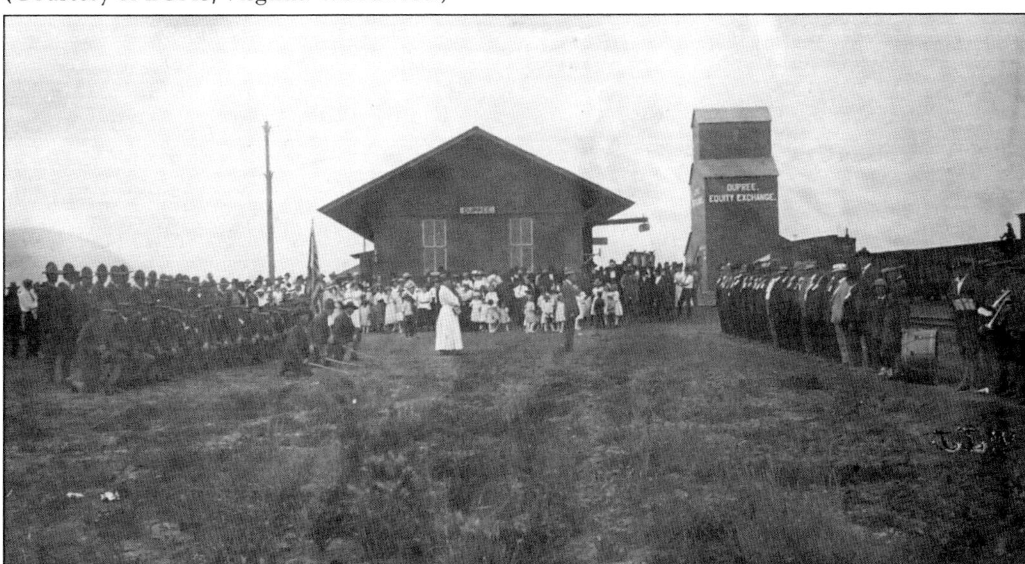

When the soldiers left for military service, the whole town would gather, including the schoolchildren and the small town band. This photograph was taken in 1916 or 1917. (Courtesy of ZCHS/Virginia Woodward.)

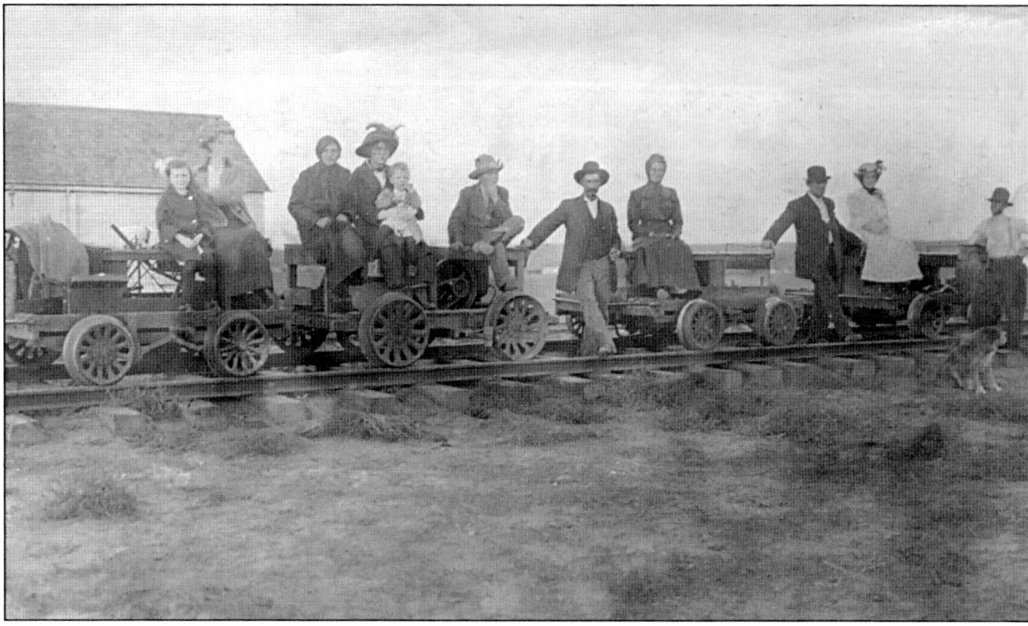

Dupree pioneers are dressed up in their Sunday best, posing on the railroad section cars. (Courtesy of ZCHS/Harold and Joan Ross.)

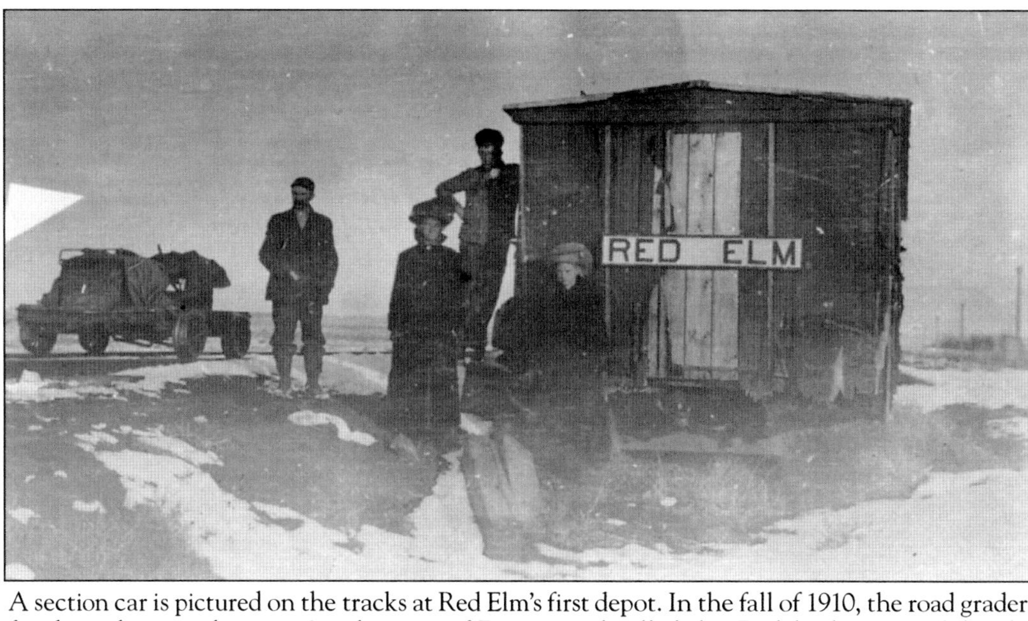

A section car is pictured on the tracks at Red Elm's first depot. In the fall of 1910, the road graders for the railway made camp 9 miles west of Dupree and called this Redelm because of the elm trees. Jake Nelson started the first lumberyard, and Burt Smith built the first general store. Later L. O. Adams built a general store. (Courtesy of ZCHS/Virginia Woodward.)

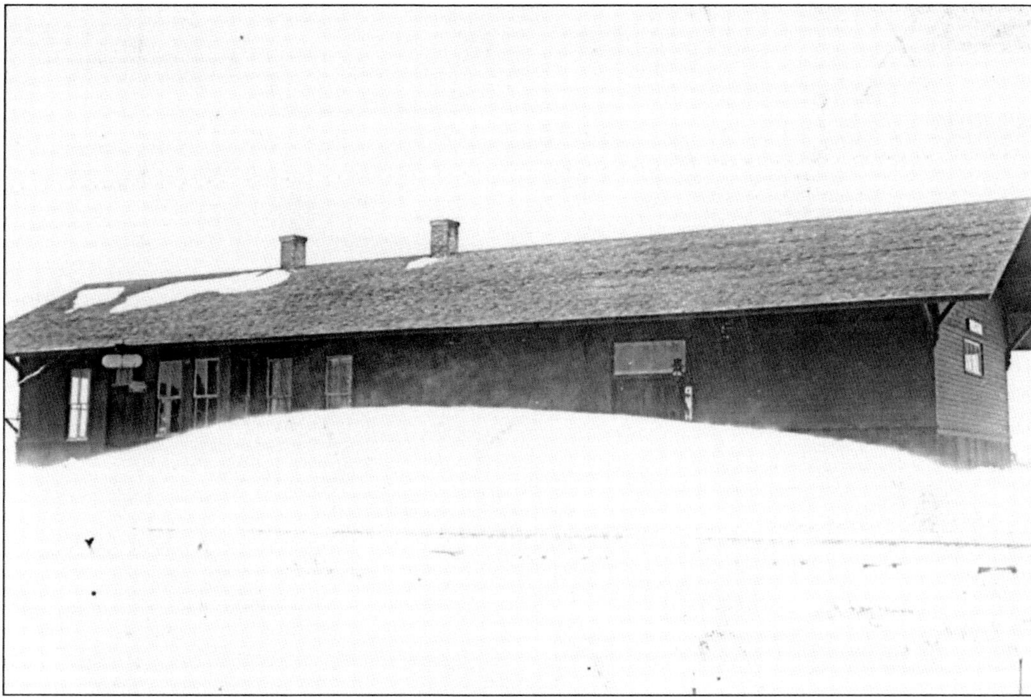

A winter snow covers the tracks on the south side of the railroad depot in Dupree in 1915. (Courtesy of ZCHS/Virginia Woodward.)

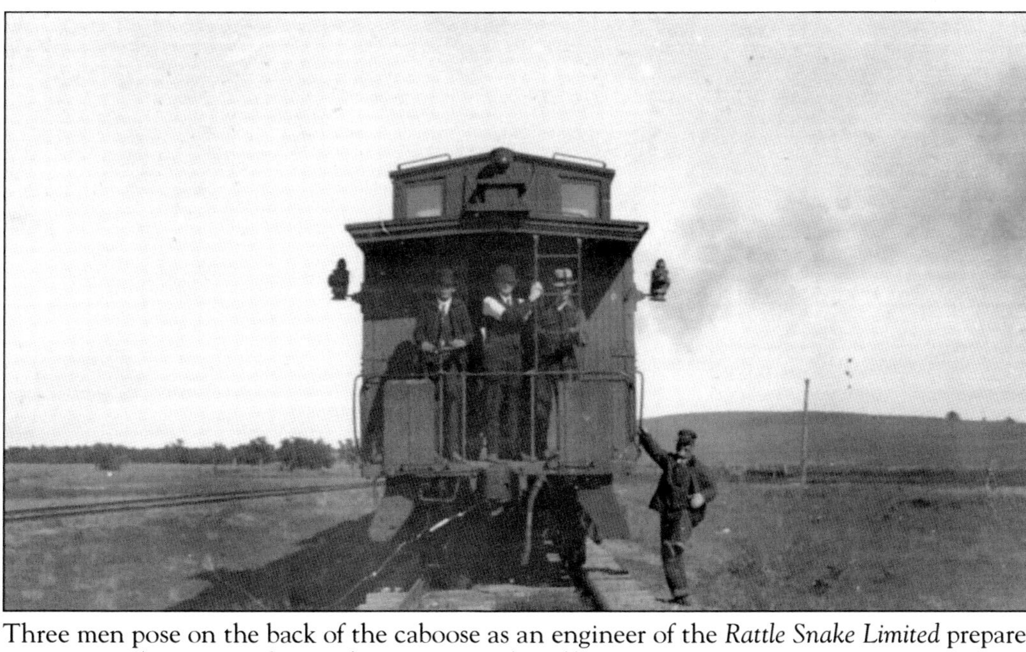

Three men pose on the back of the caboose as an engineer of the *Rattle Snake Limited* prepares to jump on. (Courtesy of ZCHS/Virginia Woodward.)

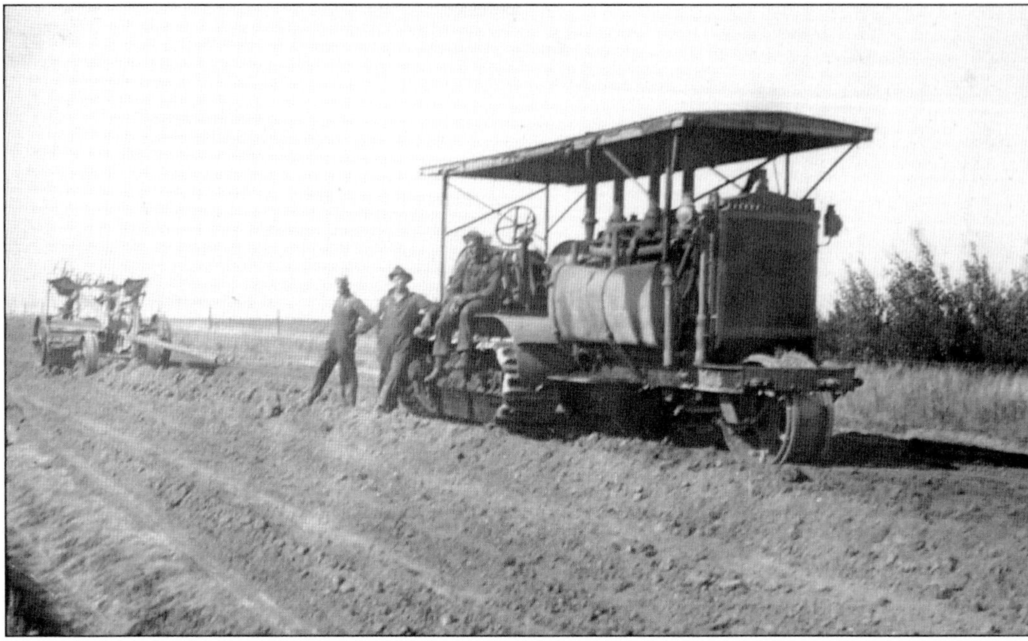

Pictured here is the first caterpillar used in Ziebach County, during the years of 1910–1920. After hours of hard work, the crew took a short break. (Courtesy of ZCHS/Virginia Woodward.)

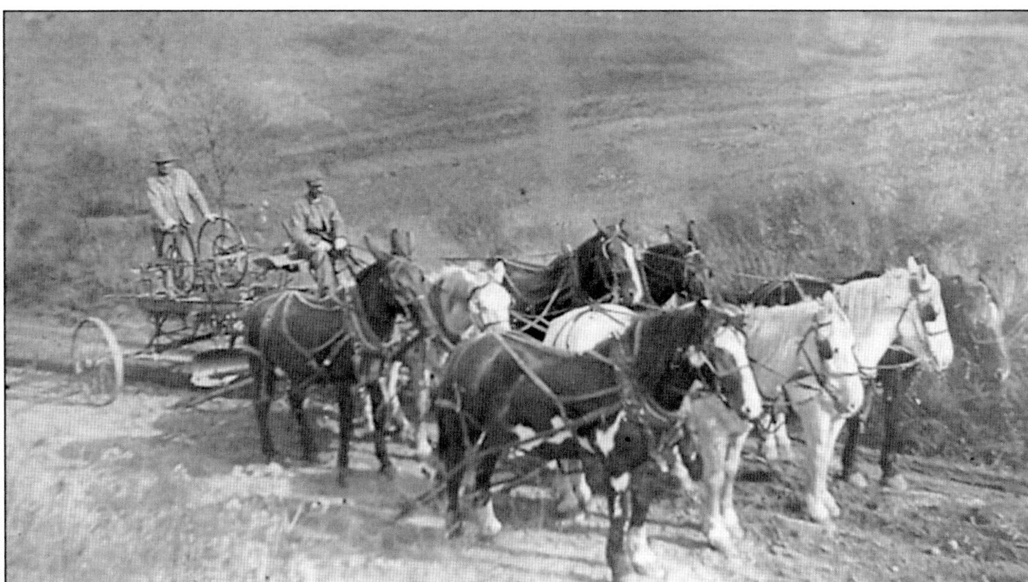

George O'Riley's road crew has a wagon drawn by seven horses and a mule. The man on the front handles the horses while the man on the back of the wagon adjusts the grader. (Courtesy of ZCHS.)

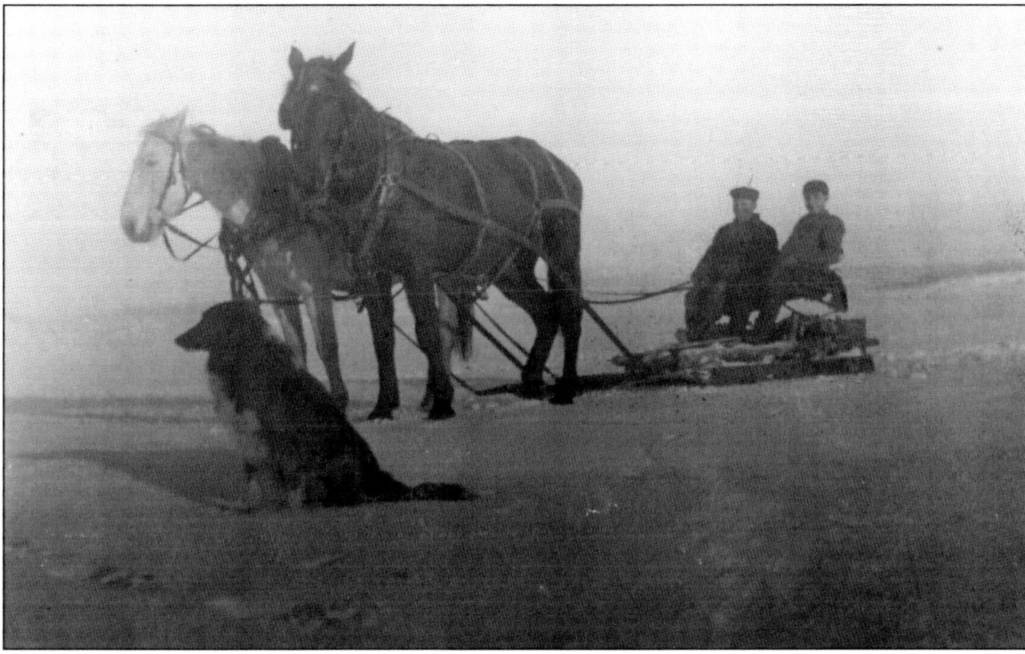

Carl and Hazel Anderson are pictured with their team, bobsled, and old Duke, the dog. Carl was the son of Bastian and Thea Anderson, and Hazel was the daughter of William and Hattie Martin. (Courtesy of Evelyn Anderson.)

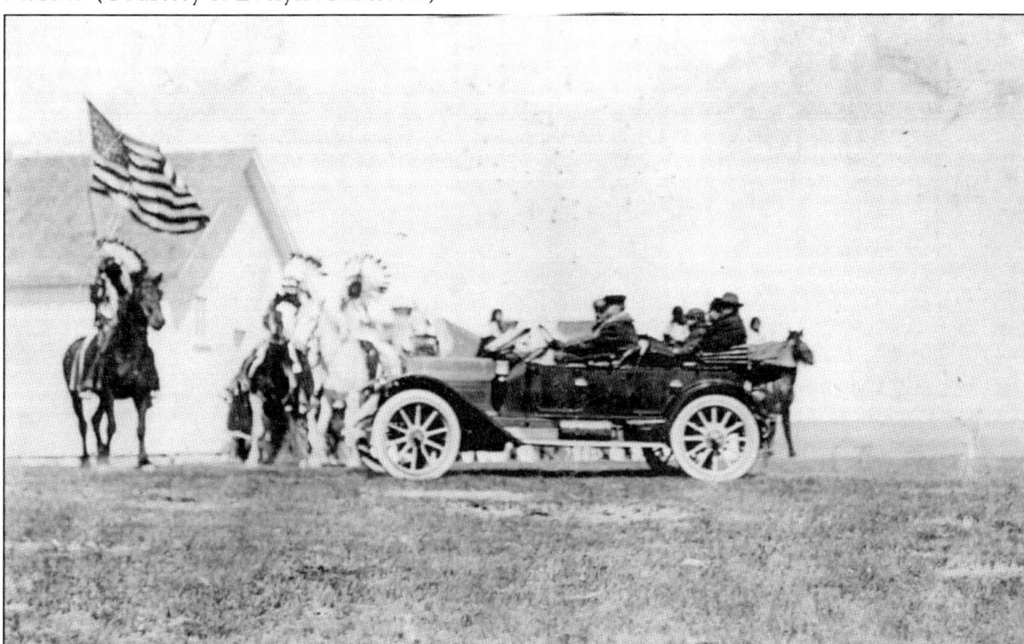

What is seen here is possibly a Fourth of July celebration in Thunder Butte, South Dakota. In the 1890s, residents had to journey to old Cheyenne Agency along the Missouri River to receive food rations. About 1900, agency substations began to be placed around the reservation, and one was at located at Thunder Butte. A school began here at Thunder Butte Station in 1904. The community is 15 miles north of Dupree. (Courtesy of Donovin Sprague.)

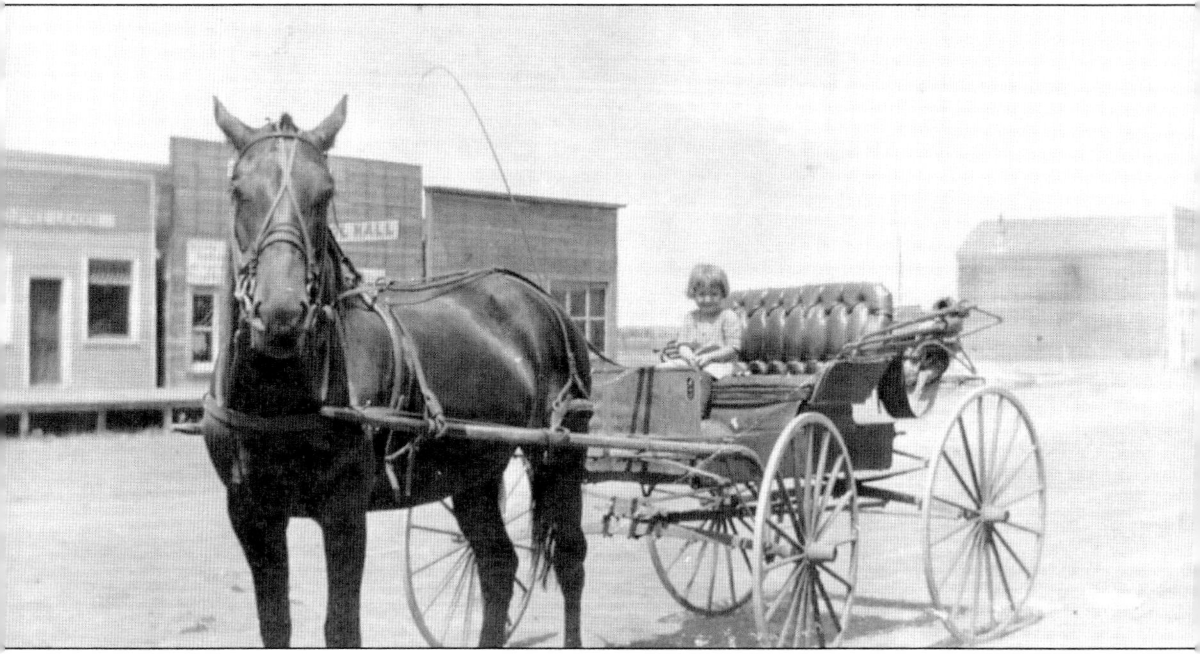

A little girl waits in this fancy wagon for her mom and dad. This is the north end of Main Street, and the wagon is facing south. (Courtesy of ZCHS.)

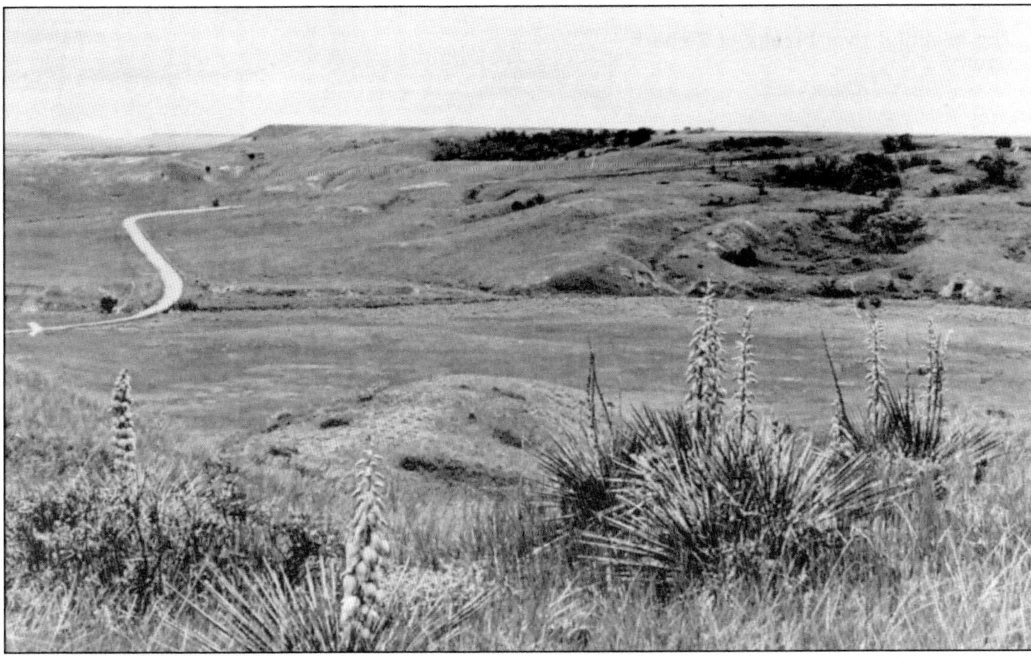

Wild yucca grows north of Cherry Creek in 1986. The gravel road running southwest goes to Bridger. (Courtesy of ZCHS.)

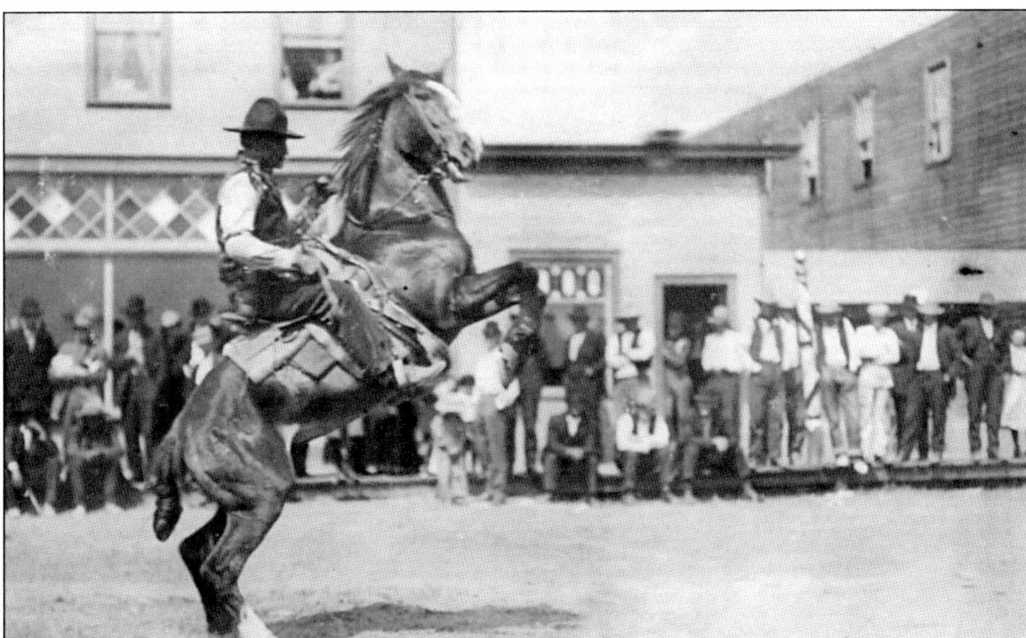

John Bald Eagle is performing and showing horsemanship in a parade at a neighboring town. (Courtesy of Thelma Frame.)

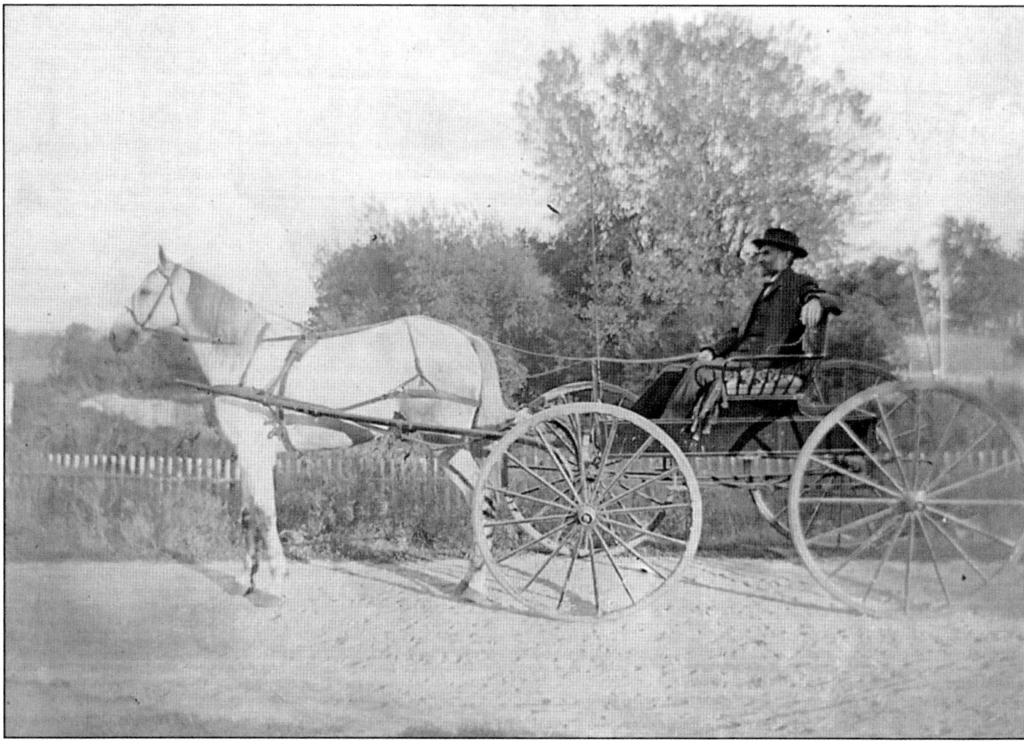

Dr. Henry Matter is pictured in the buggy he used for medical calls. He was a retired doctor from Iowa but found his services in demand when he moved to the Glad Valley area of Ziebach County. He was assistant postmaster until he retired again at age 85. Later the Witte's General Store and Glad Valley Post Office were located where the old cream station had been. (Courtesy of Thelma Frame.)

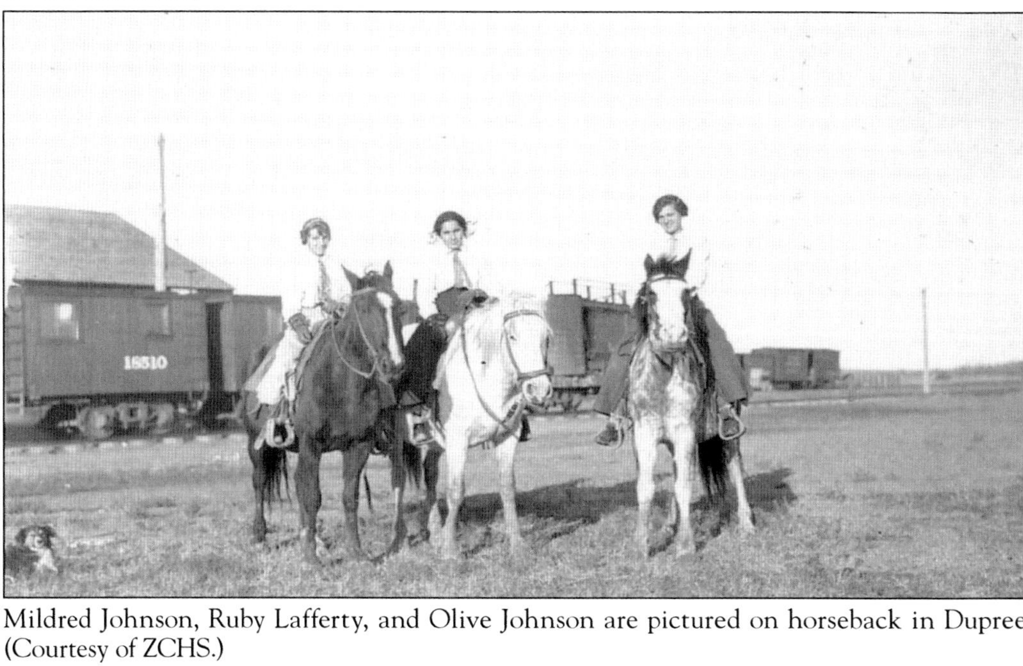

Mildred Johnson, Ruby Lafferty, and Olive Johnson are pictured on horseback in Dupree. (Courtesy of ZCHS.)

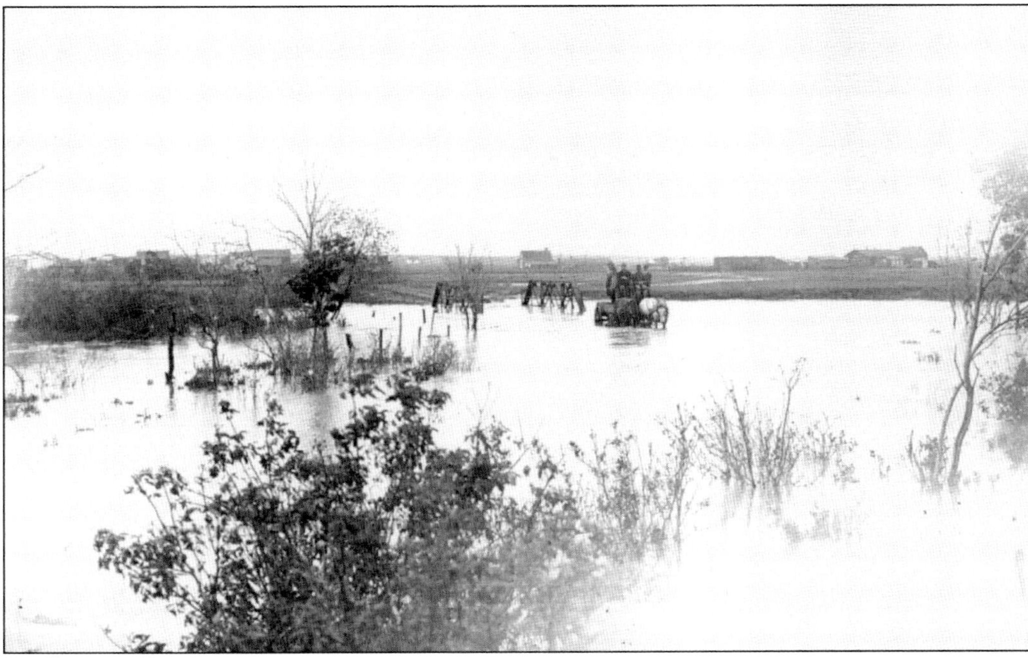

High water has caused flooding on Elm Creek north of Dupree as men stand in their wagon. (Courtesy of ZCHS/Virginia Woodward.)

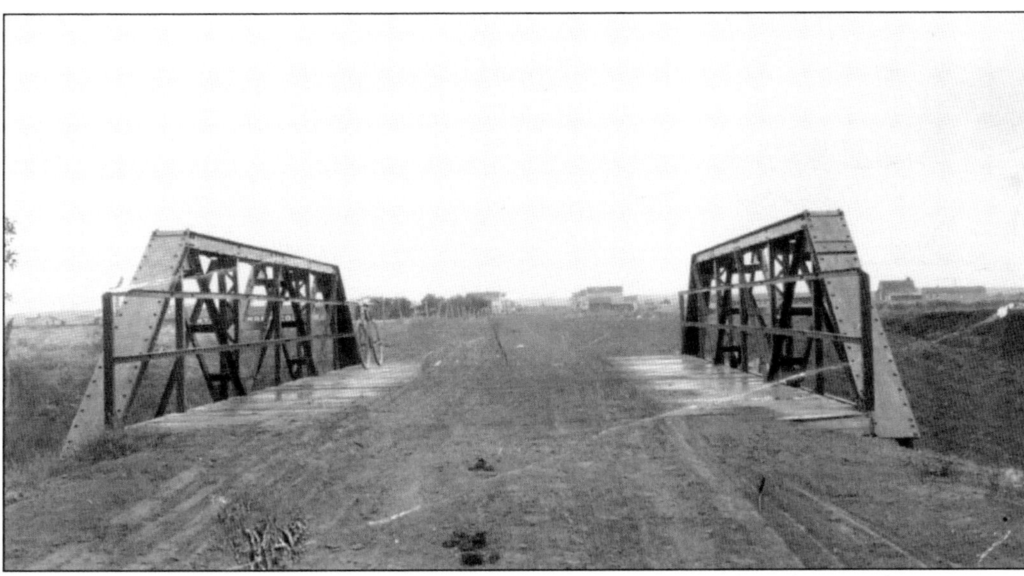

This is the iron bridge looking south into the town of Dupree. South Dakota Highway 212 now runs east and west between the iron bridge and the entrance into town. (Courtesy of ZCHS/ Virginia Woodward.)

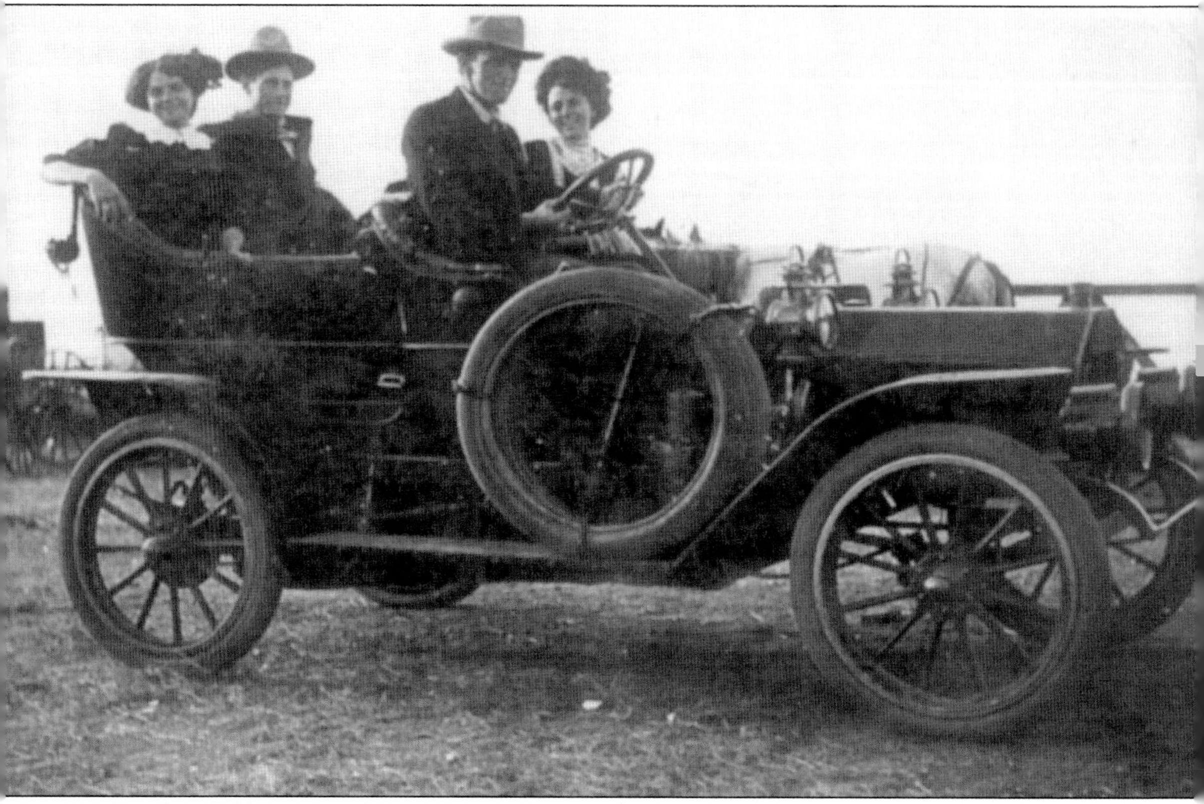

Frank Bull (driving) and Lota Ralston are in the front seat of this car, with an unidentified couple in the back. (Courtesy of Irean Jordan.)

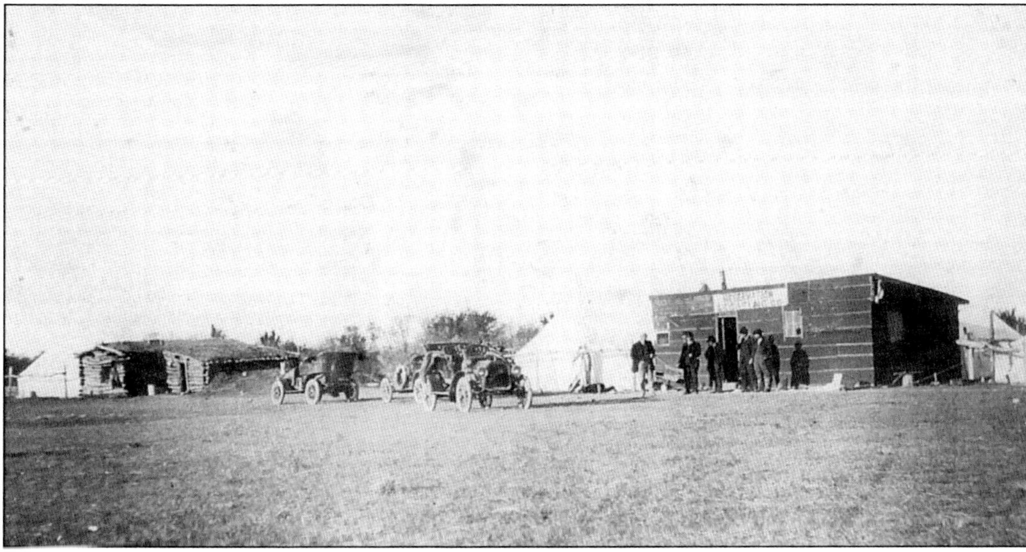

This may be the first location of Dupree, 2 miles east of the present location. At right is the Reservation Locating Company, which assisted people in finding land claims. (Courtesy of Irean Jordan.)

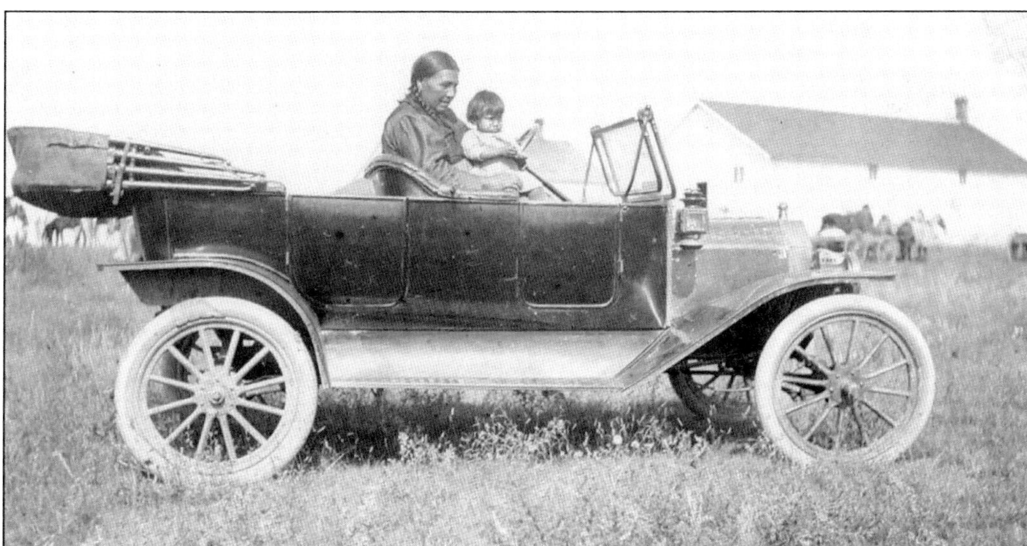

An unidentified Lakota woman and *takoja* (grandchild) are in this car in front of what appears to be Dupree Legion Hall, before the front porch was added. (Courtesy of ZCHS.)

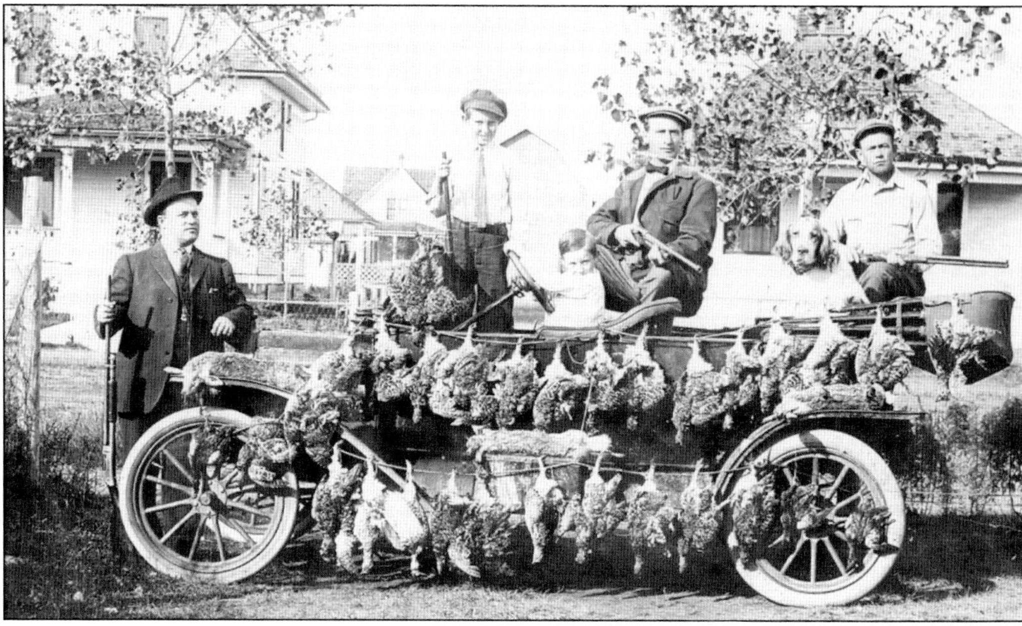

The men and boys posing with shotguns and rifles return with what appears to be a successful grouse hunt. A hunting dog is also posing. Three fur-bearing animals appear to have been also taken in the hunt. (Courtesy of ZCHS.)

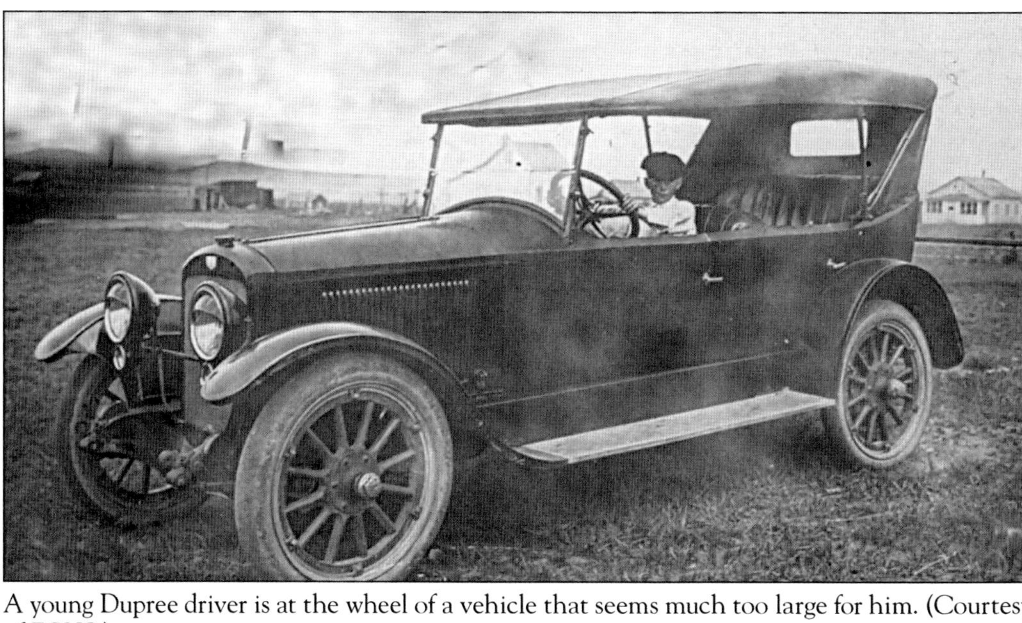

A young Dupree driver is at the wheel of a vehicle that seems much too large for him. (Courtesy of ZCHS.)

Three

Homesteads on the Prairie

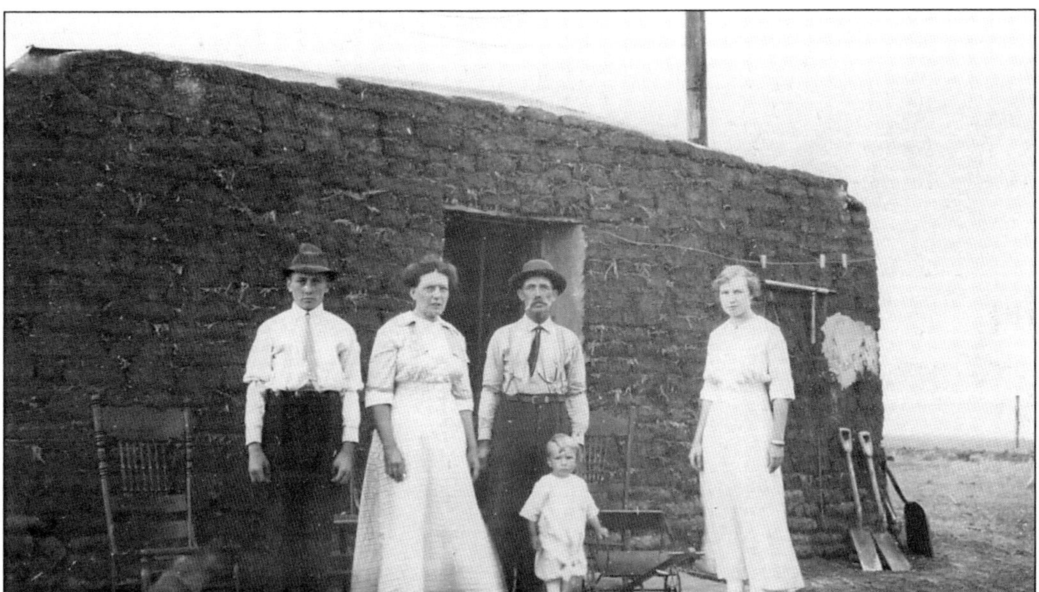

A family of homesteaders is pictured by their sod home. A dog also poses in front of the chair at left. (Courtesy of ZCHS/Harold and Joan Ross.)

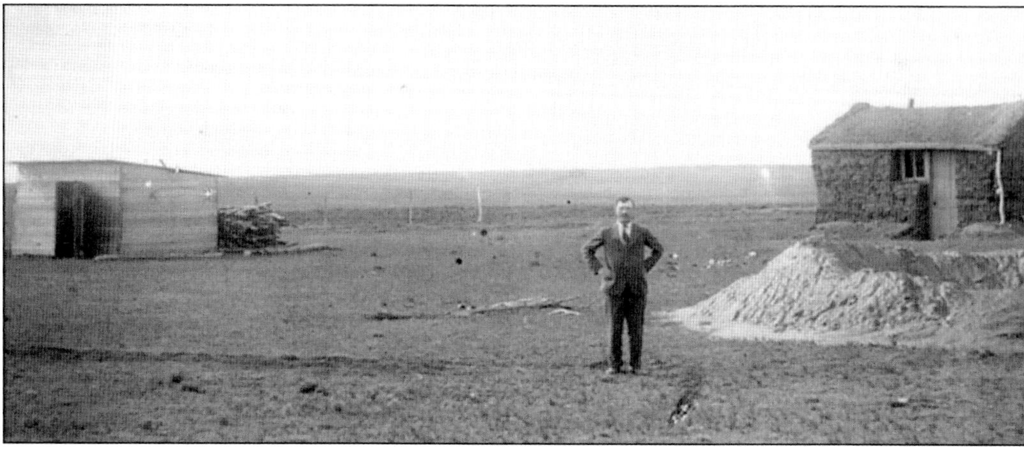

Reinold Heinz homesteaded 4 miles north of Dupree in the early Ziebach County years. (Courtesy of ZCHS.)

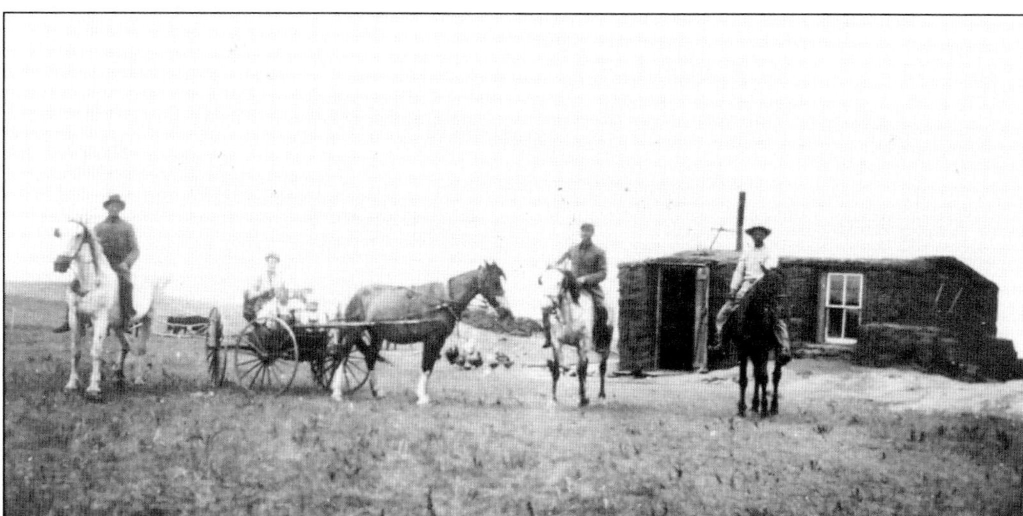

This is the sod house and homestead of the parents of Barney Meland. Three men are on horseback and an adult and two children appear to be in the wagon. (Courtesy of Edith Meland.)

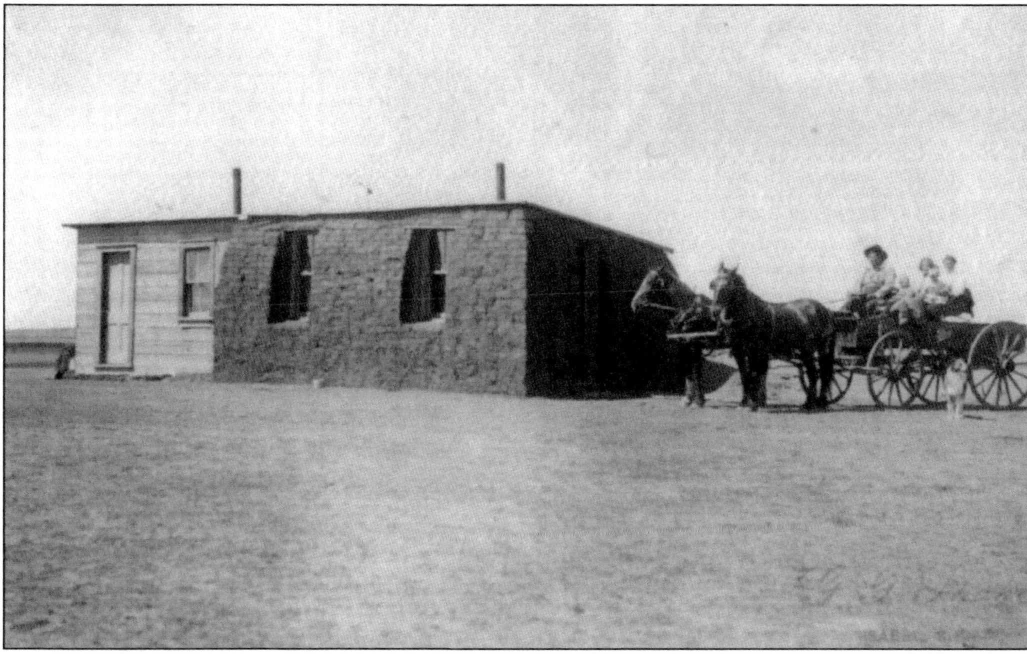

The family of C. Eliason is pictured in a wagon drawn by a team of horses, with a dog in the foreground. The house is a combination of sod and wood construction. The sod house is the homestead of Myron Eliason's grandfather C. Eliason. The picture was taken by a photographer from Isabel, South Dakota. (Courtesy of Myron Eliason.)

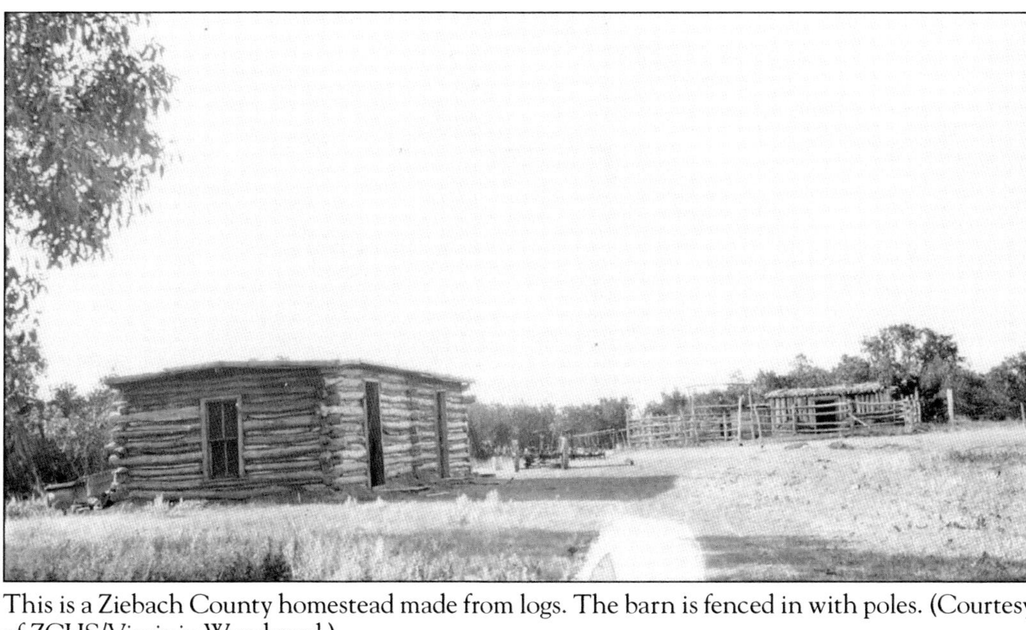

This is a Ziebach County homestead made from logs. The barn is fenced in with poles. (Courtesy of ZCHS/Virginia Woodward.)

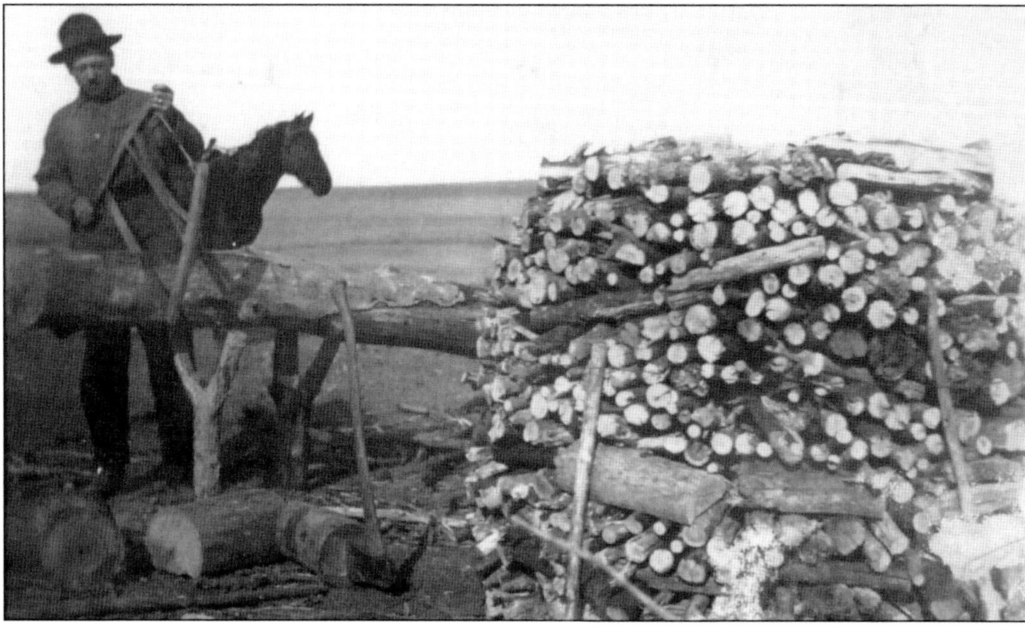

This picture was taken in the fall of 1918. Carl Anderson is sawing wood with an old hand saw. Carl was an experienced carpenter, and he was also a member of the first board of directors of the Farm Security Administration. He helped organize the Dupree Farmers Elevator and served on the community hospital board. (Courtesy of Evelyn Anderson.)

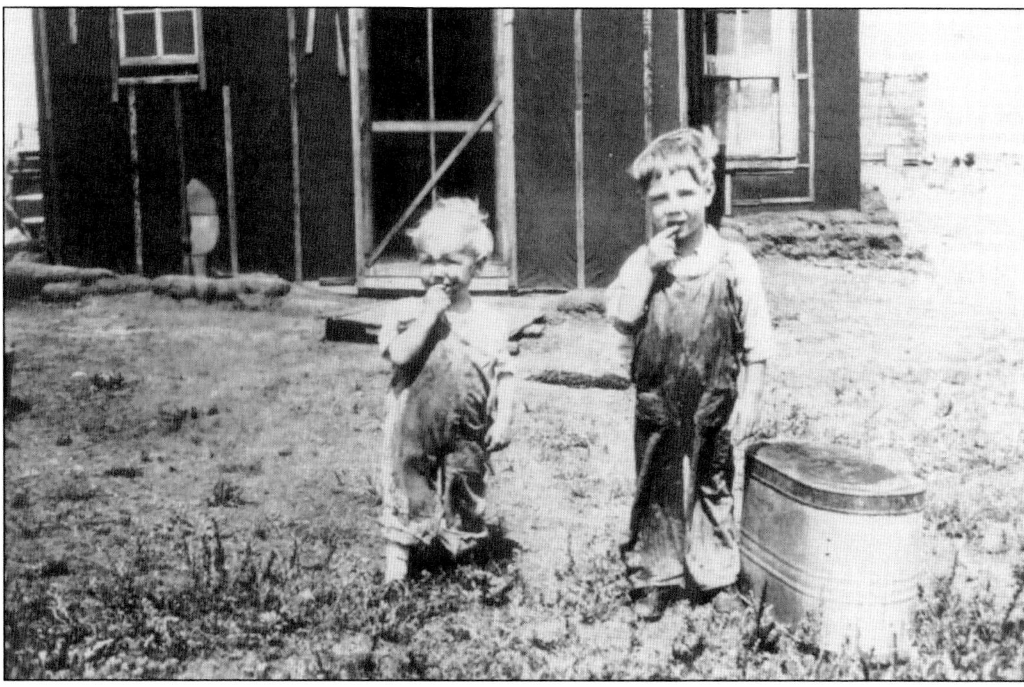

From left to right are Ralph (Doc) and Pat Pesicka, pictured in front of their family's tarpaper shack. Their parents were George and Edna Pesicka. Doc and Pat's other sisters and brothers are Barbara Eaton, Philo (Mike), Lawrence, Frances Holder, Richard (Dick), and Lee. (Courtesy of Pesicka family.)

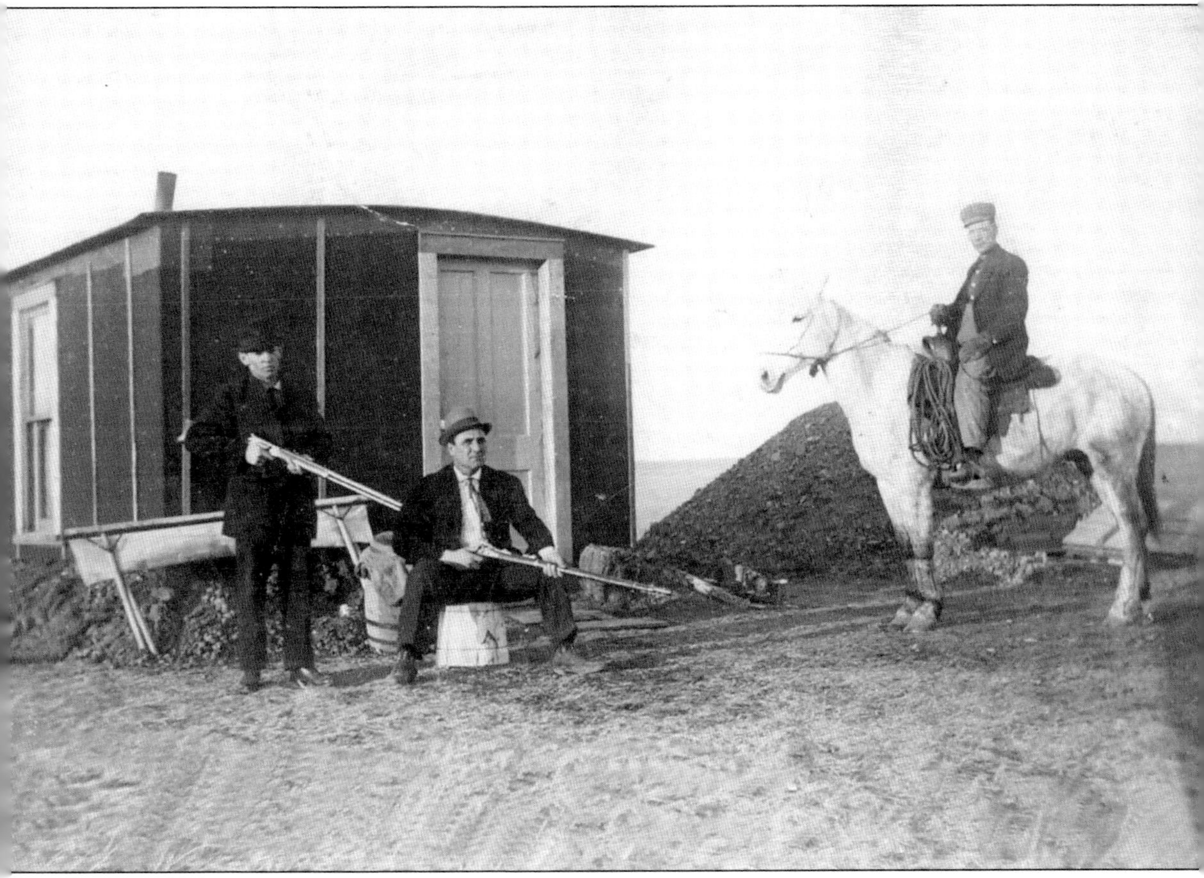

The C. Brown homestead is shown here, with a one-room house covered with tarpaper. "Joe Brown" is written on the back of the photograph, and the rider on horseback is labeled as "brother-in-law." (Courtesy of ZCHS.)

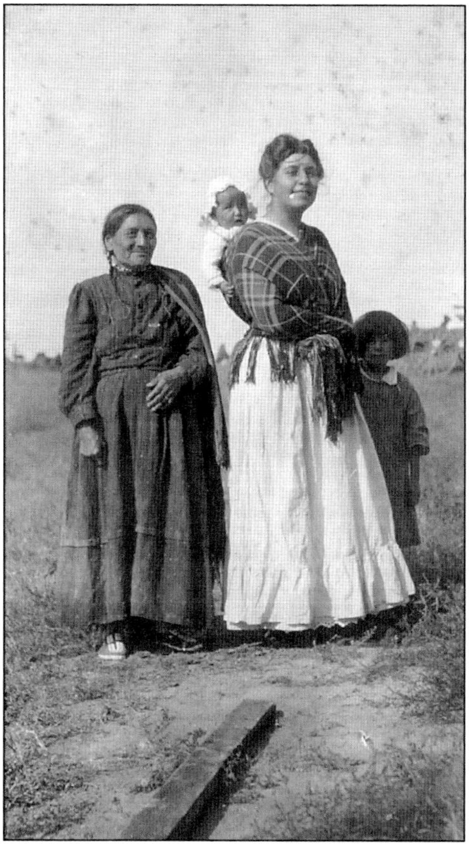

Four unidentified people are shown here, with a woman carrying her baby on her back. (Courtesy of ZCHS/Harold and Joan Ross.)

William and Gertrude Searson were early pioneers in Ziebach County and their homestead was 3.5 miles north of Dupree. Gertrude is pictured in front of their house after a blizzard in March 1920. William Searson was the Ziebach County treasurer in the late 1930s, and they were neighbors of Oscar and Etta Hurst. (Courtesy of Howard Hurst.)

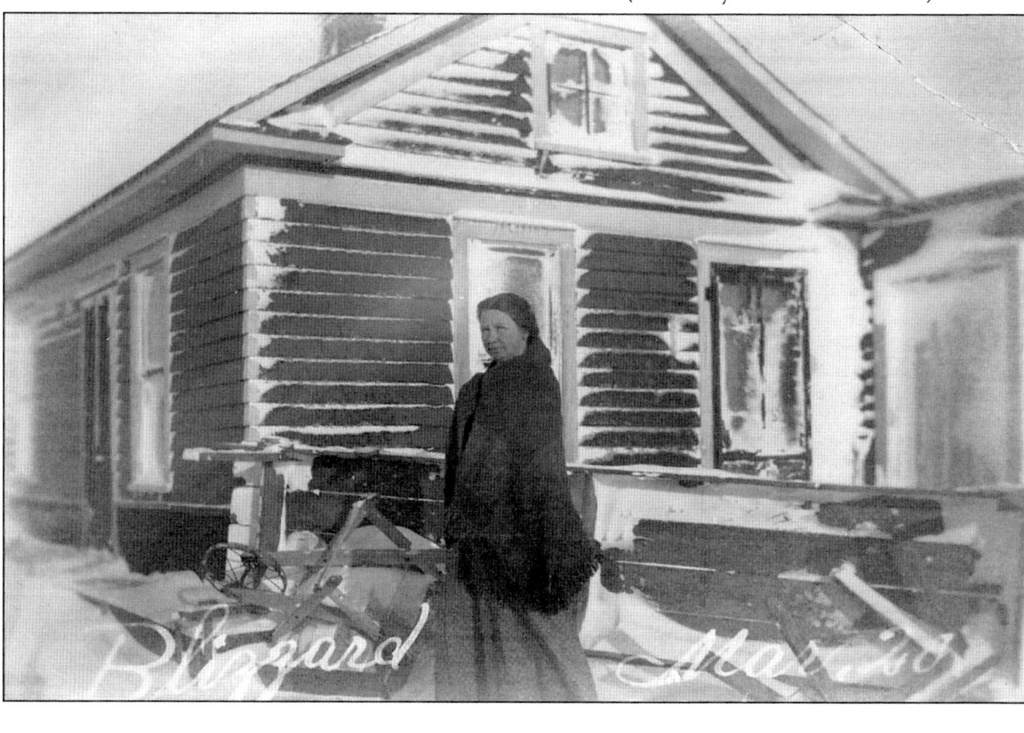

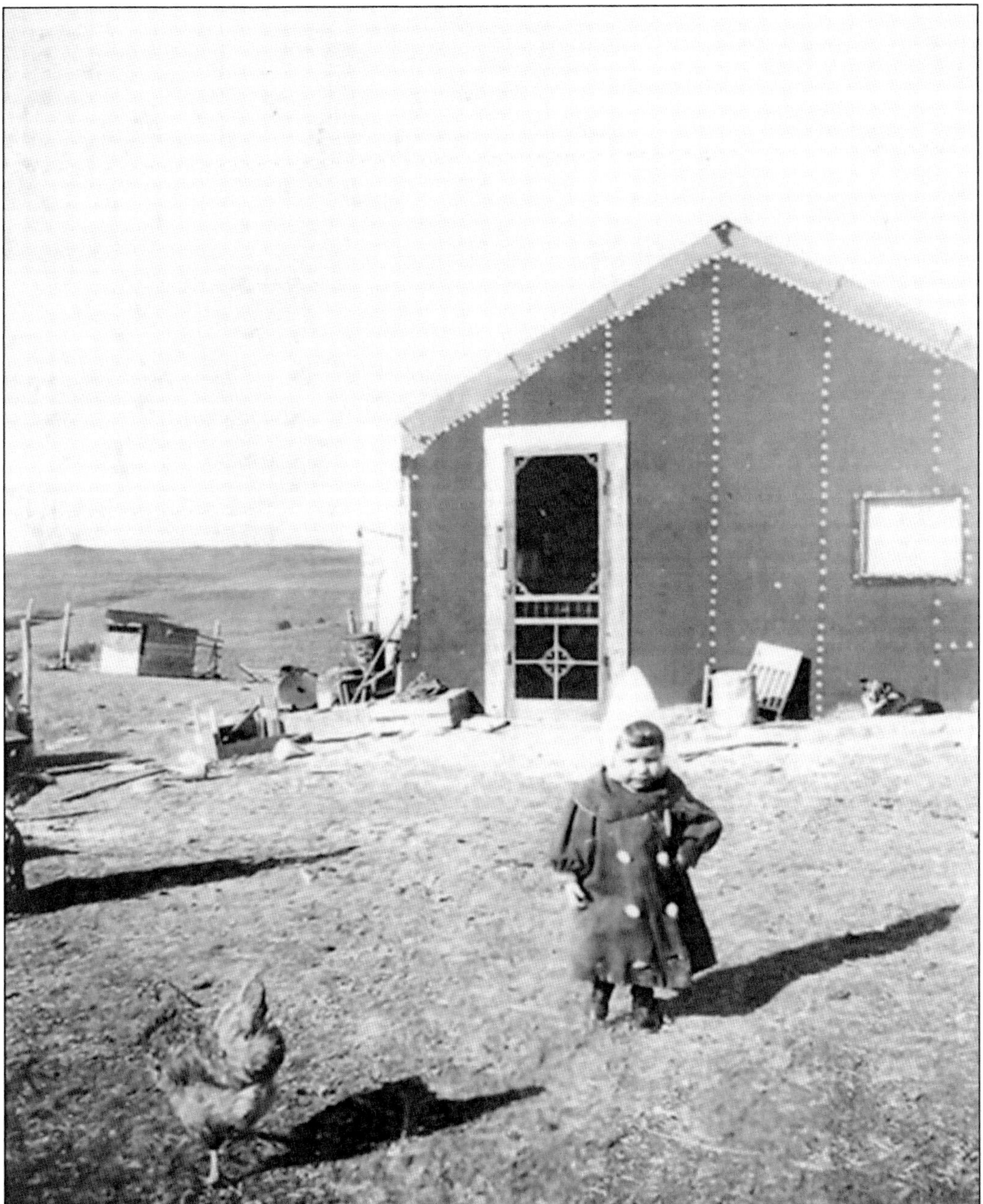

Bernice Vrooman Zacher is standing in the yard of her parents' homestead claim, which was southwest of Eagle Butte, South Dakota. The claim was filed in Ziebach County in 1916, and this claim shack was built in October of the same year. (Courtesy of ZCHS.)

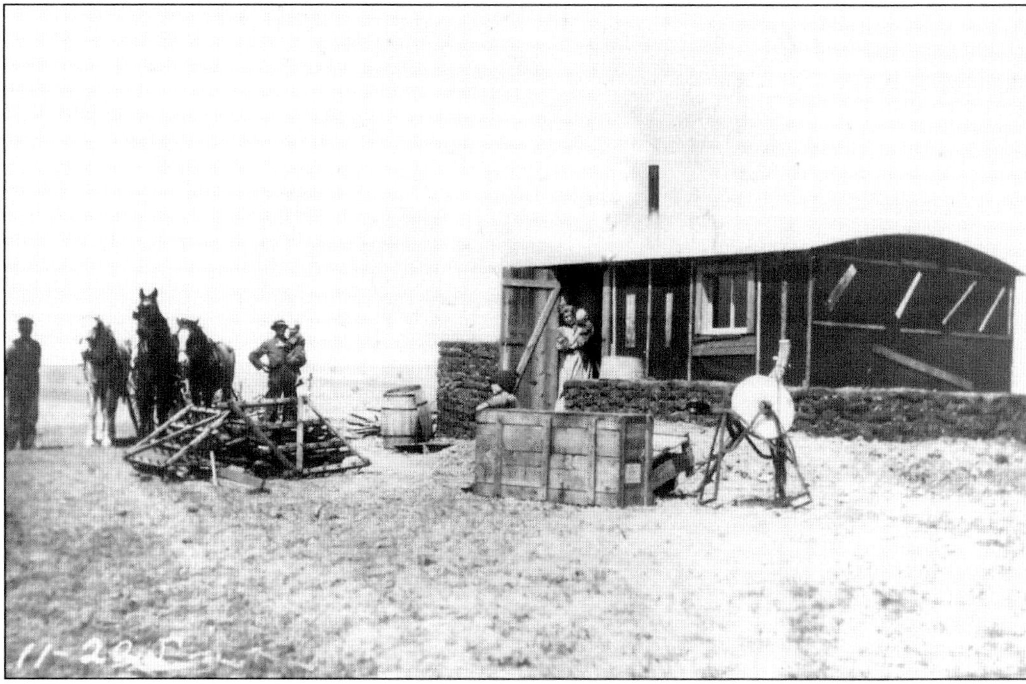

From left to right are an unidentified man, Barney Meland (holding child), Ted Meland (boy standing with stocking cap), and Edith Meland (holding child in doorway). (Courtesy of Edith Meland.)

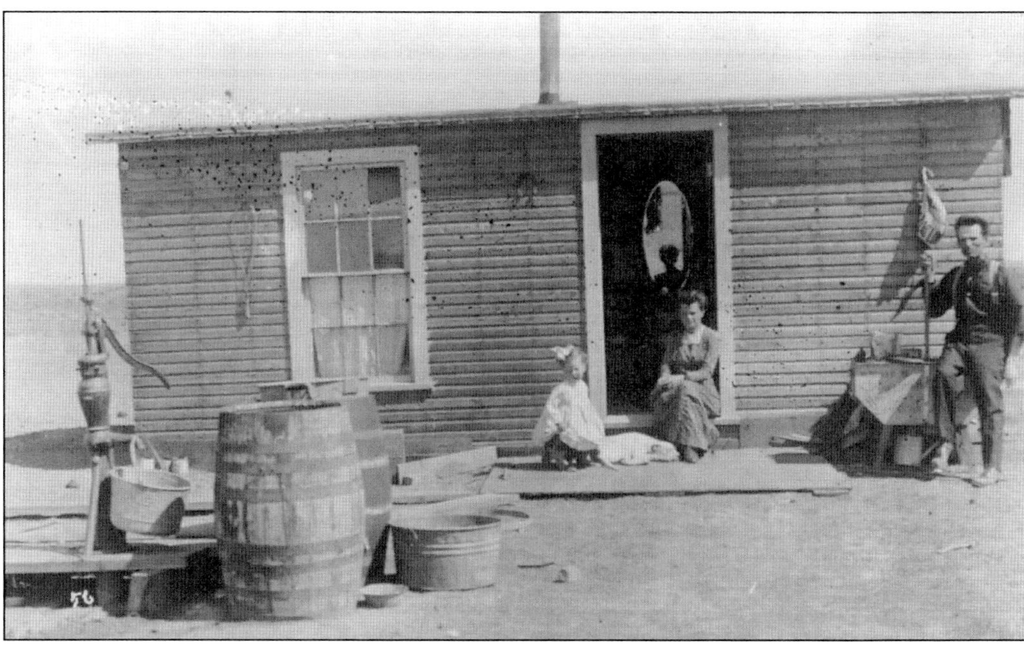

This family of three is pictured in front of their one-room homestead shack with their dog. Their water well was not far away. (Courtesy of ZCHS/Harold and Joan Ross.)

Four

SODBUSTERS AND COWBOYS

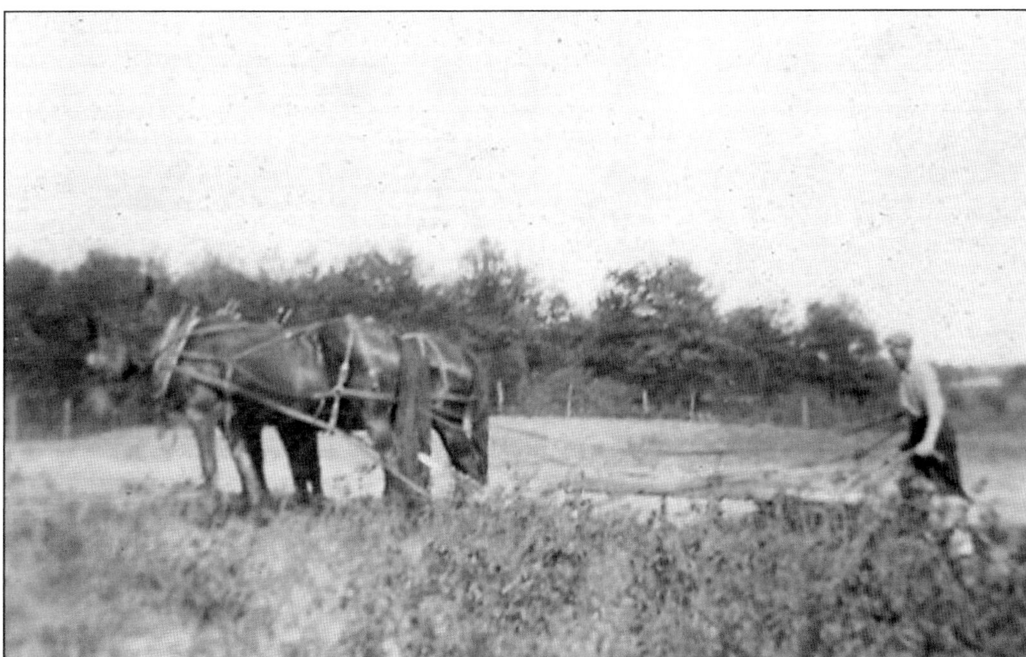

Benhard Anderson breaks sod on his homestead in 1916 with his team and walking plow. (Courtesy of Evelyn Bierman.)

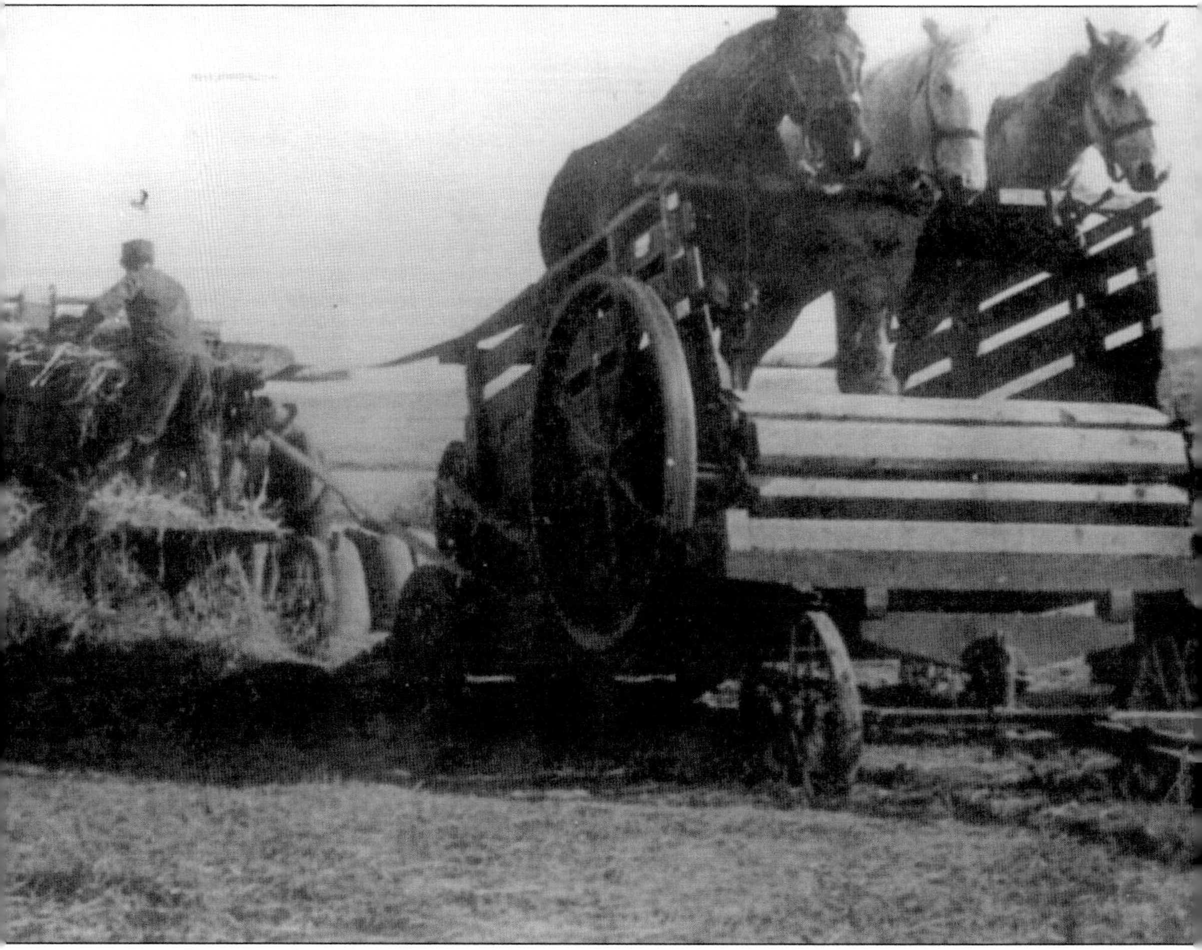

The Albers family called this "Three Horse Power." This is the horsepower for the threshing machine. (Courtesy of ZCHS/Virginia Woodward.)

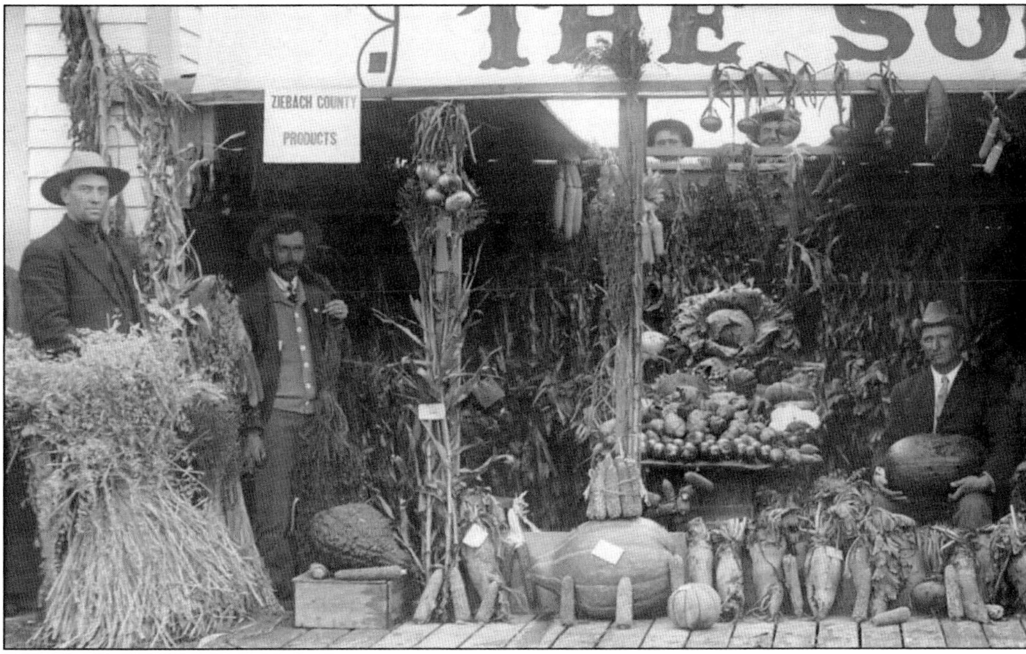

Five men are pictured at this market stand with a variety of produce. A sign reads "Ziebach County Products." (Courtesy of ZCHS.)

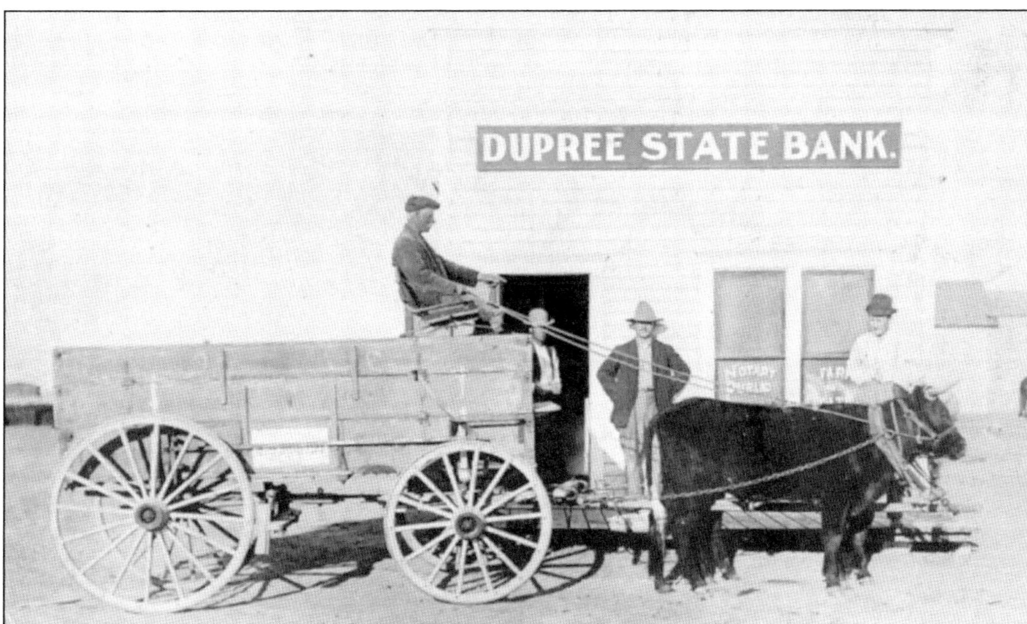

Dupree State Bank opened for business in 1910 with a capital of $10,000. The *Dupree Leader* noted that the Dupree State Bank moved to a new location in 1910. This is the present location of the First Financial Bank USA, formerly Farmers State Bank, which purchased the Dupree State Bank. (Courtesy of Irean Jordan.)

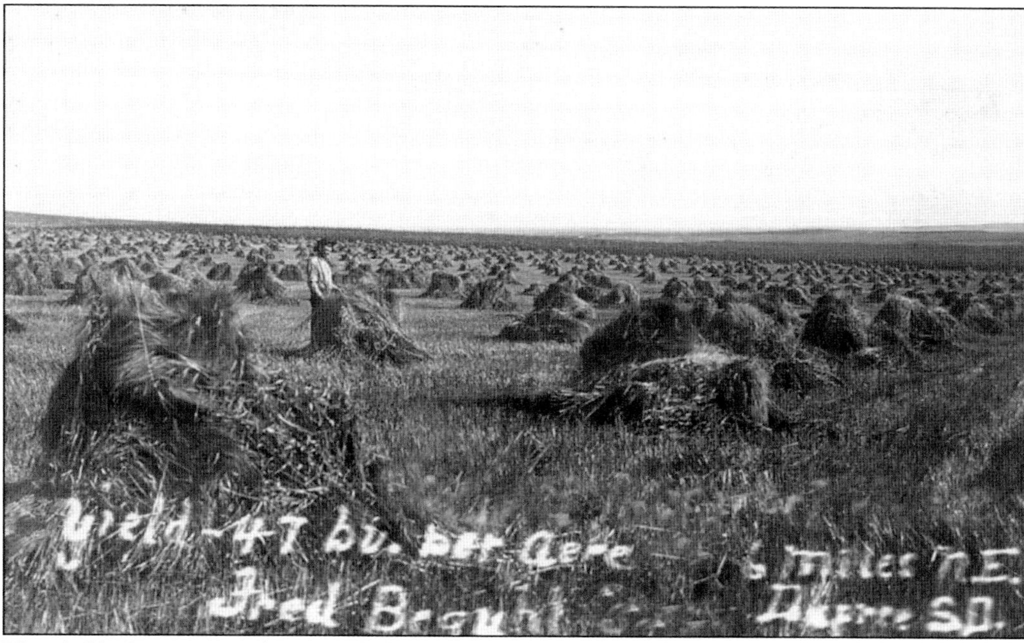

This field of macaroni wheat yielded 47 bushels per acre. Fred Beguhl's place is 6 miles northeast of Dupree. A relative of the Beguhl family was Emery Lightfield. (Courtesy of ZCHS.)

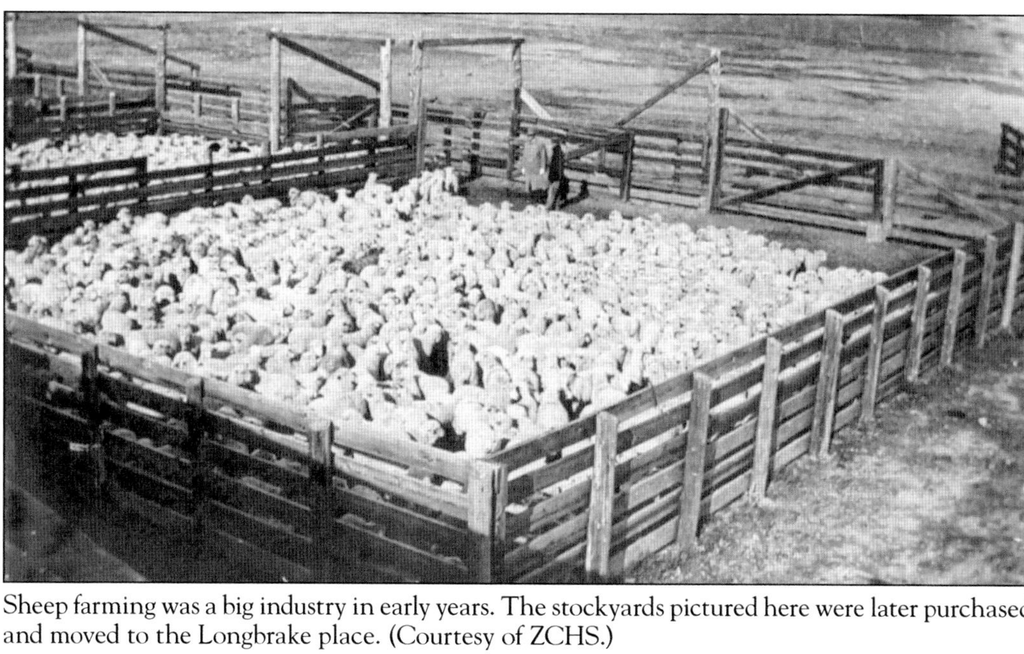

Sheep farming was a big industry in early years. The stockyards pictured here were later purchased and moved to the Longbrake place. (Courtesy of ZCHS.)

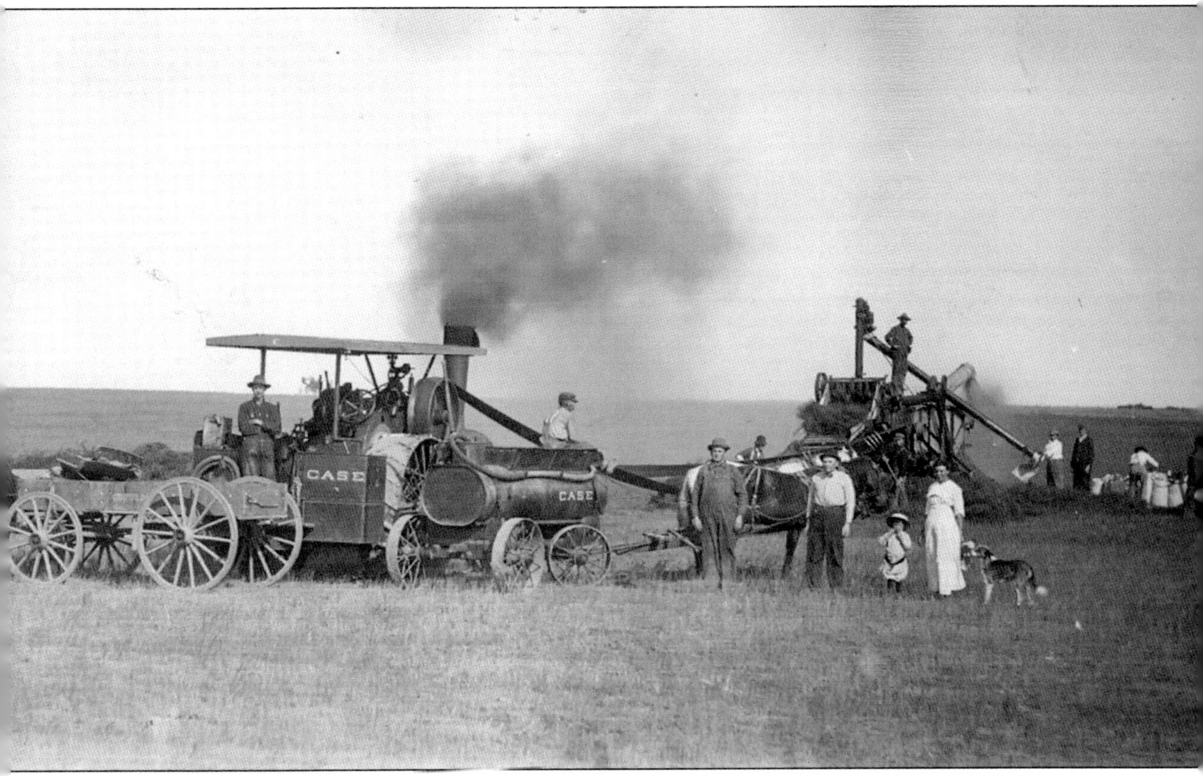

This 1912 photograph is labeled, "The Dirty Dozen threshing crew. Pete Christiansen, water monkey." The 12 people include men, women, and children. In the foreground is Case equipment, and it is threshing time. (Courtesy of ZCHS.)

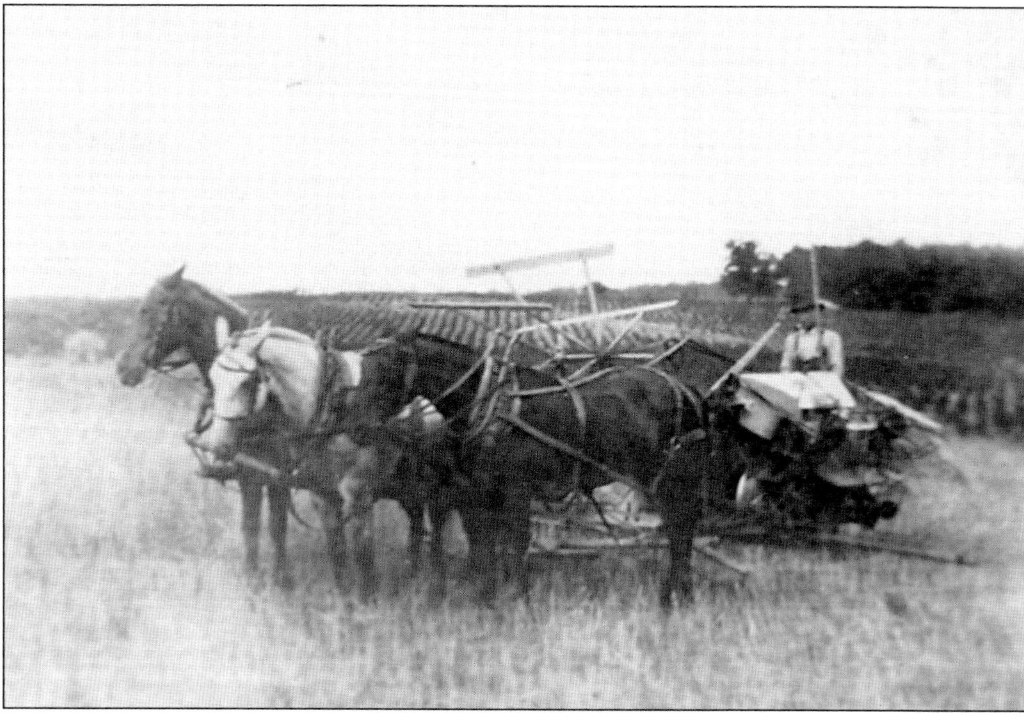

This is the Benhard Anderson homestead in northern Ziebach County, where rye is being cut with a team of three horses. (Courtesy of Evelyn Anderson.)

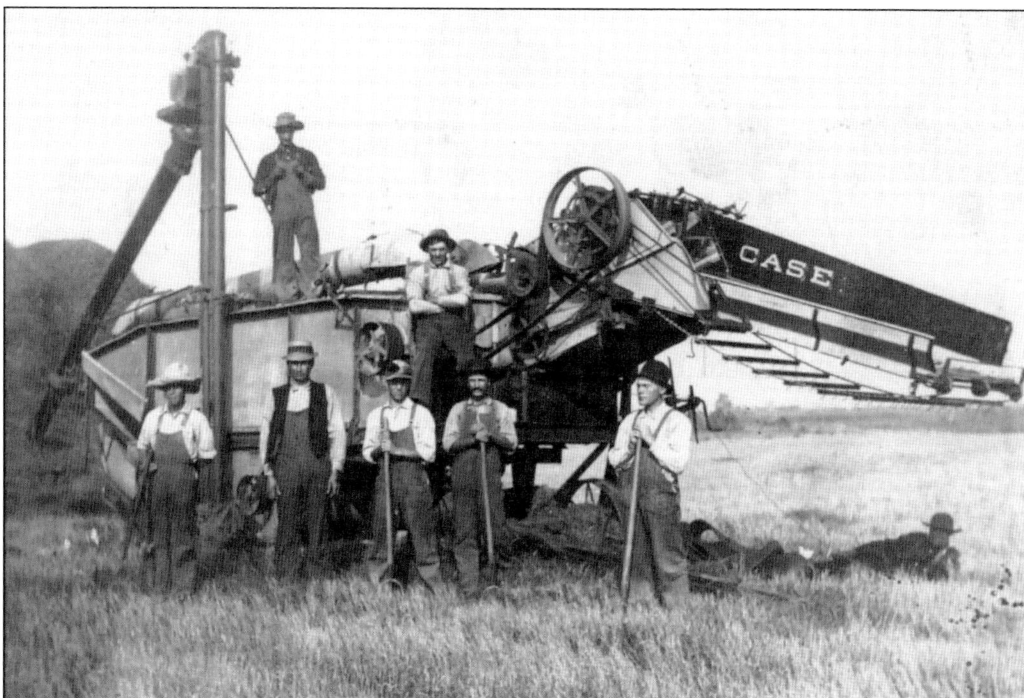

Carl Anderson's threshing crew is pictured here in 1916 with a Case rig. (Courtesy of Evelyn Anderson.)

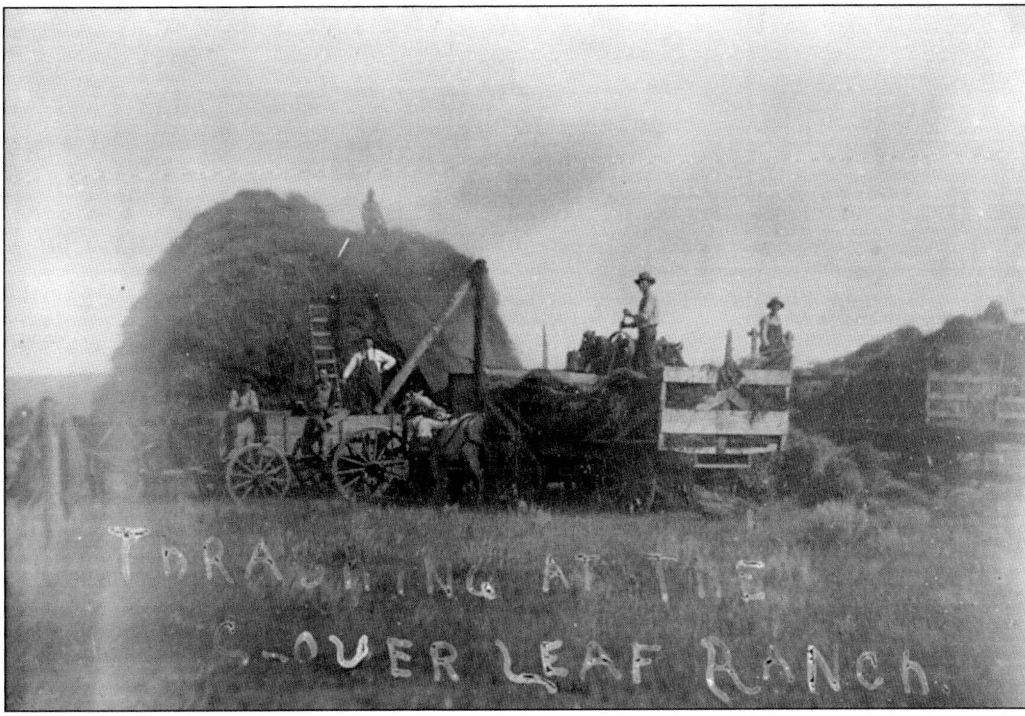

Threshing day at the Cloverleaf Ranch, north of Dupree, is depicted here. Carl Anderson, his cousin Gust Anderson, and Casper Texley each received homesteads. These three homesteads stood on adjoining land corners forming the hub of the settlement known as Clover Leaf. (Courtesy of Evelyn Anderson.)

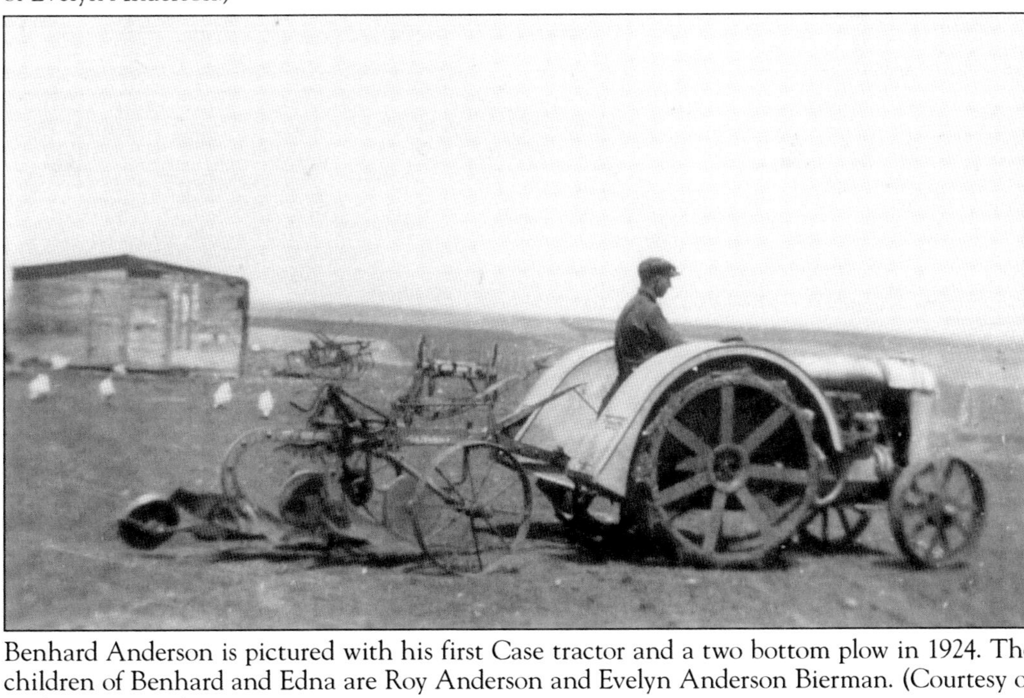

Benhard Anderson is pictured with his first Case tractor and a two bottom plow in 1924. The children of Benhard and Edna are Roy Anderson and Evelyn Anderson Bierman. (Courtesy of Evelyn Bierman.)

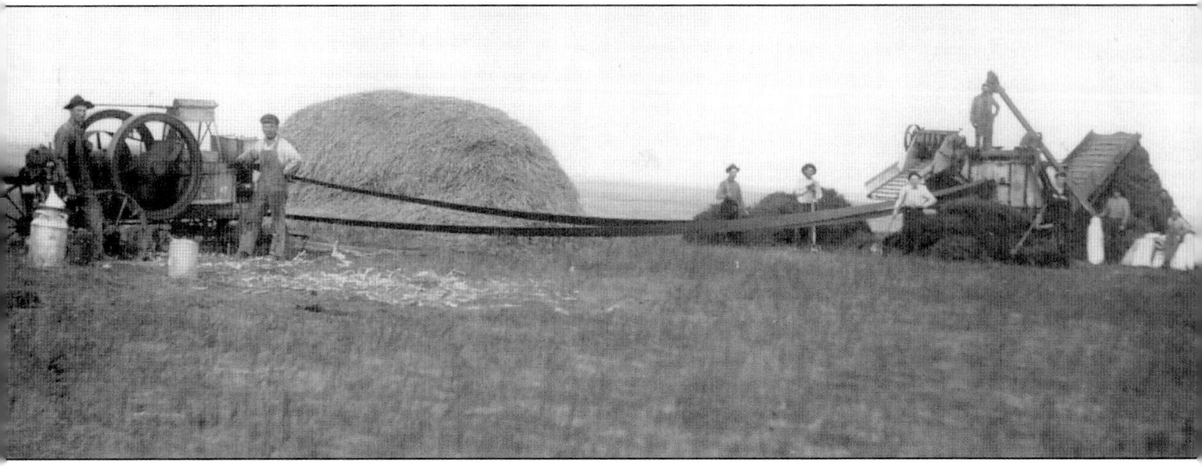

The "Big Four" (the owners of the equipment pictured) purchased this threshing rig in 1912. This picture was taken at the A. G. Davis place. A. G. Davis, his wife, and children came to Dupree by team and wagon from LeBeau. The Davis children were Hazel E., Herbert P., Hattie J. (Burke), and George. (Courtesy of ZCHS/Virginia Woodward.)

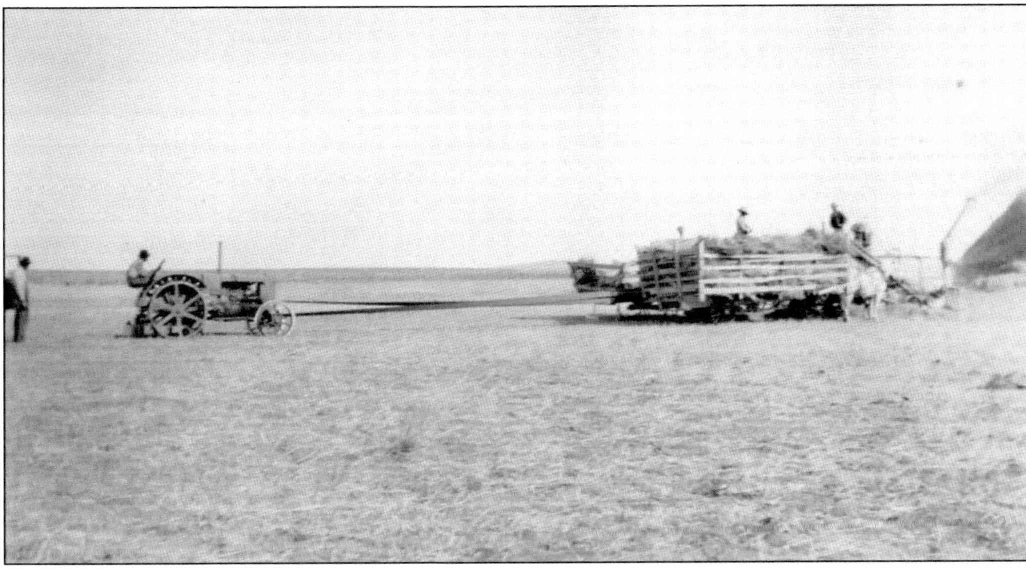

Brothers Carl and Benhard Anderson are threshing oats at the Carl Anderson homestead in 1924 with a crew. (Courtesy of Evelyn Bierman.)

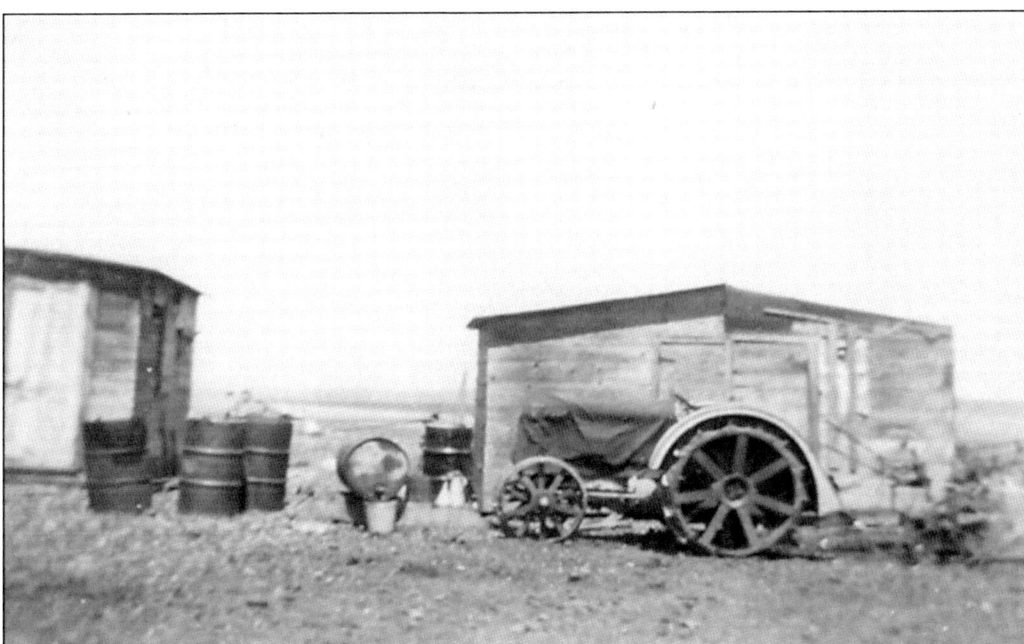

This is a photograph of Benhard Anderson's first tractor, bought in 1924. Benhard was born in Deuel County, South Dakota, and moved to Minnesota in 1915. He moved back to South Dakota in 1923, married Edna Reich in 1924, and they lived in a log house on the Moreau River the first winter. (Courtesy of Evelyn Bierman.)

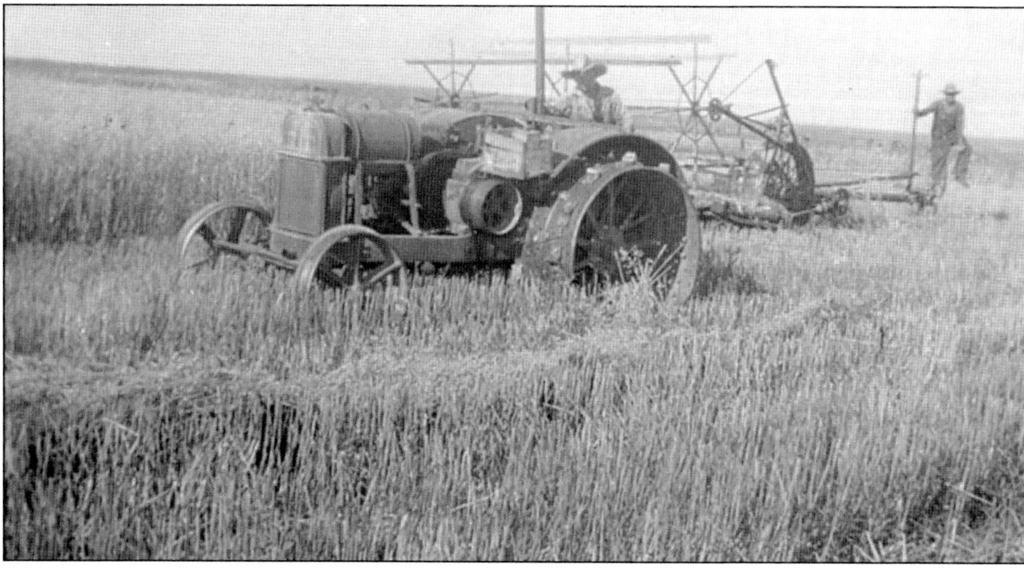

Ross and Gordon Wince are pictured here swathing grain in 1948. Their place is southwest of Dupree and southeast of Redelm. Gordon is driving the tractor, and Ross is on the swather. (Courtesy of Gordon and Carole Wince.)

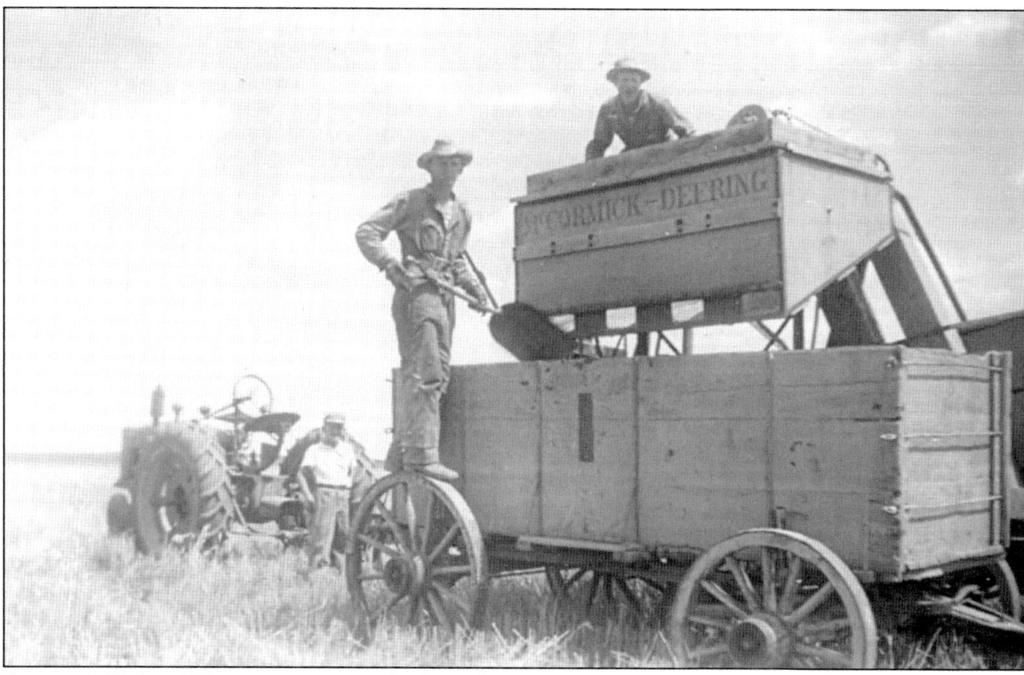

Ross and Esther Wince's sons Donald (standing behind tractor), Sherman (standing on wagon wheel), and Gordon (on tractor) Wince are shown here dumping grain into a grain wagon. The Winces also have a daughter, Nyla. (Courtesy of Gordon and Carole Wince.)

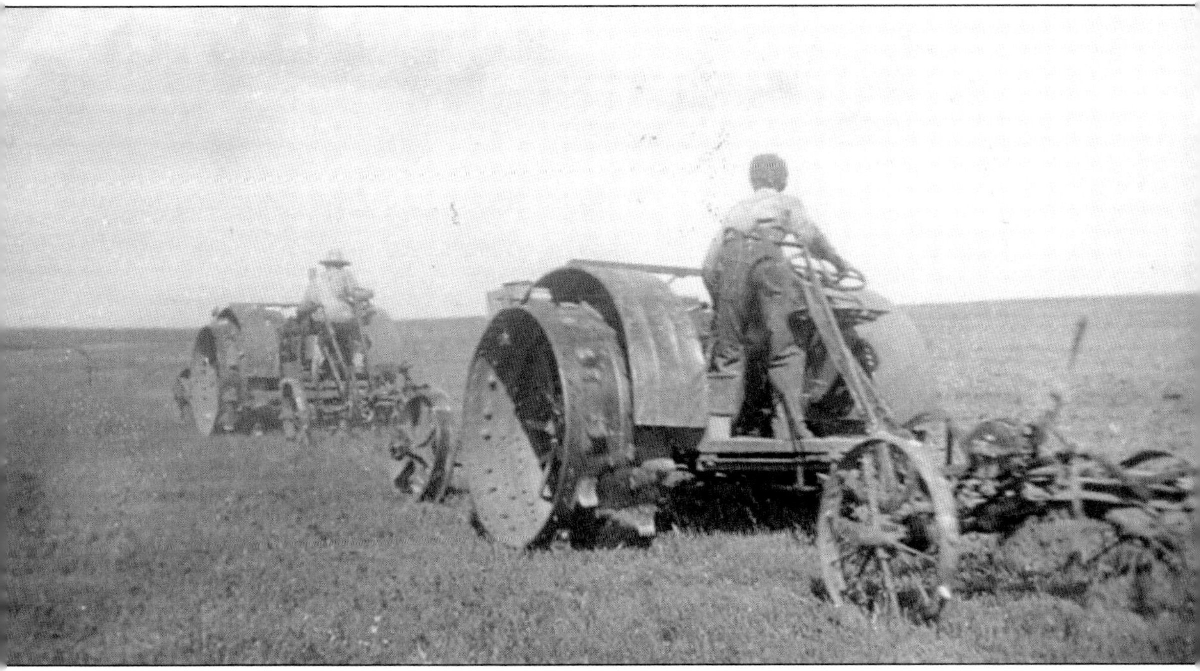

Ross Wince is pictured on the front tractor with his son Gordon following. The tractors are Hart Parr tractors, identifiable by the dual rim on the landslide. Ross Wince arrived in Redelm in Ziebach County in the spring of 1911. He was probably the second homesteader to unload there. Earl Moore was the first to arrive, in the first days of 1911. Ross married Esther Fuller in 1927. (Courtesy of Gordon and Carole Wince.)

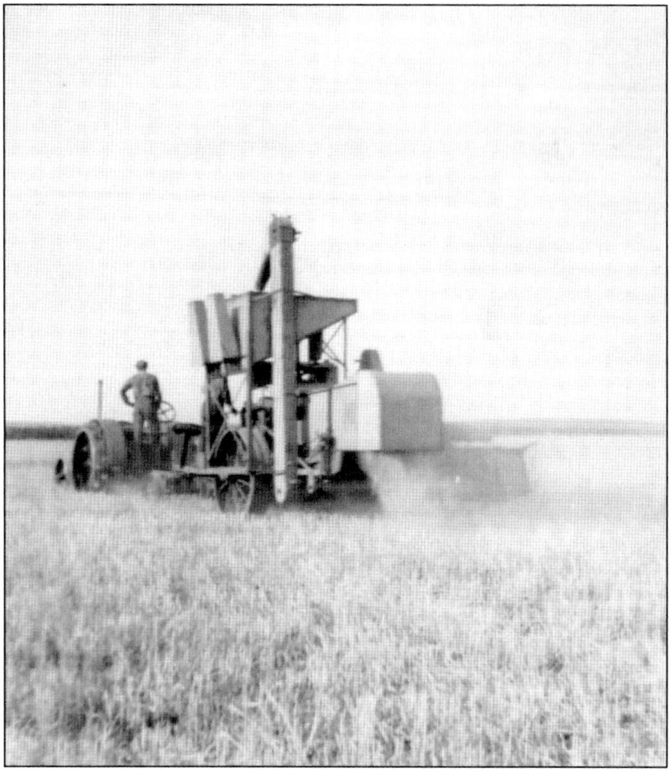

Carl Anderson is seen here with his International combine in 1942, seven miles northeast of Dupree. Carl and his wife, Hazel Martin, had five children: Carol, Thelma, Ethel, Calvin, and a first son who lived only three days. All five children were delivered by Dr. Frank Creamer. (Courtesy of Evelyn Anderson.)

Sherman and Gordon Wince bring in the hay crop in this photograph taken the first week of July 1949. Sherman is driving, and Gordon is riding on the hay wagon. (Courtesy of Gordon and Carole Wince.)

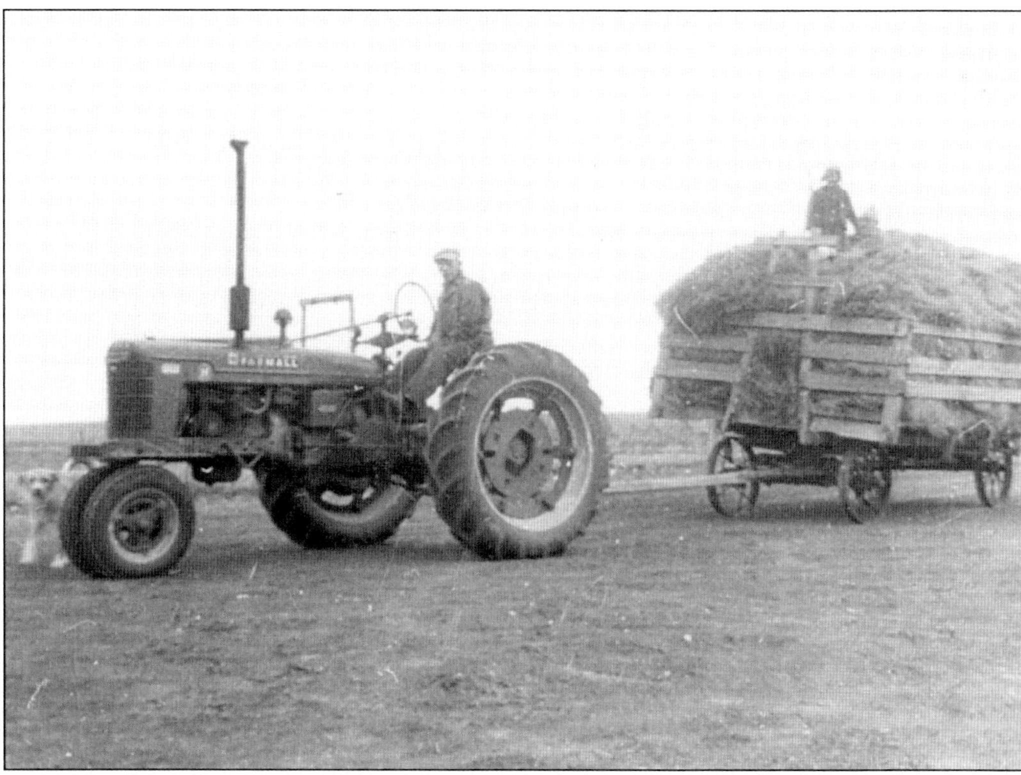

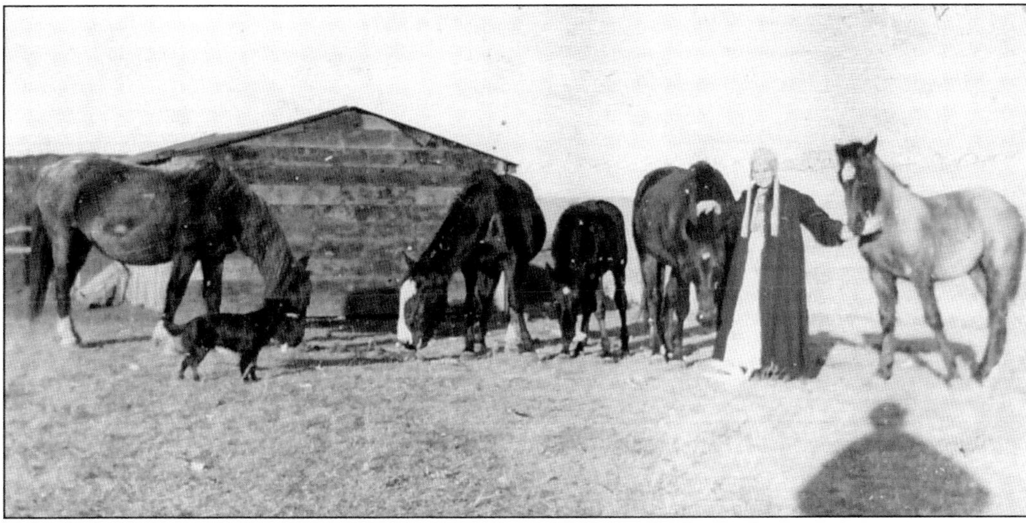

Mrs. Armentrout is pictured with horses. The Armentrouts lived southwest of Dupree, and their son was Ed Armentrout. Ed later sold his land to the Winces, Ritters, and Graslies. (Courtesy of Thelma Frame.)

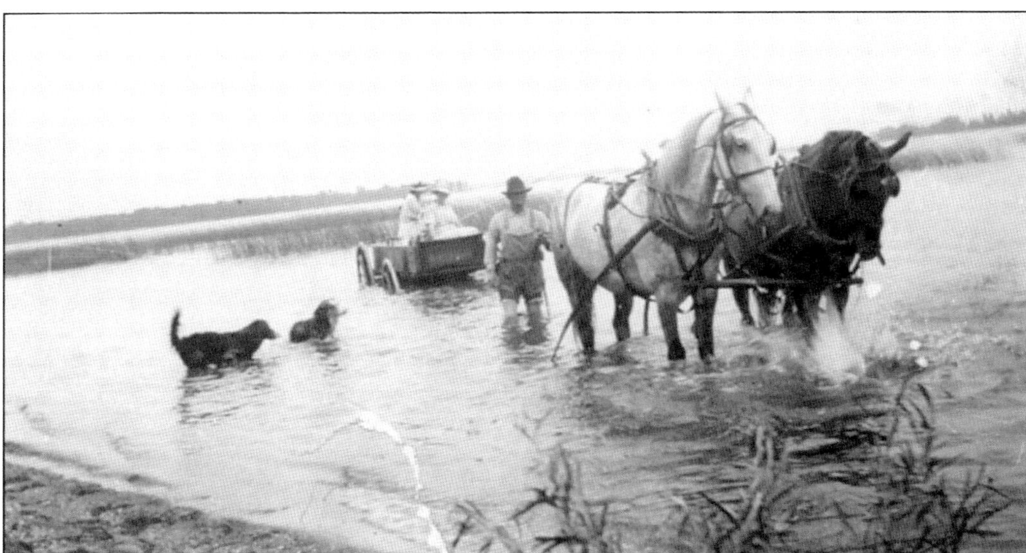

Attempting to cross high water, a man has freed the team of horses from the wagon. The wagon has two women aboard and appears to be stuck. Two dogs are coming to the rescue. (Courtesy of ZCHS/Virginia Woodward.)

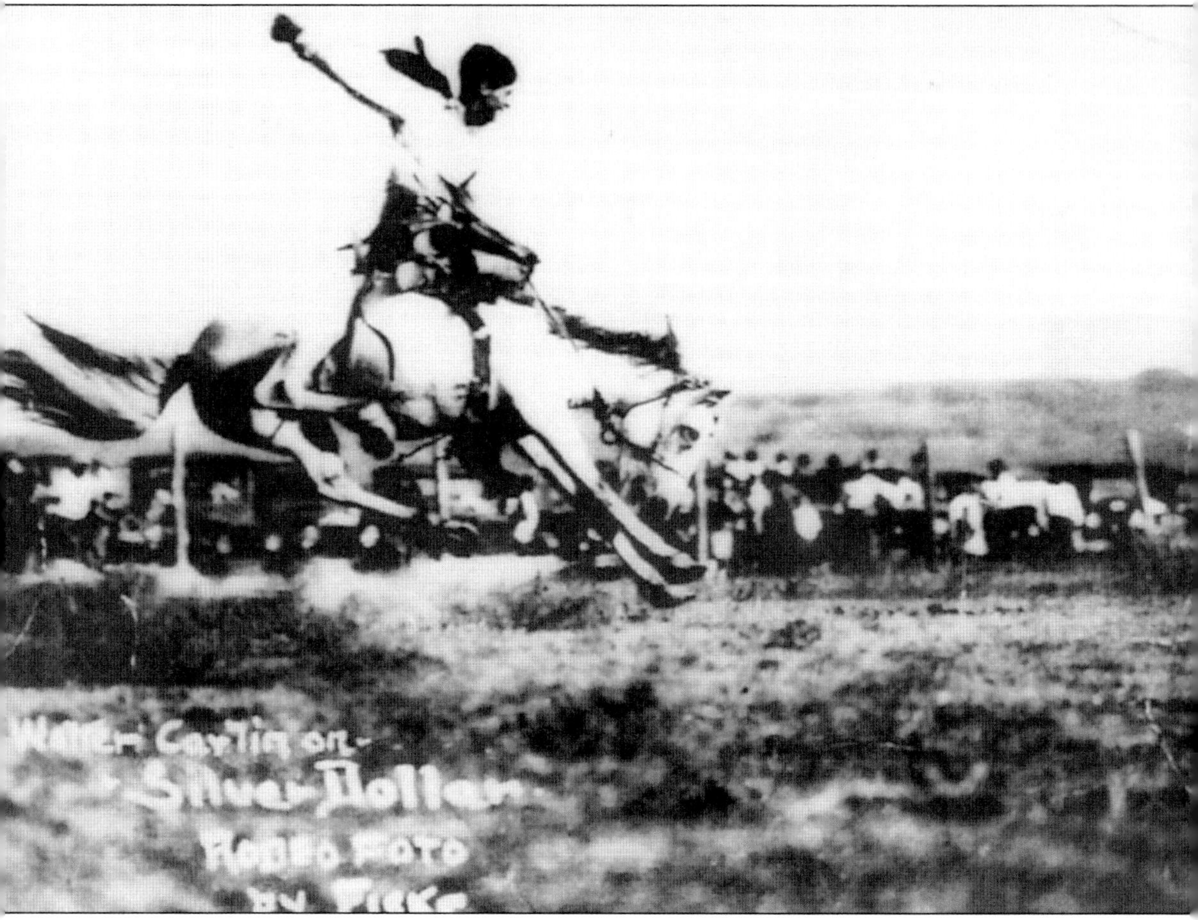

Walter "Hap" Carlin flies high on the horse Silver Dollar. Hap was born in 1909 and was the son of Walter Carlin Sr. and Mae Lablau. Walter Sr. later married Bessie in the Woods and their daughters were Hazel and Catherine "Kitty" Carlin. The family lived on Rudy Creek and raised cattle, horses, pigs, turkeys, guinea hens, peacocks, and purebred bulldogs and hounds. Following the 1929 stock market crash, they moved to Eagle Butte. (Courtesy of Donovin Sprague.)

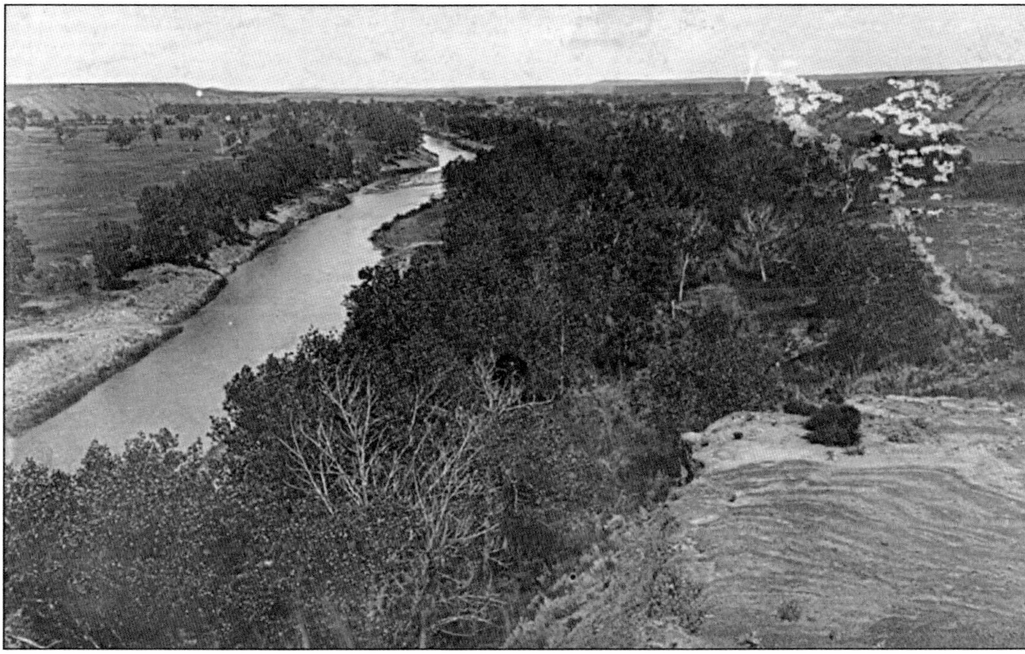

The original name of the Moreau River was Owl River. According to legend, a Lakota was hunting alone and came upon this river and decided to camp for the night. As he cooked, he heard an owl hoot, which he soon recognized was not a real owl. Preparing his weapons, he found it to be an enemy Crow Indian. The Crow said, "You surprised me, so in a gesture of defeat you take my clothing back to your people and I will go back to mine." After that, it was called the Owl River until its name changed to the Moreau River. (Courtesy of ZCHS.)

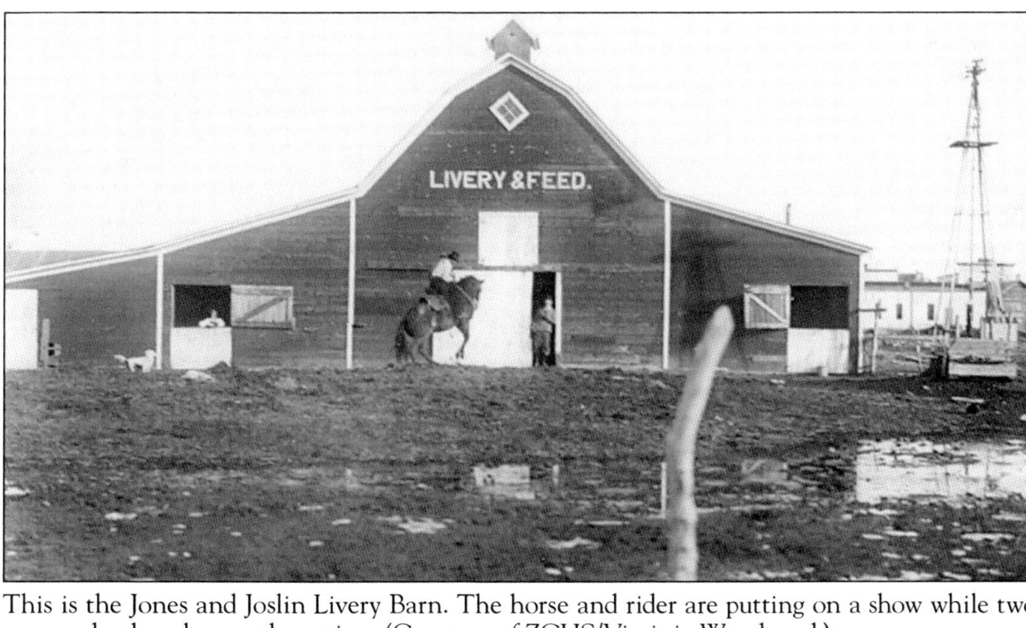

This is the Jones and Joslin Livery Barn. The horse and rider are putting on a show while two men and a dog observe the action. (Courtesy of ZCHS/Virginia Woodward.)

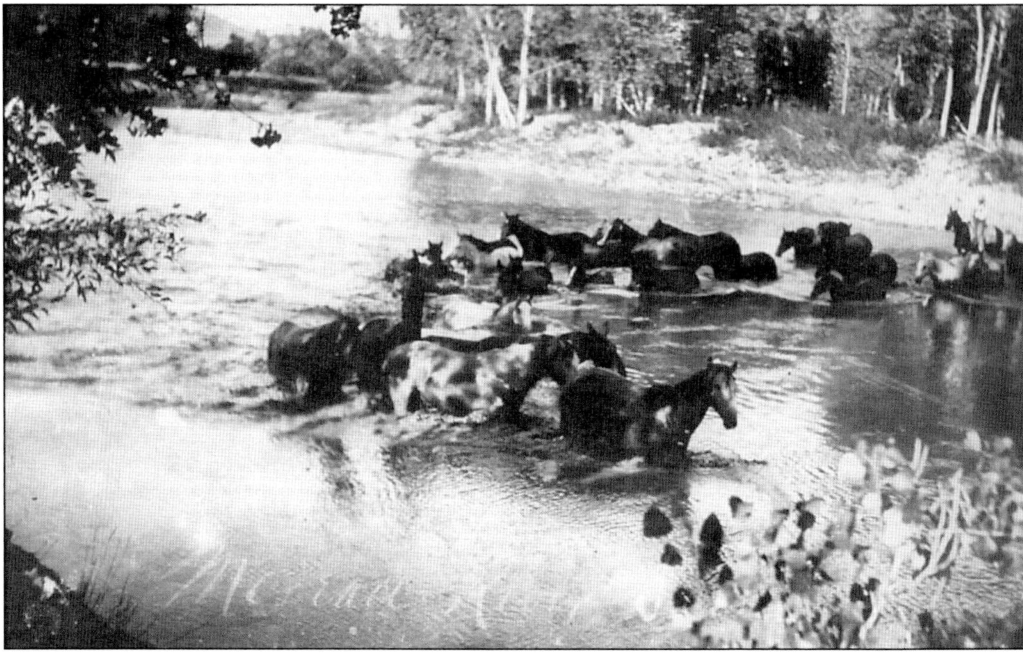

A herd of horses is being moved across the Moreau River, which crosses Ziebach County east to west and flows into the Missouri River. The Sword and Dagger outfit identified their herd with a sword brand on the left side by the shoulder and a dagger on the hip of the animal. Owners of this herd are not identified. (Courtesy of Irean Jordan.)

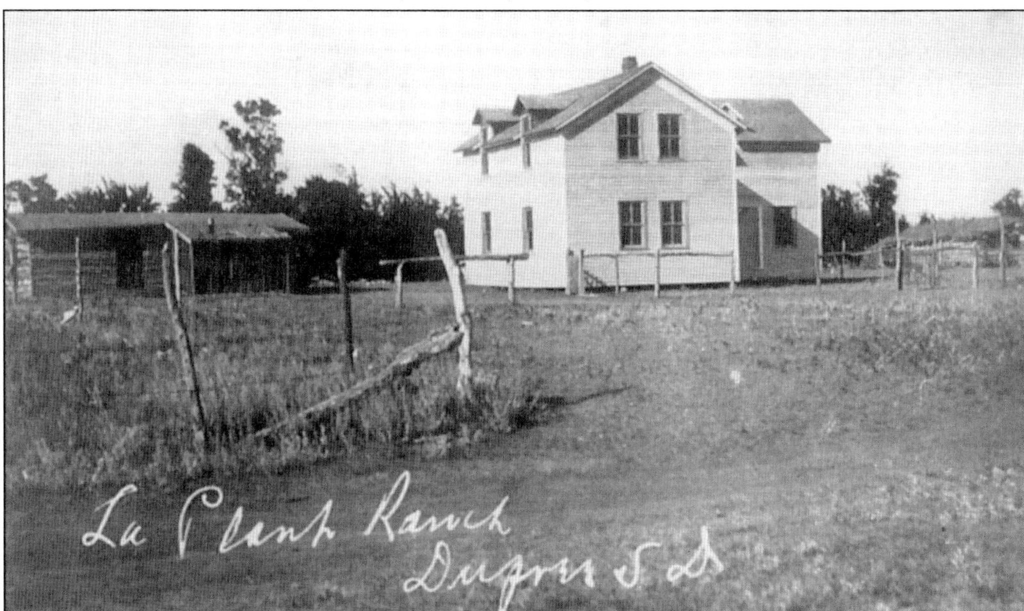

This is the Babe LaPlante Ranch on Bear Creek, west of the Bear Creek community of the same name. The Bert Libolt place was nearby, but the house later burned in what was believed to be arson. The LaPlantes were a noted family of early French traders. One family photograph of them shows Charles, Babe, Louie, Alex, Fred, Louie Sr., and George together. (Courtesy of Irean Jordan.)

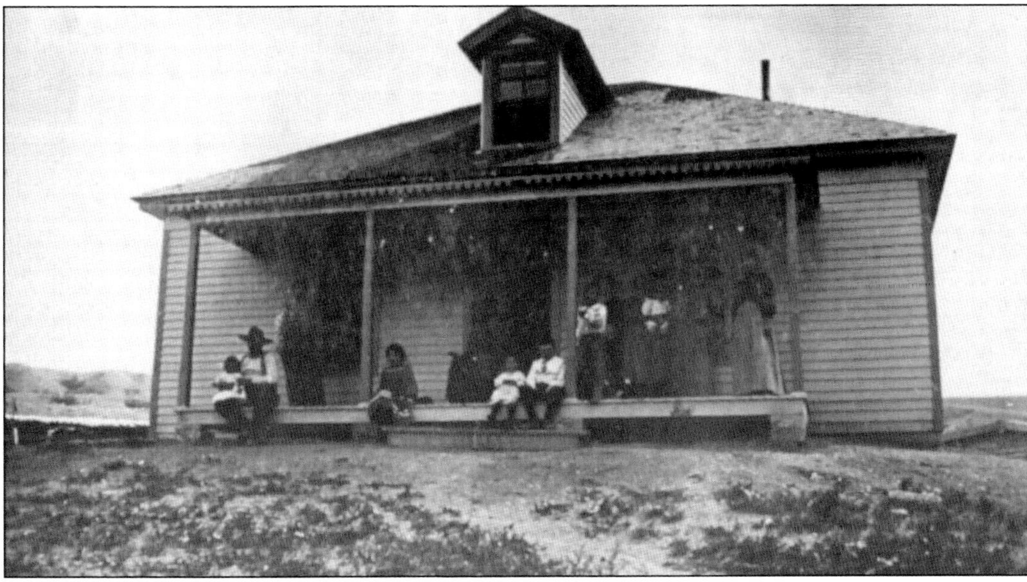

This is the home place of Ed Narcelle, who once ran a big range in the Cherry Creek country for cattle outfits such as the 70, NSS, and Spur. Ed also ran cattle for Scotty Philip before the big cattle leases came. The NSS was known as the Running N Double S and was owned by Narcisse Narcelle until his death. A son-in-law of Narcisse's was Kid Rich, who gained notoriety from his unsolved murder. (Courtesy of Donovin Sprague.)

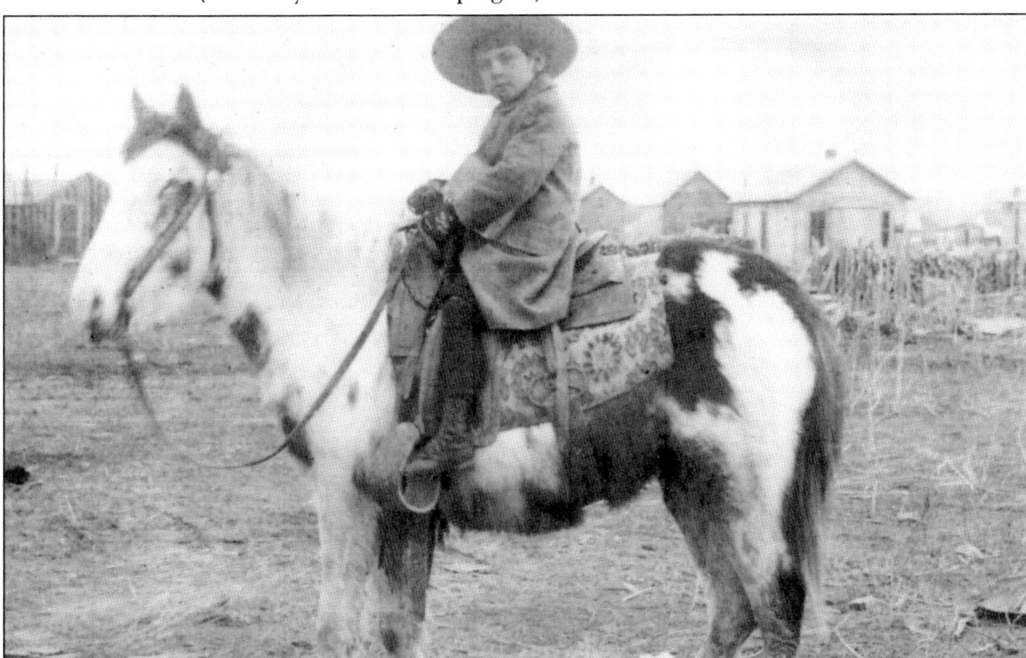

This photograph was taken at Fort Pierre and shows the oldest son of Narcisse Narcelle, who died as a boy. Narcisse was born in 1849, and during the late 19th and early 20th centuries, he reportedly had the largest cattle operation not only in the state, but in the country, with stock ranging over the entire Cheyenne River Sioux Reservation. In 1892, he was admitted into the Western South Dakota Stock Growers Association. (Courtesy of Donovin Sprague.)

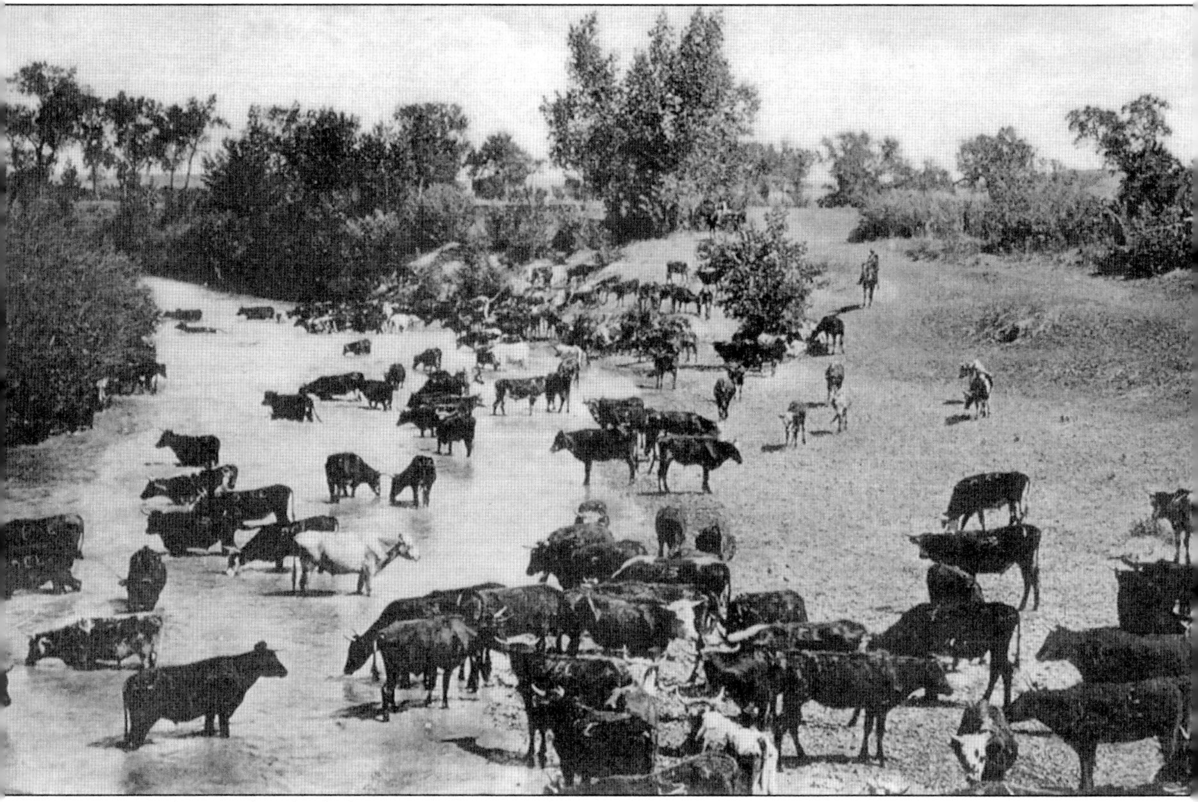

A cattle roundup fords the Moreau River. The Diamond A Cattle Company, established in Colorado, was the largest cow outfit to operate during the open range days in South Dakota, covering all of Ziebach and part of Dewey County. The Matador Cattle Company, owned by Murdo McKenzie, leased the other part of the reservation. (Courtesy of Irean Jordan.)

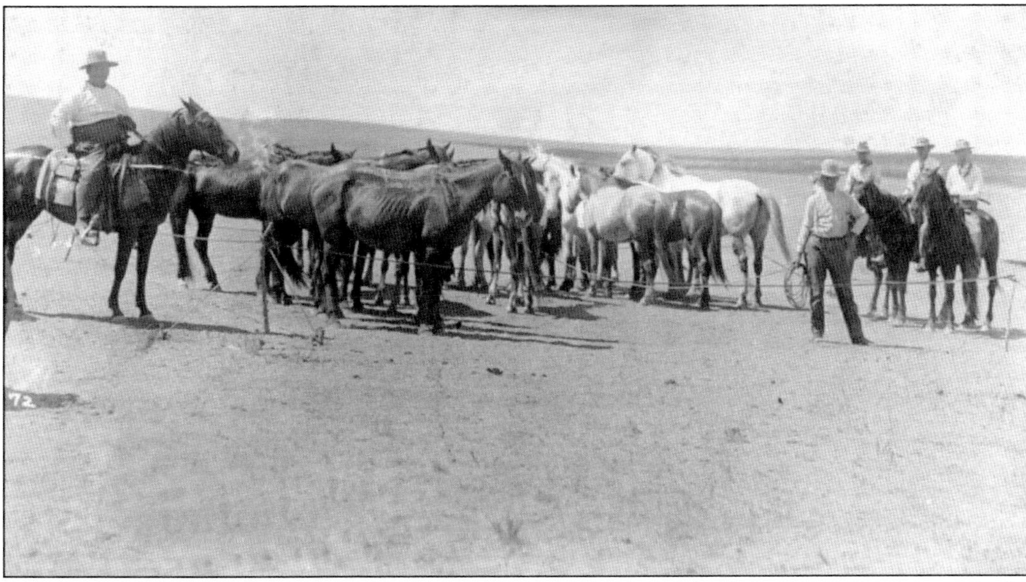

Five cowboys are gathering horses, with Jim Swan on the left. The horses at center are underfed and the grassland looks very sparse, probably from hot and dry weather conditions. (Courtesy of ZCHS.)

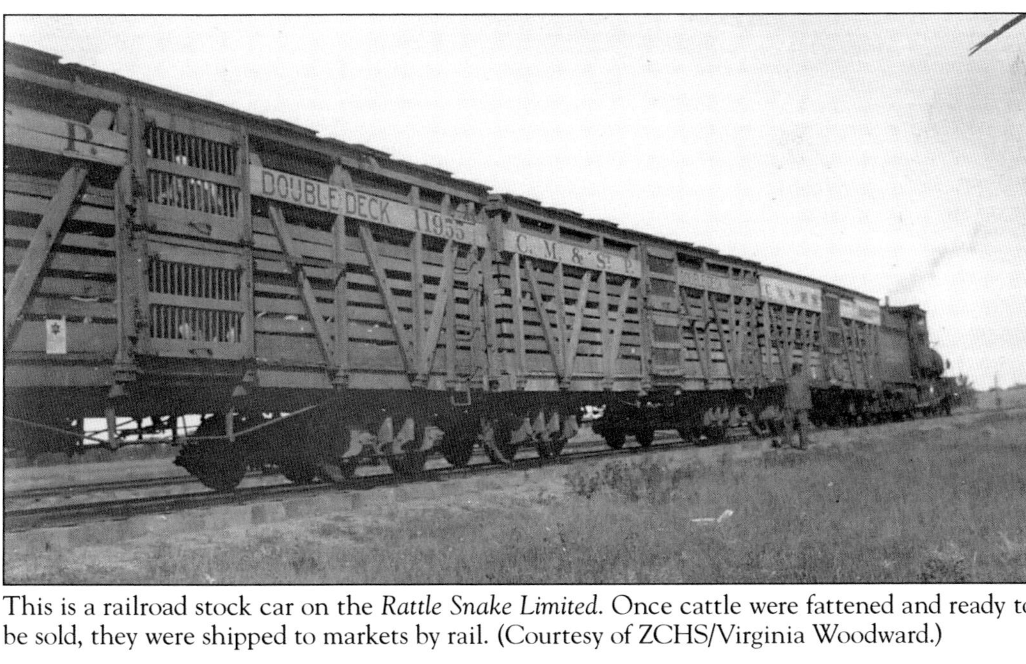

This is a railroad stock car on the *Rattle Snake Limited*. Once cattle were fattened and ready to be sold, they were shipped to markets by rail. (Courtesy of ZCHS/Virginia Woodward.)

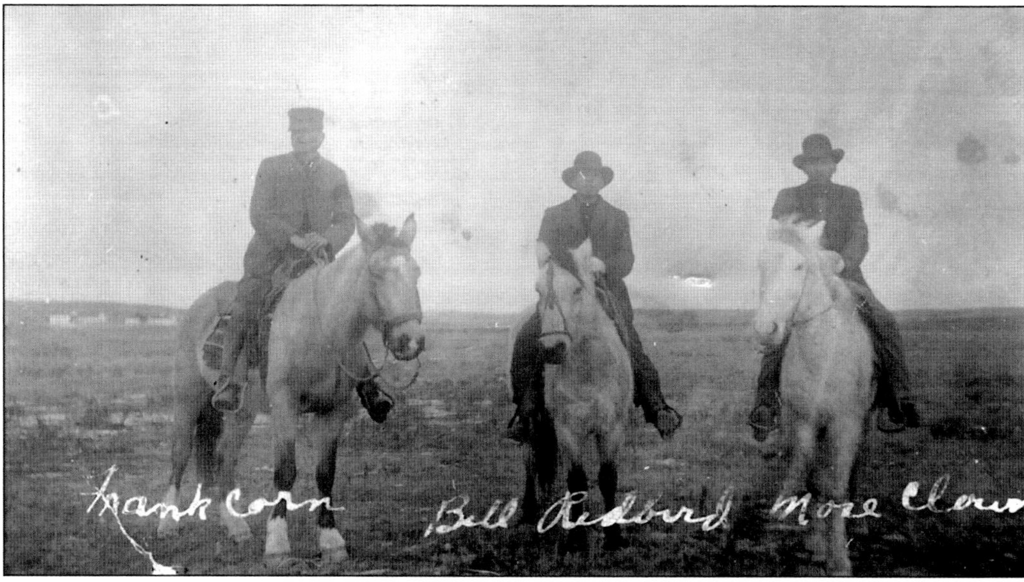

Paul Red Bird had two children, Bill and Mollie, who later married Frank Corn. Moses Clown was the son of Amos Clown and Julia Iron Cedar Woman of Thunder Butte; he died of wounds he received 10 days before the end of World War I. The Redelm newspaper recorded that his funeral was the greatest gathering of people ever assembled in the history of Ziebach County. (Courtesy of Thelma Frame.)

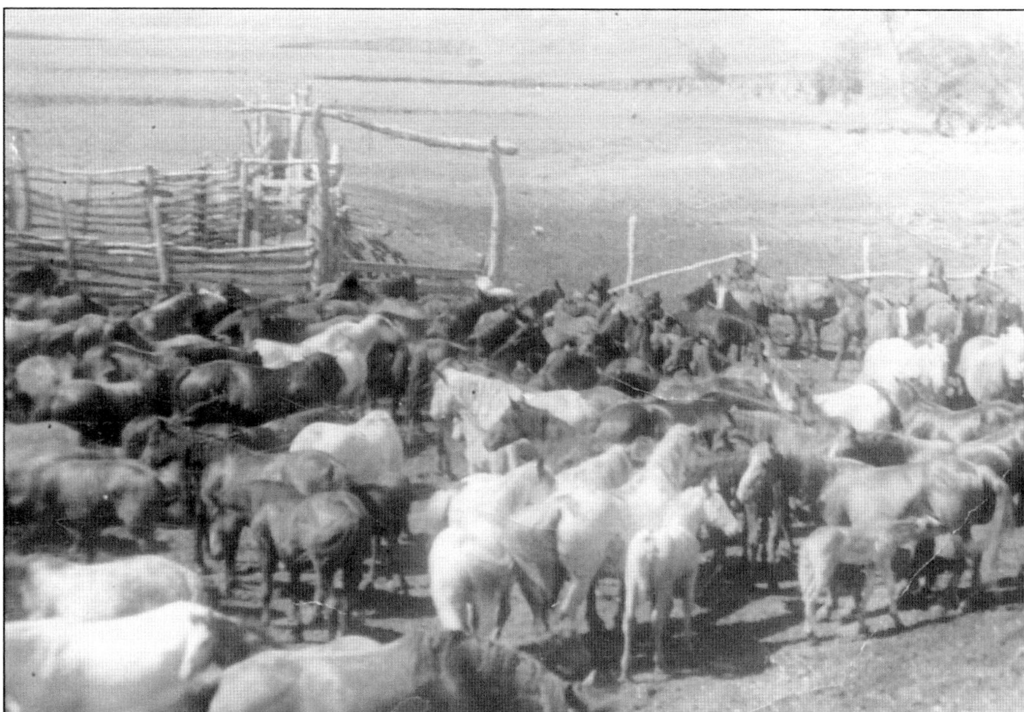

This picture was taken in 1941 at Jack Hunt's ranch on Dupree Creek south of Dupree. Jack Hunt married Jennie Annis, and their sons include Geno and Everett Hunt. (Courtesy of Faye Longbrake.)

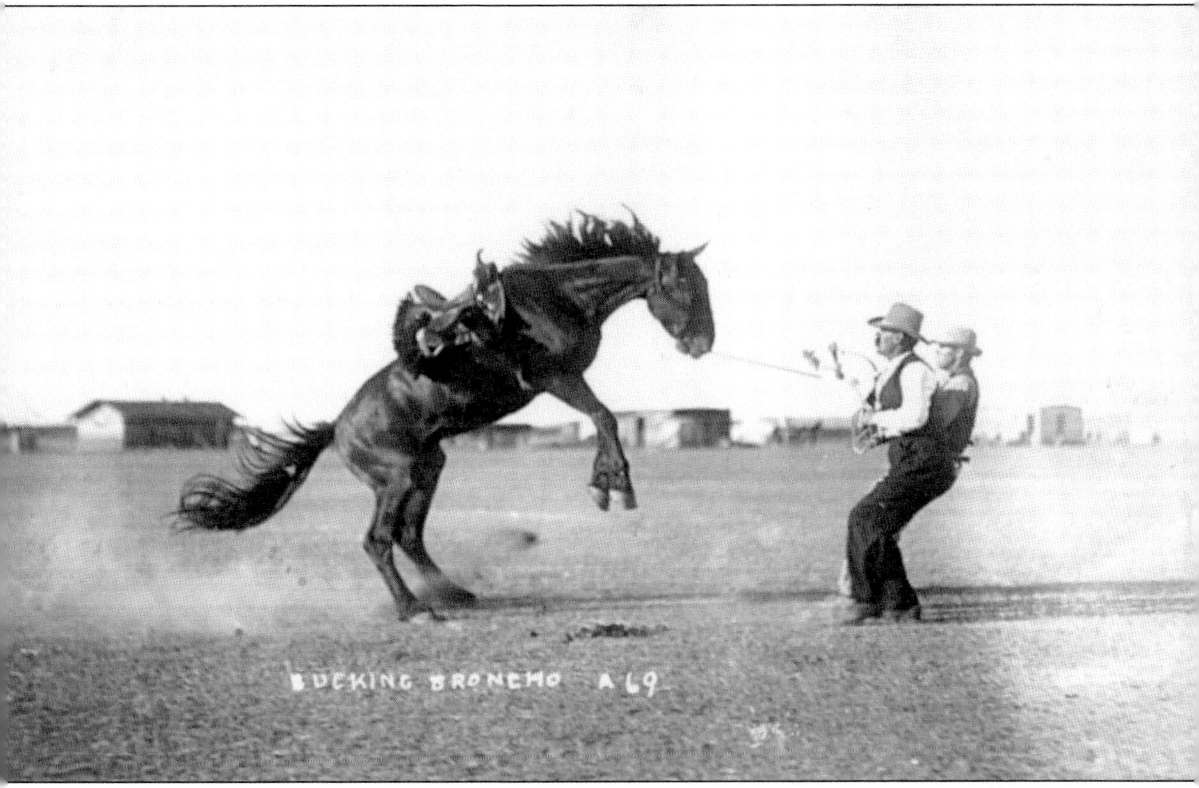

Pictured here are Babe LaPlante and Hank Oakes attempting to settle down a saddle horse. (Courtesy of ZCHS.)

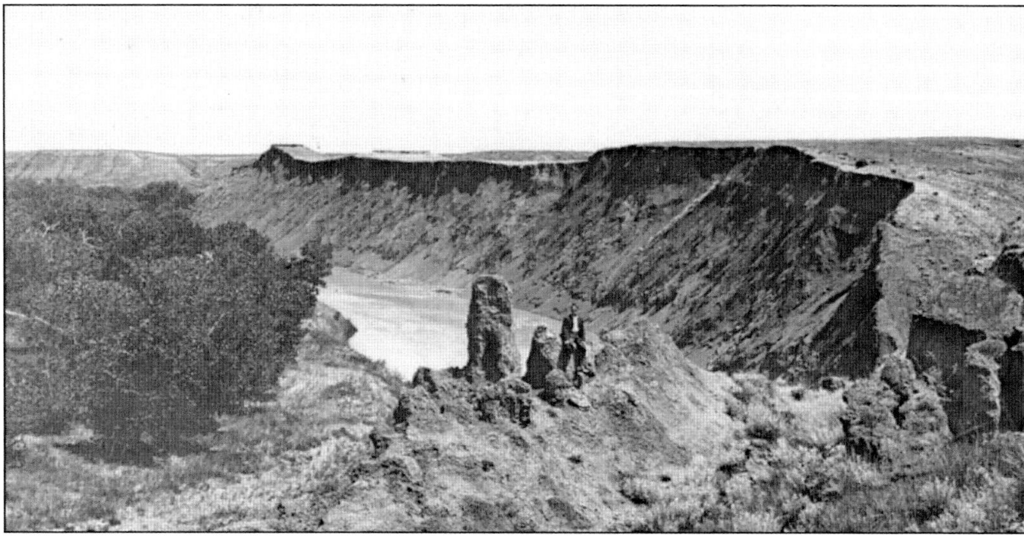

Along the banks of the Moreau River, a man poses for a photograph. The Moreau River crosses Ziebach County and flows into the Missouri River. (Courtesy of ZCHS.)

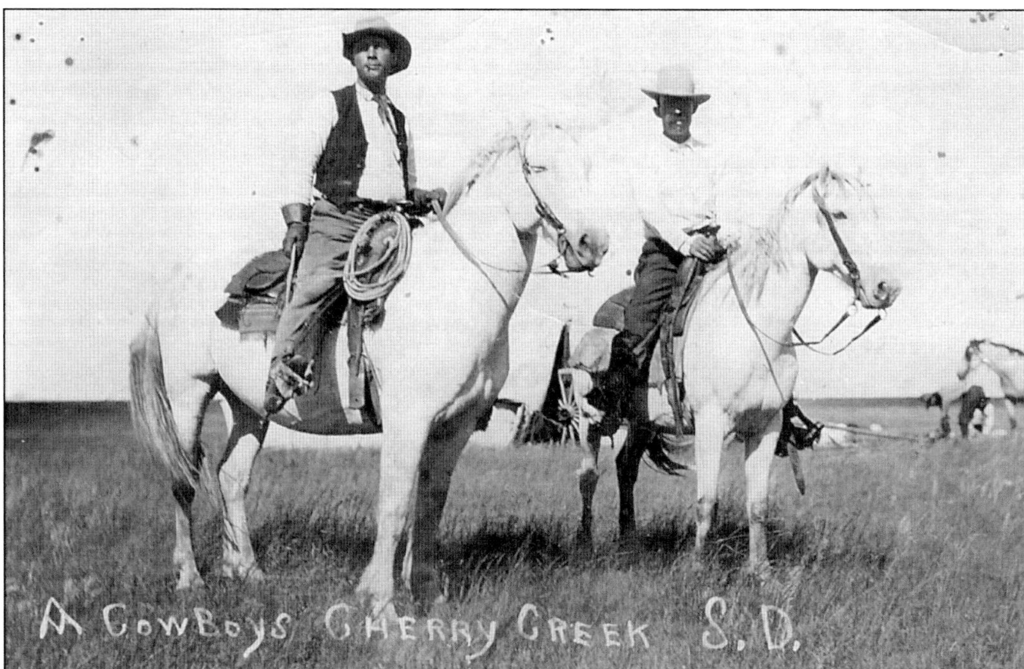

This photograph was taken at Cherry Creek, South Dakota. The Diamond A Cattle Company was the largest cattle outfit during the open range days in South Dakota. It was established by Frank Bloom about 1870 in Colorado. Burton "Cap" Mossman joined the Diamond A Cattle Company as general manager until the company sold in 1944. Mossman leased 1 million acres on the reservation for 4¢ an acre. Cattle were shipped from Evarts, South Dakota, to Chicago. (Courtesy of Thelma Frame.)

Felix Benoist Sr. is pictured as a student at Hampton Institute in Virginia in 1877. Upon his return, he moved from the family ranch near Evarts to the Cherry Creek area where he worked as foreman for his brother-in-law Narcisse Narcelle. He was agency interpreter between Si Tanka (Big Foot) and Colonel Sumner just prior to Si Tanka leaving with his band to Wounded Knee in 1890. Benoist and Narcelle had large ranching operations, before fences. (Courtesy of Donovin Sprague.)

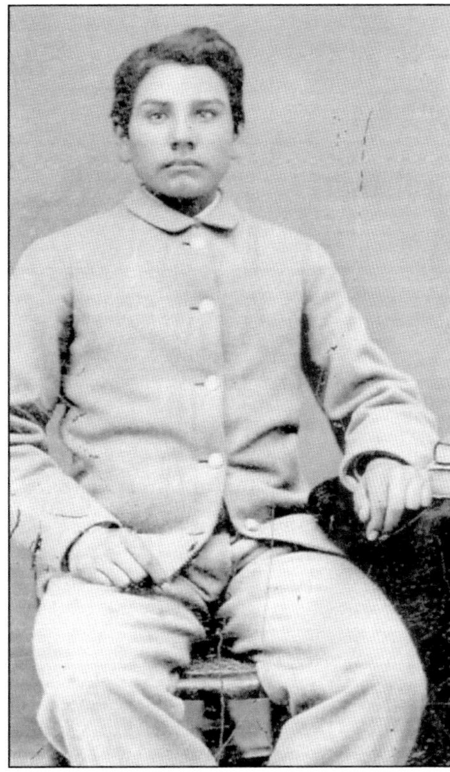

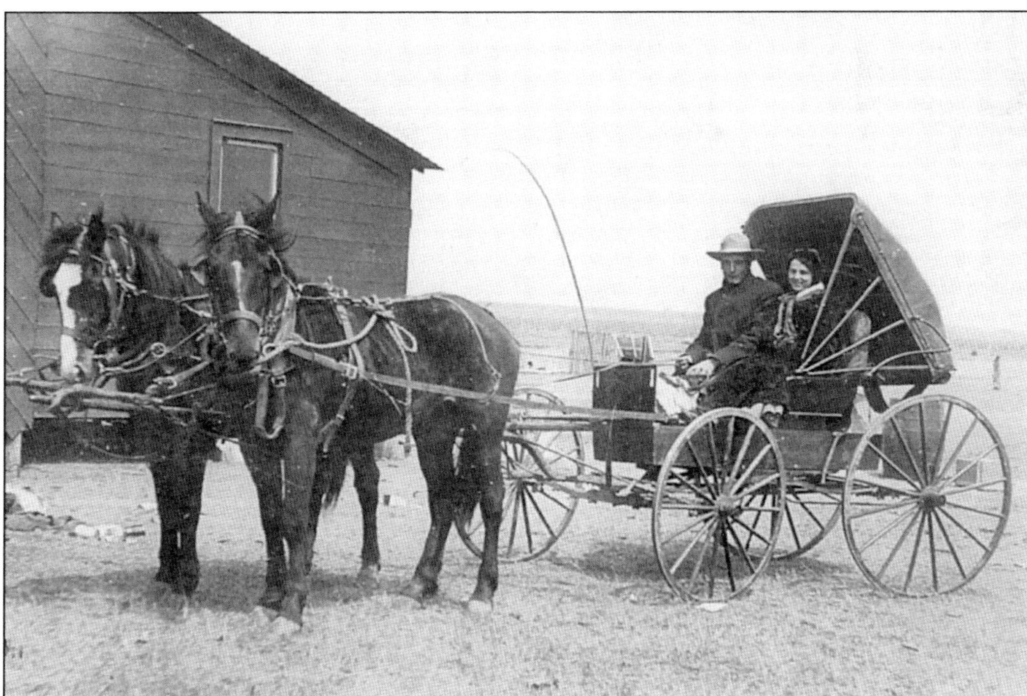

This is Frank Bull and Lota Ralston ready to travel with their buggy and team of horses. (Courtesy of Irean Jordan.)

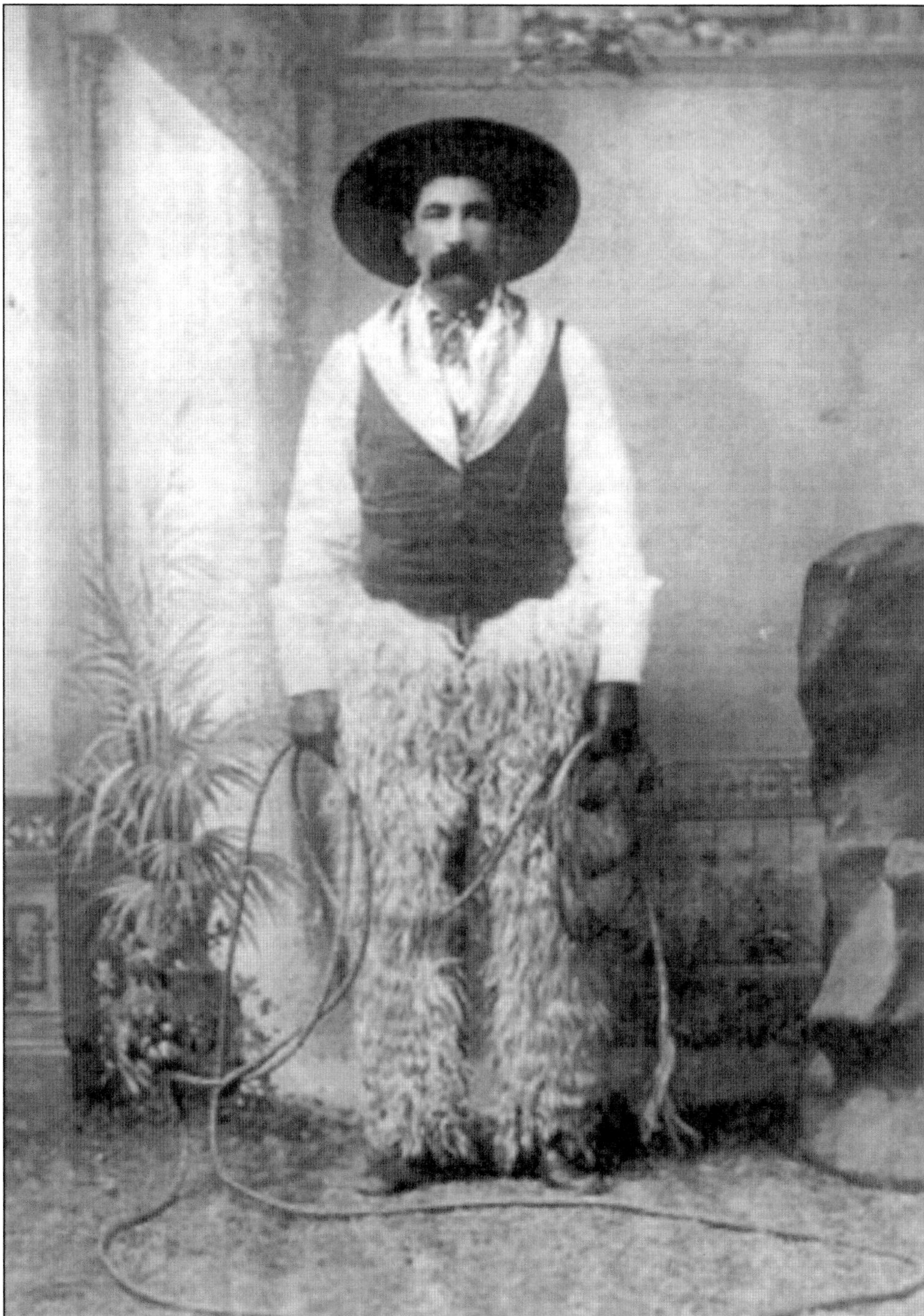

Edward Narcelle sports fancy chaps and a rope. Edward was the husband of Julia LeCompte and brother of Edward and Narcisse Narcelle. Edward and Narcisse were some of South Dakota's very first beef producers and supplied Fort Sully with beef. Edward based his operations where Eagle Butte is today, and the cattle also ranged onto the Standing Rock Reservation. Narcisse also had a son named Edward. (Courtesy of Donovin Sprague.)

Five

DEVELOPMENT IN ZIEBACH COUNTY

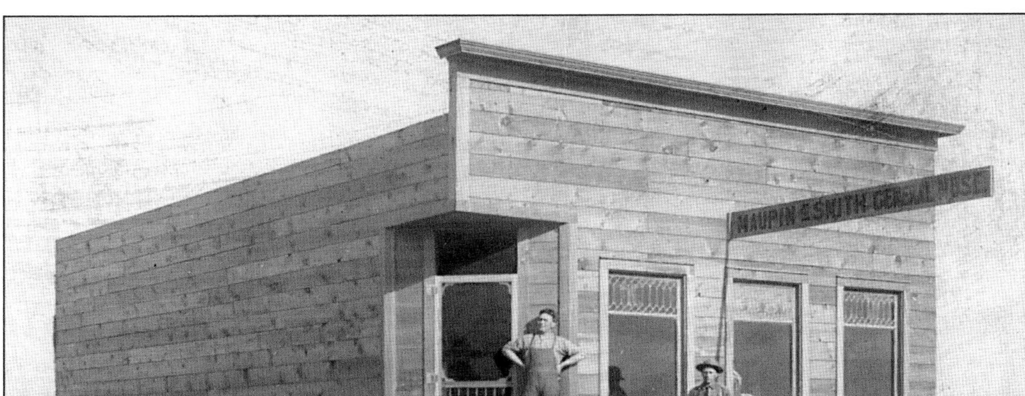

This is the Maupin and Smith store. The Maupins originated in France as de Maupin (pronounced moe-peen). The name likely indicates the area of France they came from, with *de* meaning "edge," *mau* meaning "mouth or head of," and *pin* meaning "pine forest." The Maupin coat of arms shows pineapples, which is what pinecones were once called in England. At least two of the Maupins—Tolbert "Tollie" and William "Henry"—operated stores in Dupree. (Courtesy of ZCHS.)

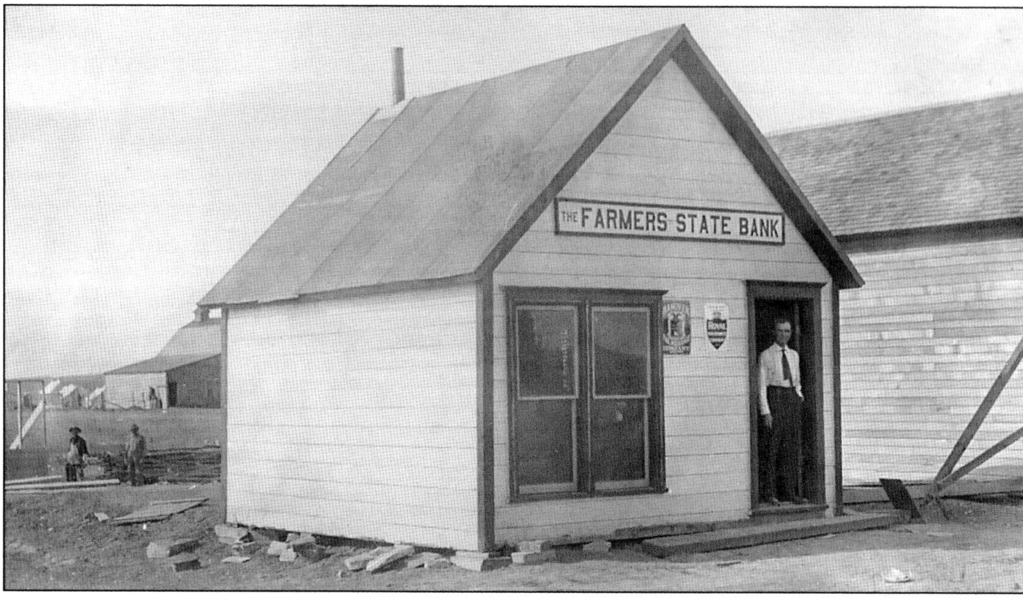

A man is pictured in the doorway of the Farmers State Bank in Dupree. (Courtesy of Thelma Frame.)

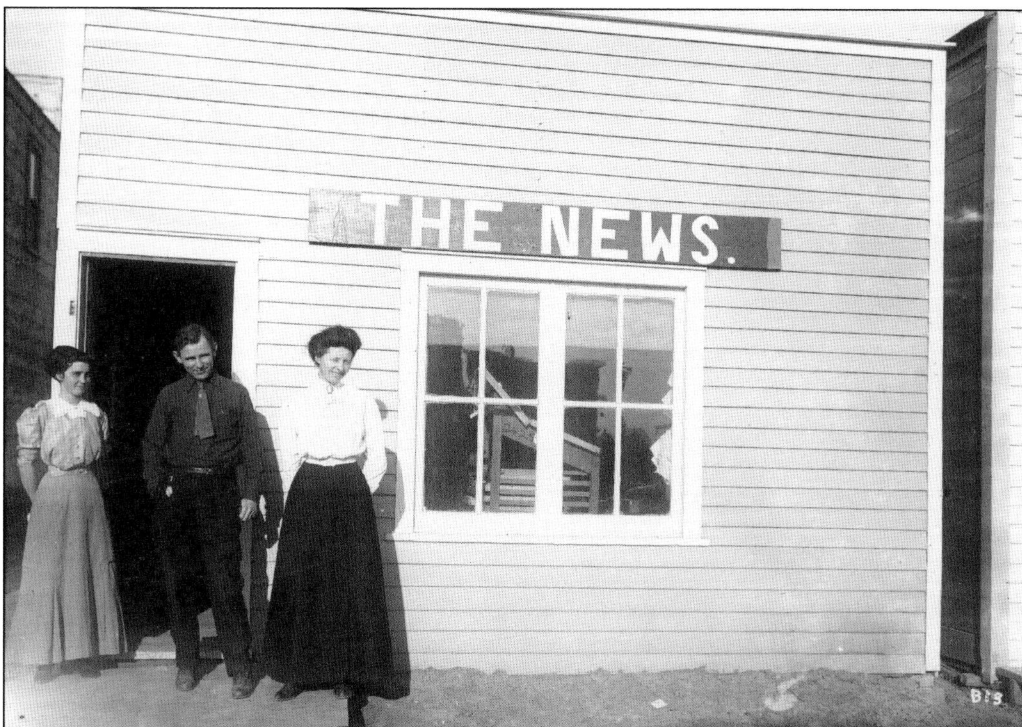

Editor Frank Riley is pictured in front of the newspaper office with unidentified women. The first paper in Ziebach County was the *Dupree Leader*, published in May 1910 by James Stewart of Selby and Pete Hoven of Hoven, South Dakota. The *Ziebach County News* was published by Lottie Kruckman and Eb Jones in 1911. They sold the paper to Frank E. Riley in 1911, and he continued with the business until 1932. (Courtesy of ZCHS.)

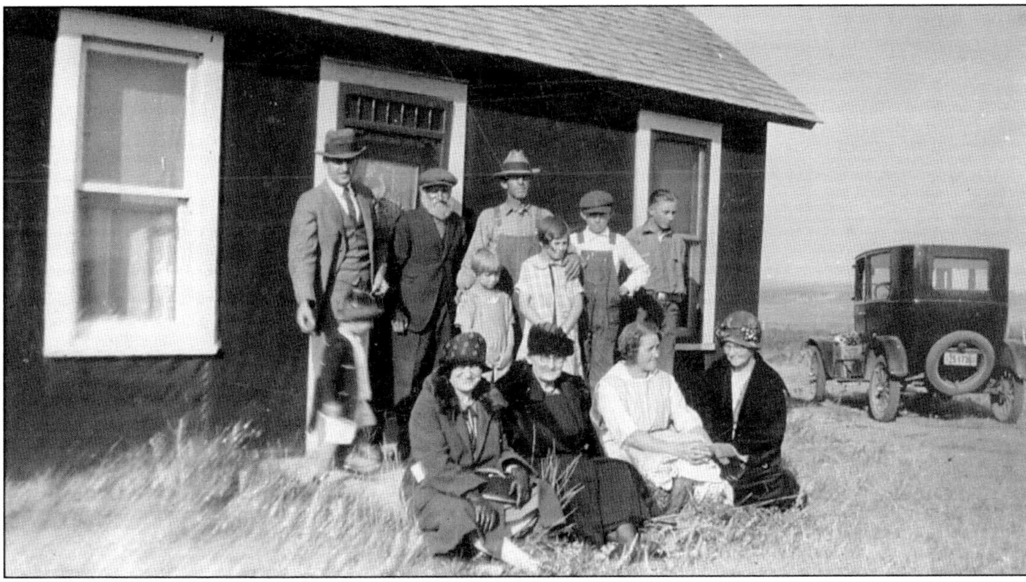

V. F. Matter and family stand in front of their house. Vic Matter named their place Glad Valley Farm in 1910. Nearby was Pickerville, the present site of Glad Valley. Vic became the local postmaster, so the post office at Pickerville changed its name to Glad Valley Post Office, and the community became known as Glad Valley. (Courtesy of ZCHS.)

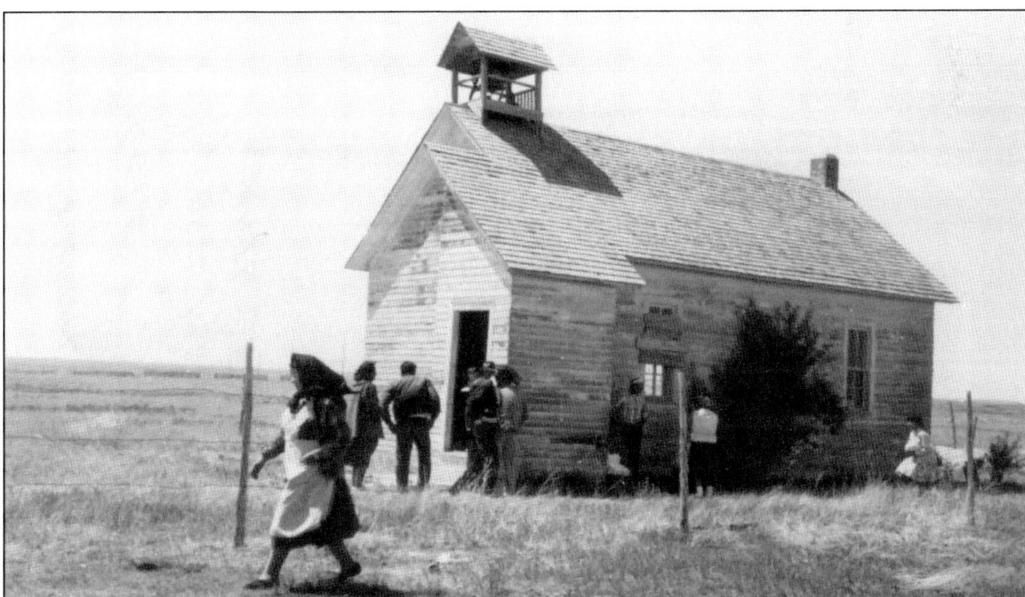

The woman walking in the foreground is Mary "Mollie" D. Rivers, mother of Eugenia Burgee, and Emma Lambert is among those in the background. The Dupree Family Buffalo Church is located east of Cherry Creek near the Carlin Bridge over the Cheyenne River. Fred Dupris Sr. and Good Elk Woman settled here and the Dupree family cemetery is next to the church. The photograph was taken May 24, 1959. (Courtesy of Donovin Sprague.)

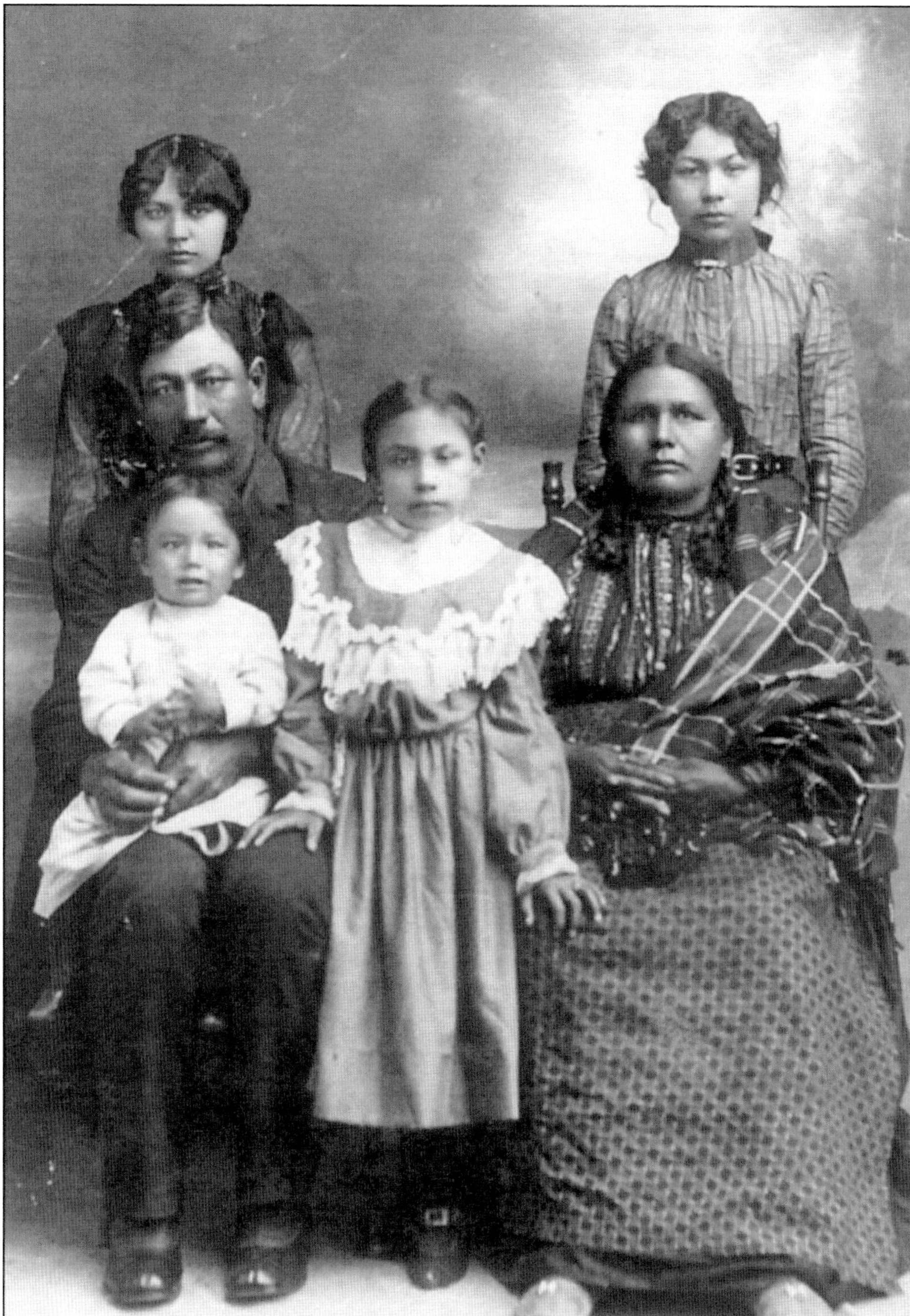

Fred Dupris Jr. holds his infant son Johnny as one of his daughters, Susie, stands between him and his wife, Emily Eagle Shield Dupris. Emily and Fred's other daughters, Edna (left) and Mary, stand behind them. Two sons died in childhood—Philip in 1895 and Ed in 1901 at age two. Mary was known as "Molly" and was the mother of Eugenia Burgee. Molly's Lakota name was Nape Waste Win (Good Hands Woman). (Courtesy of Eugenia Burgee.)

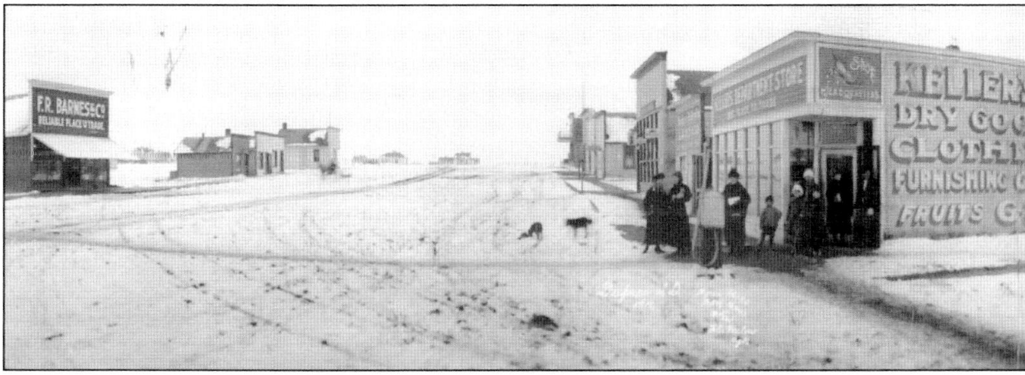

Keller's Department Store was the place to go for dry goods, clothing, household furnishings, shoes, and groceries. I bet they even had some penny candy! (Courtesy of ZCHS.)

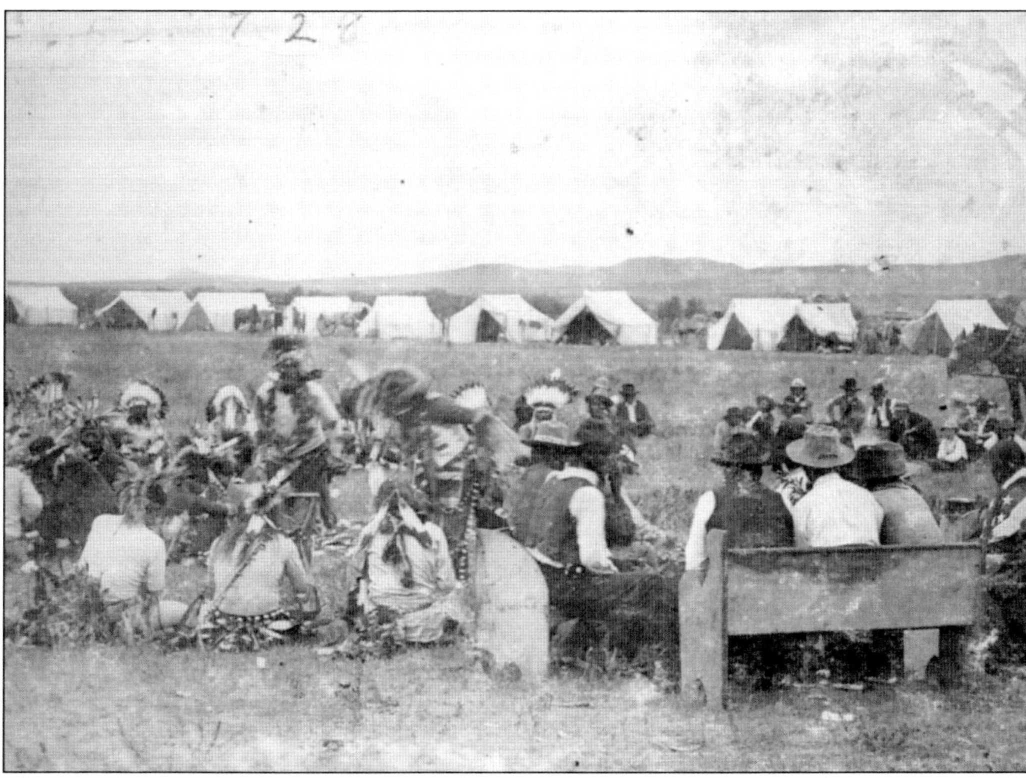
This is a Thunder Butte, South Dakota, celebration. The landmark of Thunder Butte rises to the northwest, at the left side of the photograph. (Courtesy of Donovin Sprague.)

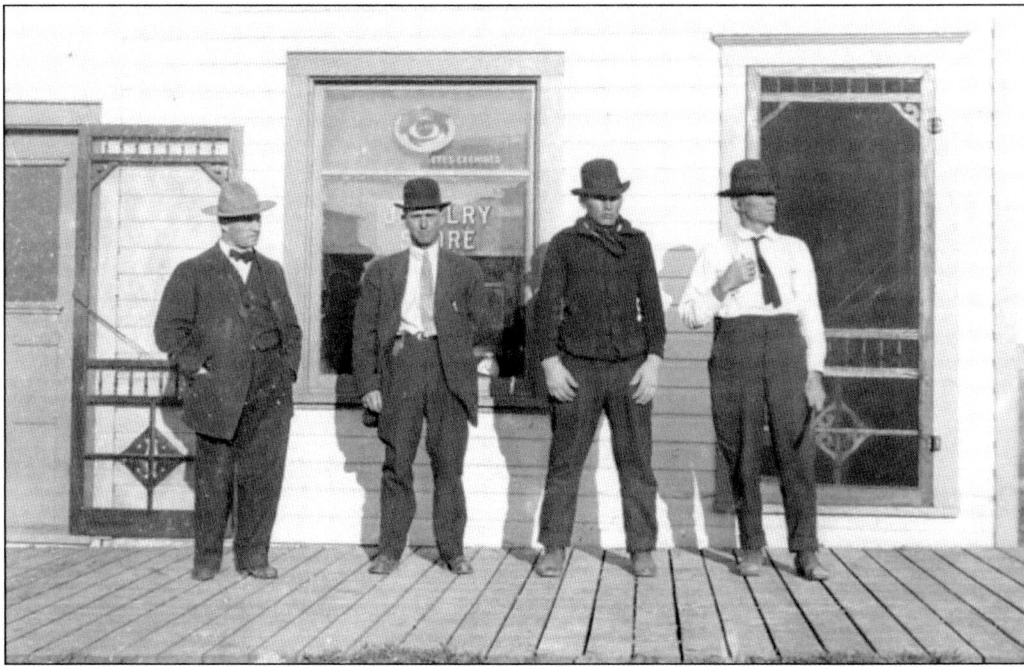

Four gentlemen stand in front of the jewelry store in Dupree. (Courtesy of ZCHS.)

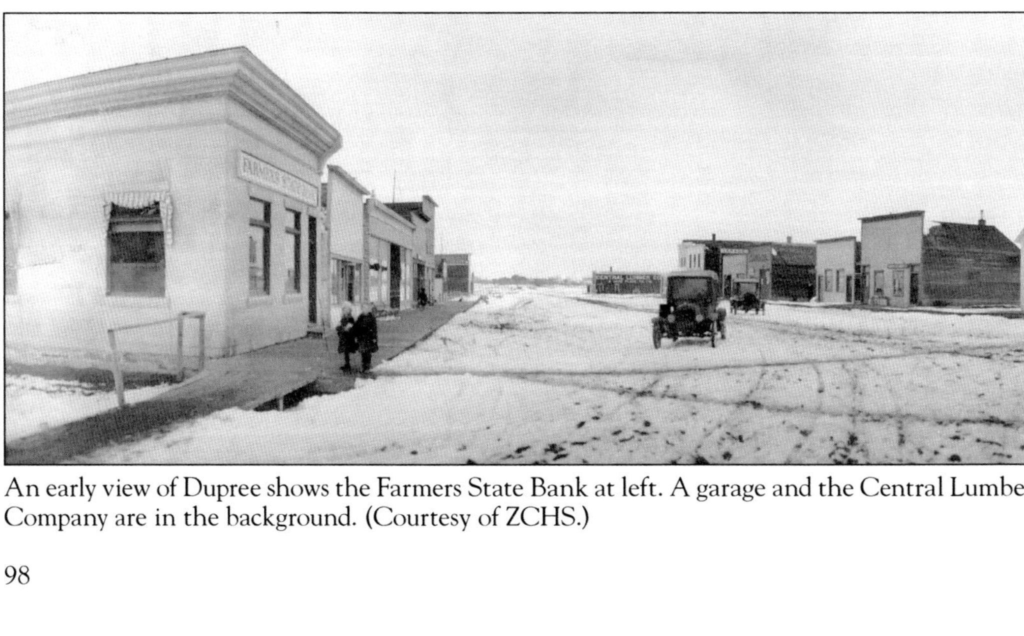

An early view of Dupree shows the Farmers State Bank at left. A garage and the Central Lumber Company are in the background. (Courtesy of ZCHS.)

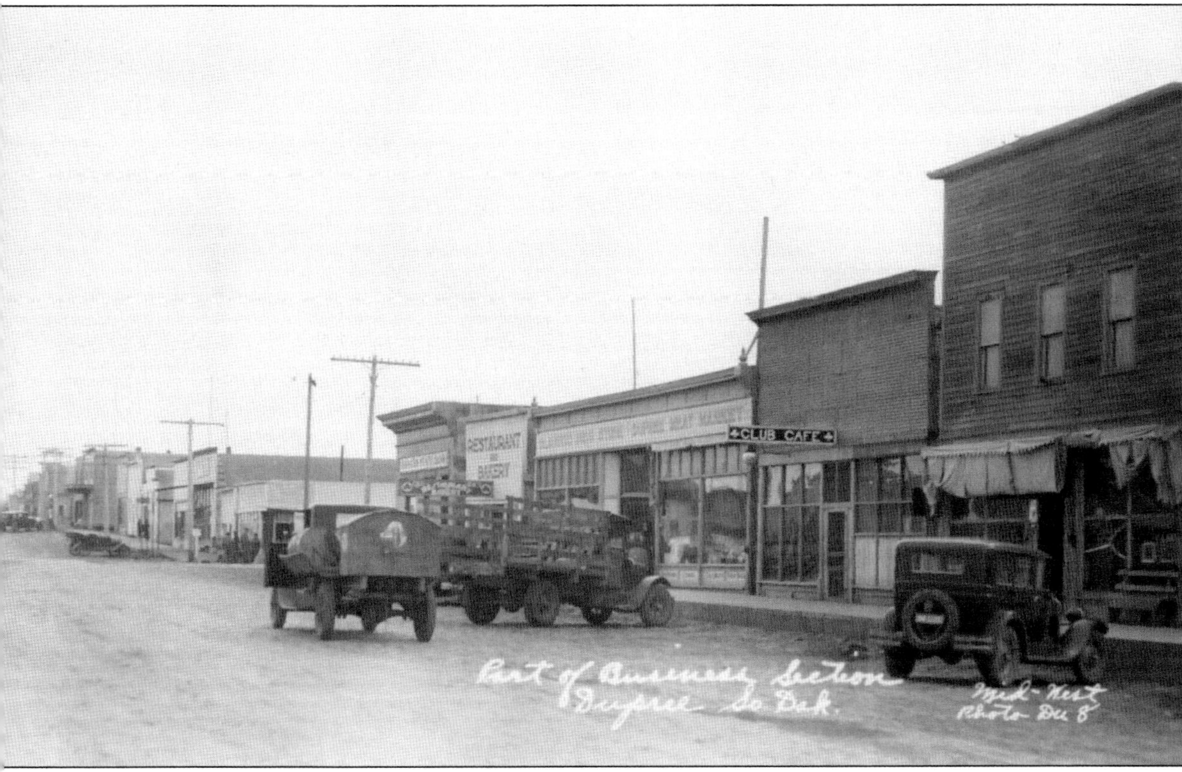

This is part of the business section on Main Street in Dupree. Pictured are a café, meat market, restaurant and bakery, and much more up the street. The photograph was made by Mid-West Photograph. (Courtesy of Robert Shannon.)

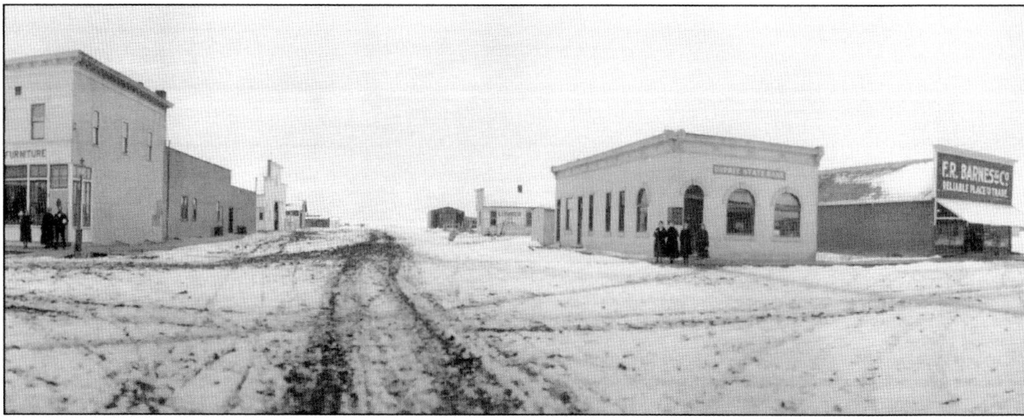

This scene looks east from Main Street in Dupree. The present lumberyard is the rear white building in view on the left side of the street. Across the street from the lumberyard a sign reads "Lumber and Coal." The width of this side street was measured and was wider than Main Street. It may have become the Main Street, but the town grew north and south instead of east and west in the beginning. (Courtesy of ZCHS.)

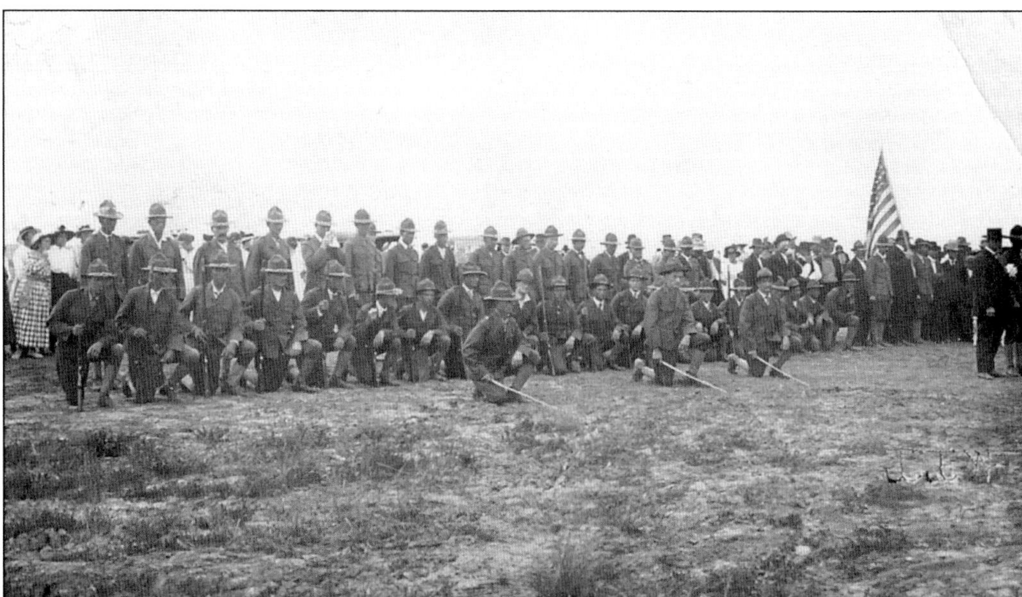

The last draft quota from Ziebach County for World War I is met. Ziebach County sent 197 men for service in World War I. The following 12 men were killed or died of diseases: Edwin Flavius Hodgdon, Charles Yousites, Oliver Leslie Roberts, Henry Lloyd Strommer, Karl Schumann, Edward F. Cors, George Diermier, Moses Clown, Jacob Christianson, George J. Pederson, Joseph Dupris, and Carl Hageman. (Courtesy of Thelma Frame.)

The L. O. Adams store at Red Elm was built in 1916 and burned down in 1929. A sign indicates the Redelm Post Office was also located here. Redelm also had a high school. Early teachers were Homar Norvald, Ruth Davis, Edith Jensen Dexheimer, and Ruth Lovelady. Music for dances was provided by the Callen Orchestra and Orbeck Brothers. (Courtesy of ZCHS.)

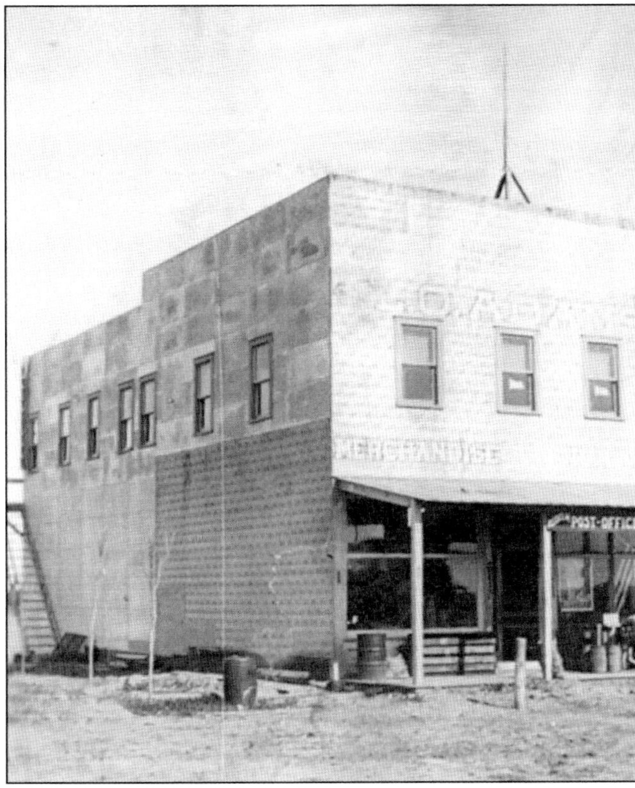

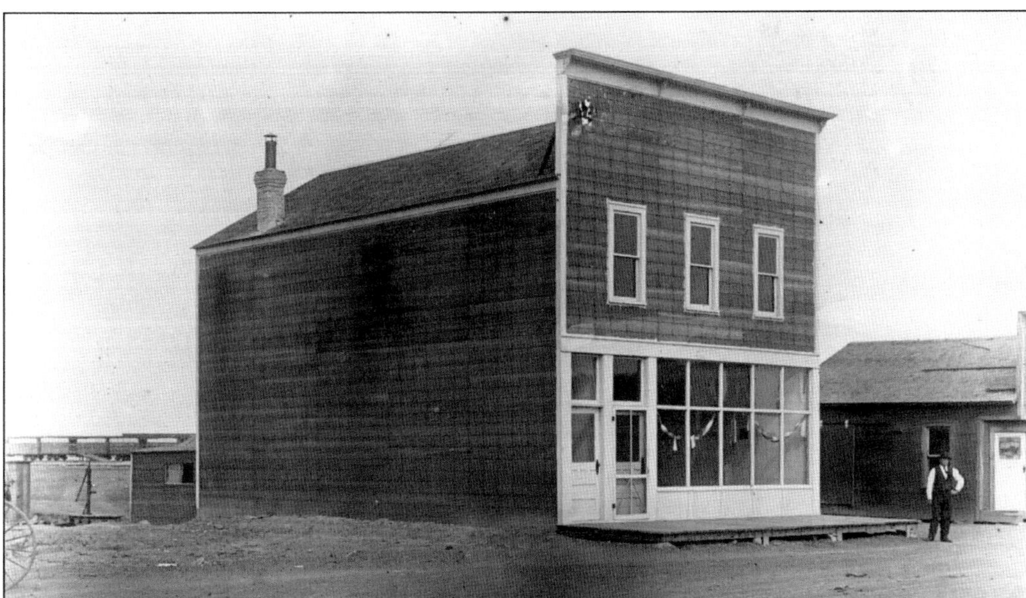

This is the first store and post office at Red Elm, South Dakota. Anderson Lumber Company and Dewey Day's Garage were also started. Later Mr. and Mrs. Day went into the grocery and creamery business until about 1940. Then Pete Reynolds bought the store and ran it until 1953 when he sold it to Francis Stocklin. Early grocers were Rosenthal, Clarence Johnson, John Sejnoha, and H. V. Nielsen. Flora Reynolds ran a restaurant. (Courtesy of ZCHS.)

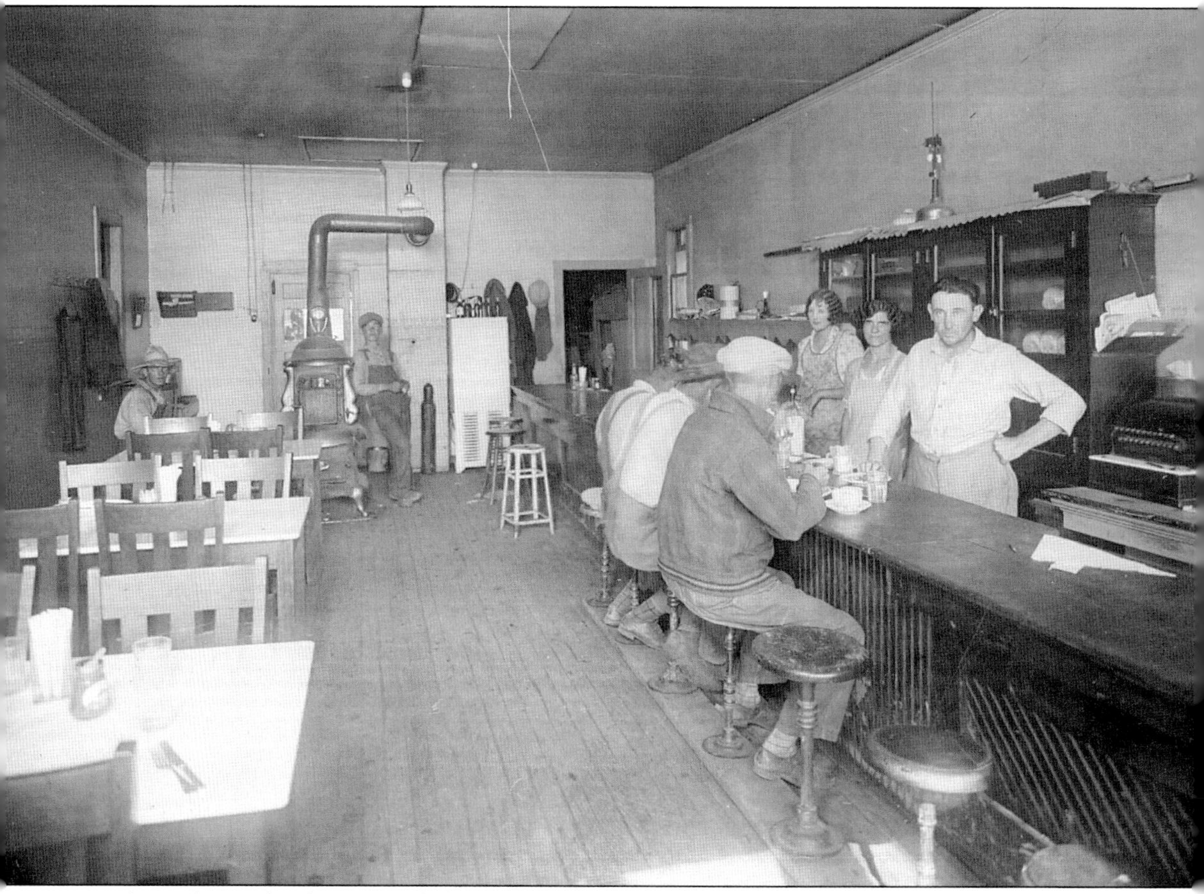

This is the inside of August Bakeberg's Café/ Restaurant in Dupree, South Dakota, about 1925. Edna Mae Marple and another woman are behind the counter. (Courtesy of ZCHS/Bakeberg family.)

Lillian Carlin Briggs was the daughter of Doug Carlin and Marcella Dupris. She married Frank Briggs and their children were "Buster," Marcella "Tet" (Souers), Marion (Laundreau), Flora (Kensler), Catherine (Leake), Bessie (Smith), Margarite, Forest, Helen "Heddy" (Laurenz), Laura (John), Melvelle, and Eva (Severson). The Briggs family lived next to Doug and Marcella Carlin, east of Cherry Creek. (Courtesy of Donovin Sprague.)

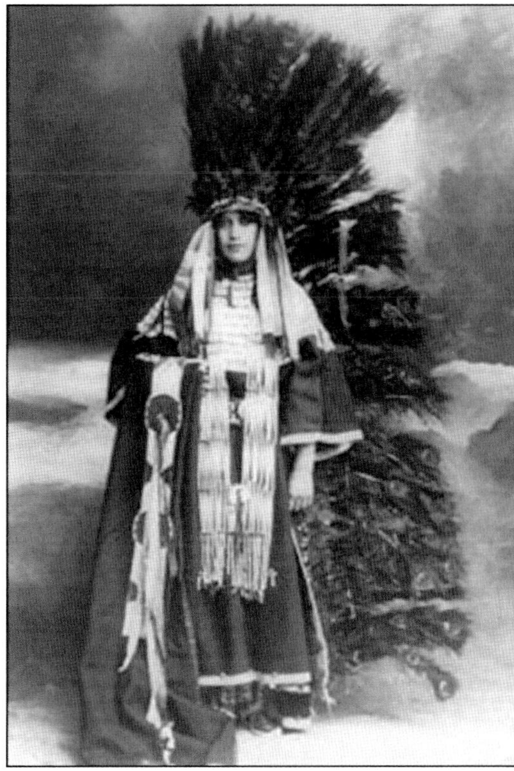

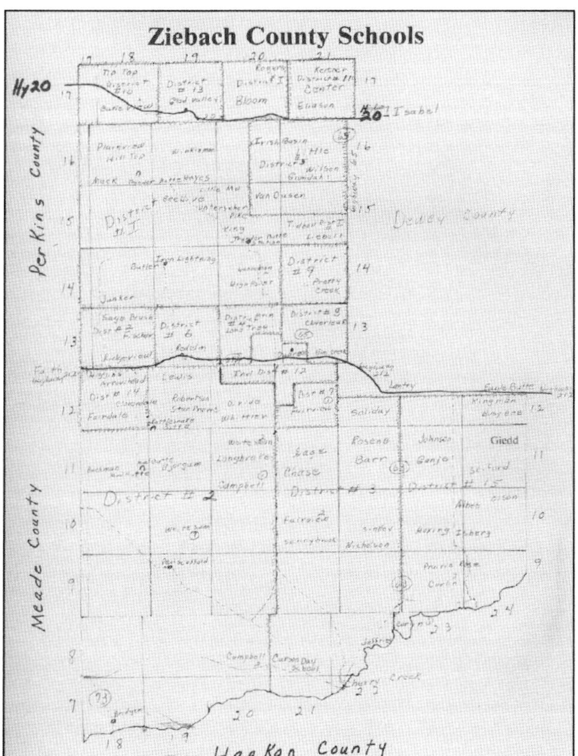

This is a map of Ziebach County schools. (Courtesy of ZCHS.)

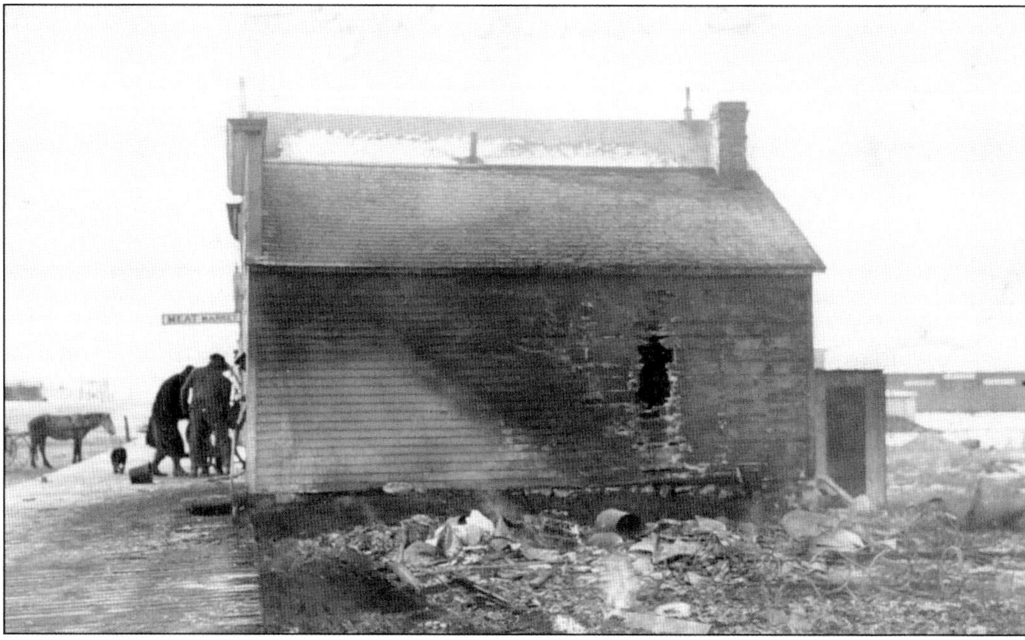

This is one of the buildings damaged from the fire in Dupree. The meat market sign remains above the men. (Courtesy of ZCHS.)

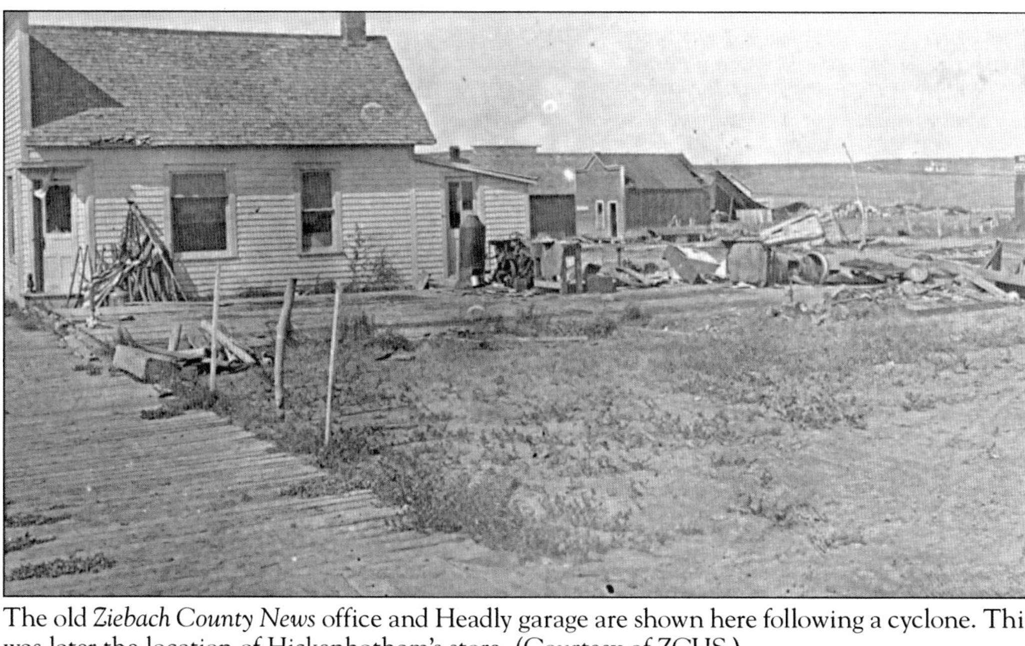

The old *Ziebach County News* office and Headly garage are shown here following a cyclone. This was later the location of Hickenbotham's store. (Courtesy of ZCHS.)

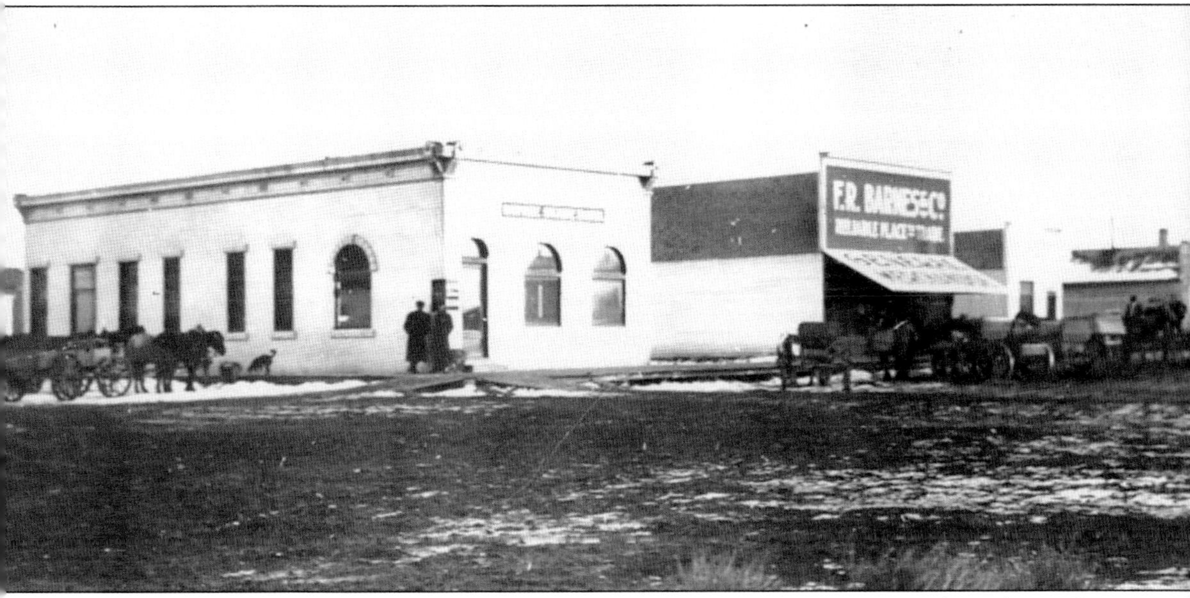

Pictured here are the Dupree State Bank (the current location of First Financial Bank USA) and the F. R. Barnes store, which boasts the logo of "Reliable Place to Trade." The Barnes store burned down in later years. (Courtesy of ZCHS/Virginia Woodward.)

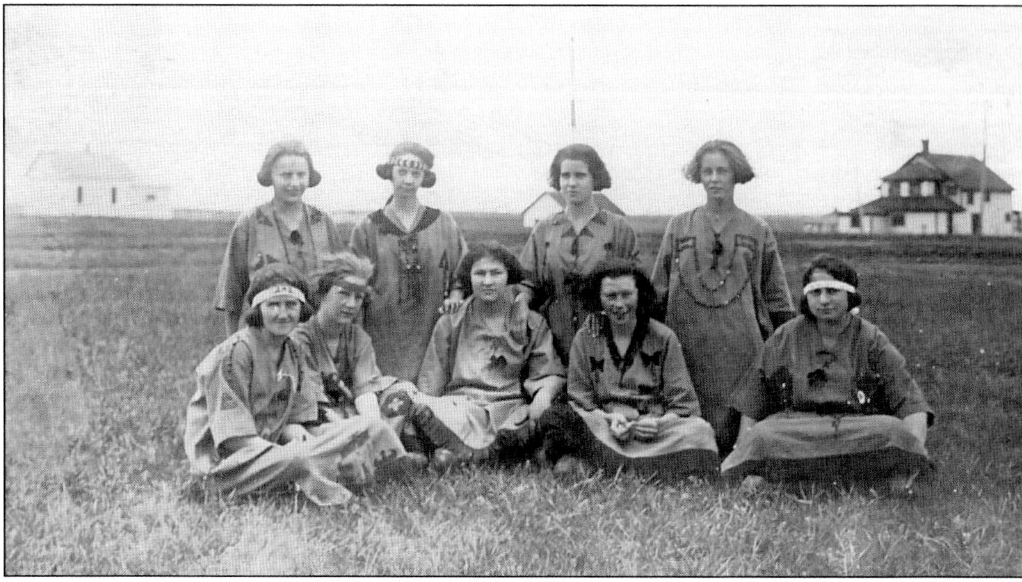

The names of these ladies are Grace Stevens Leake, Effie Pollard Hall, Louella Geesey Ferguson, Clarissa Pladsen-Price, Margaret Stephenson-Parrott-Tubbs, Liona Callen-Bickett, Freda Serr-Jones, Lucille Walters-Mauser, and Ruth Stevens-Hersey. (Courtesy of ZCHS/Harold and Joan Ross.)

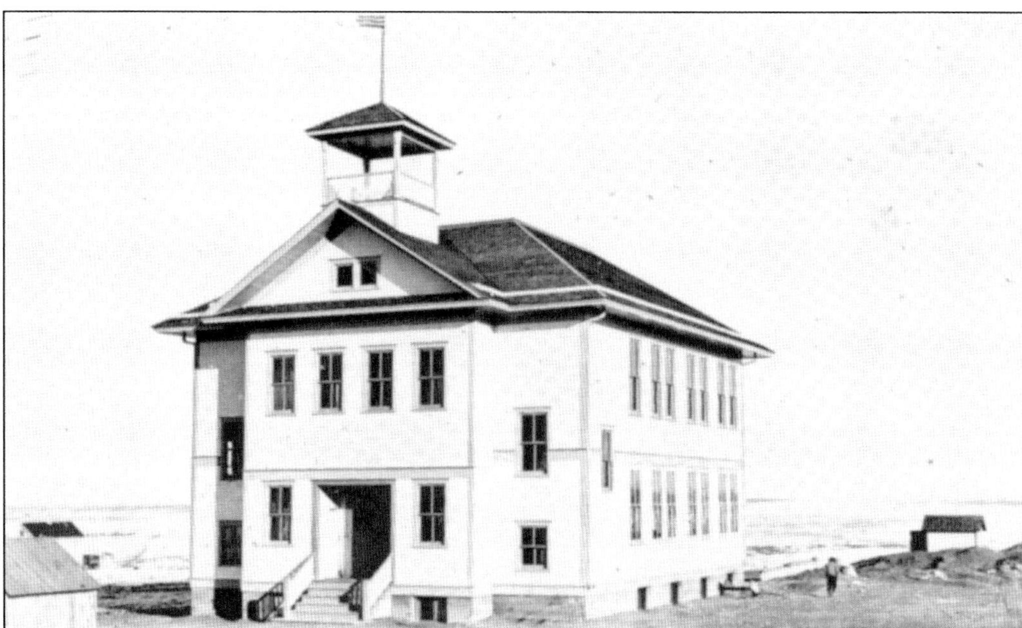

The Dupree School was built between 1913 and 1916 and served the community until 1939 in the same location where the present school now stands. Some of the wood from the building was used in the construction of the new school. The Legion Hall building was used for school activities while the new school was being constructed. (Courtesy of ZCHS.)

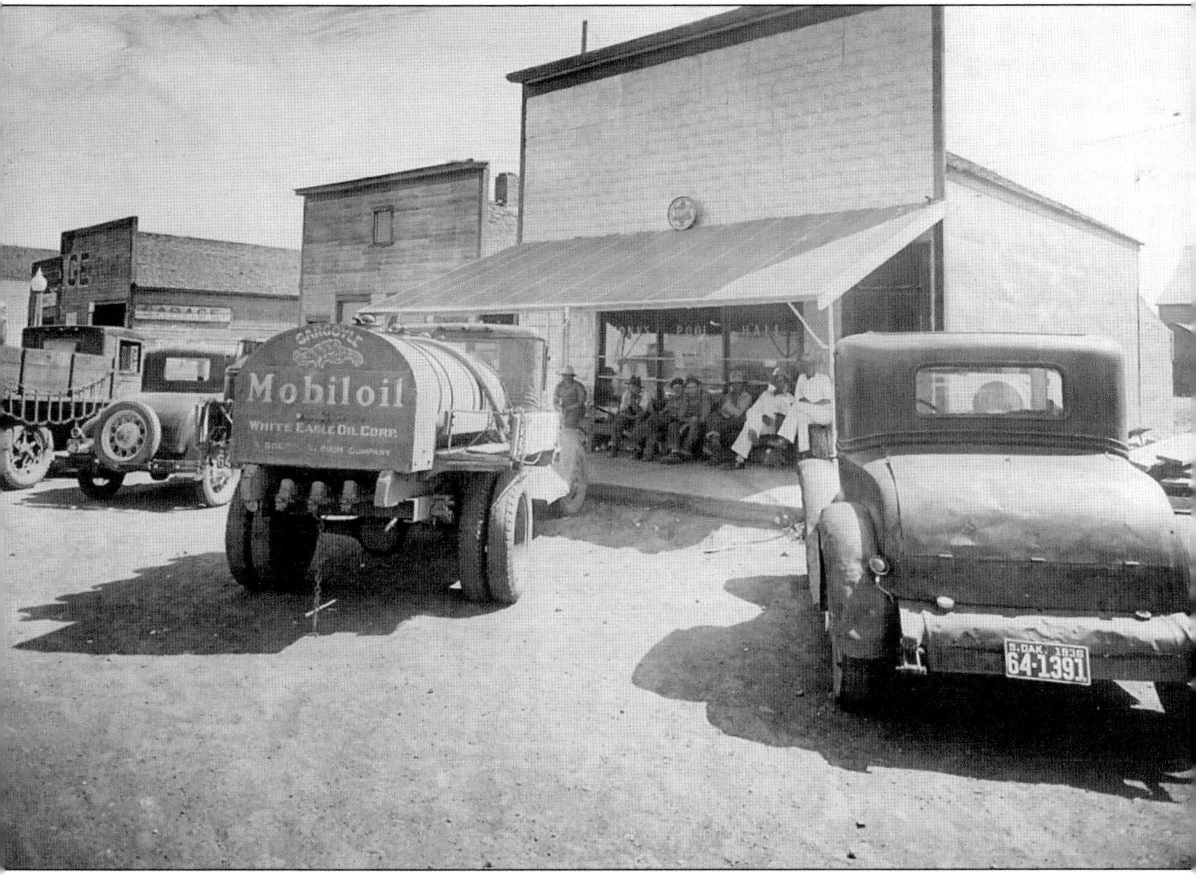

People gather at Tony's Pool Hall in Dupree, which was operated by Tony Kempf. Just to the left of the pool hall was the Tom Nelson law office, which has a truck parked in front. A garage and filling stations appear to be two buildings down from the pool hall. The roadster at right bears a license plate for the year 1938. (Courtesy of Thelma Frame.)

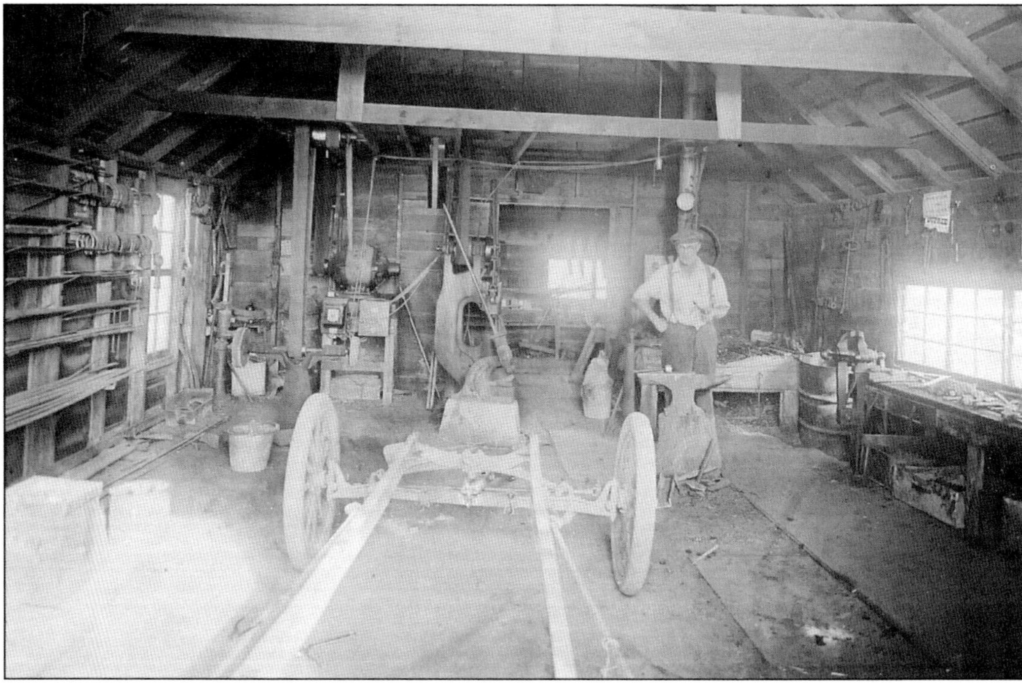

This looks like the blacksmith shop that was near the former ASC Office in Dupree, one block east of Main Street. It may be the original building, which was moved to the present farm of David and Linda Pesicka, northwest of Dupree. (Courtesy of Thelma Frame.)

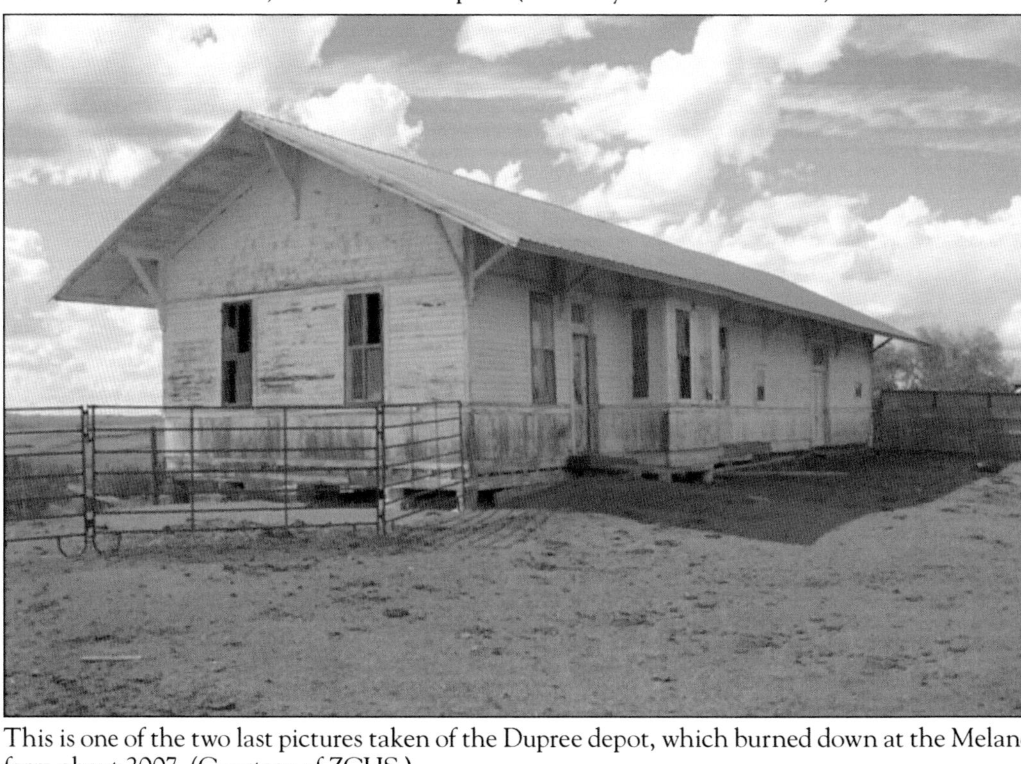

This is one of the two last pictures taken of the Dupree depot, which burned down at the Meland farm about 2007. (Courtesy of ZCHS.)

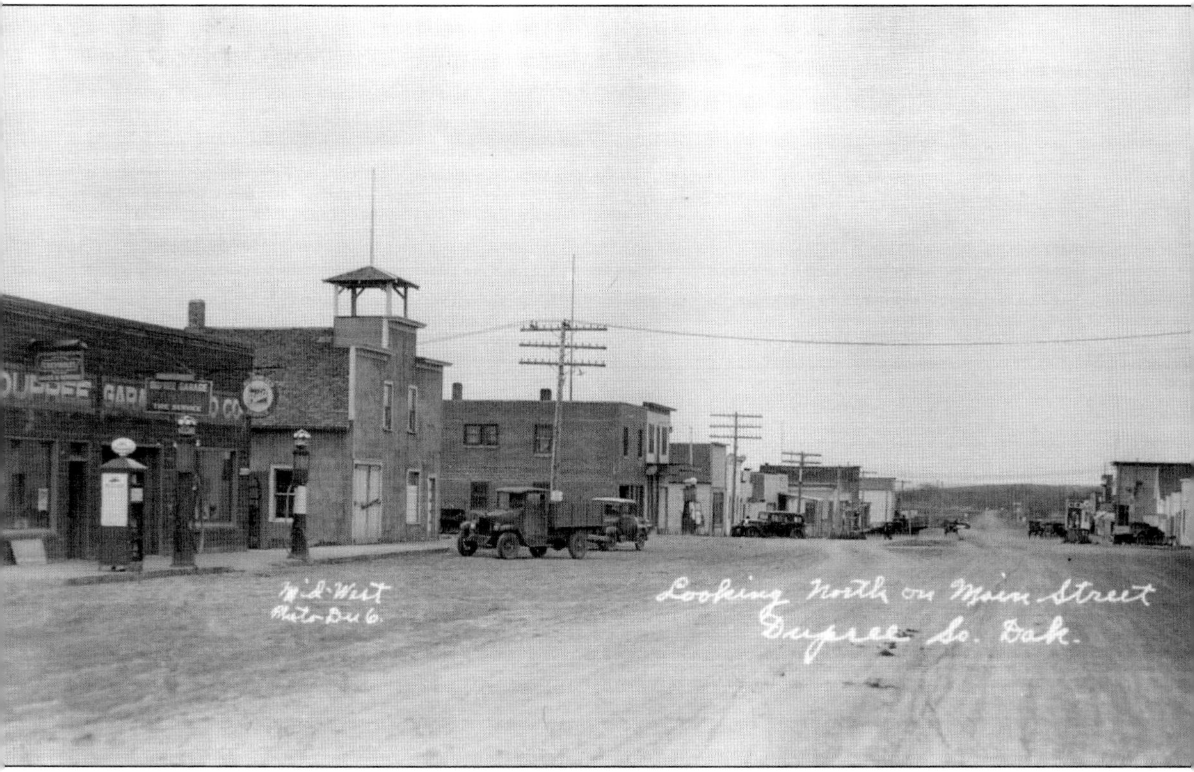

This image by Mid-West Photograph shows Main Street, Dupree, looking north. Ed Ross operated the Dupree Garage at left. (Courtesy of Robert Shannon.)

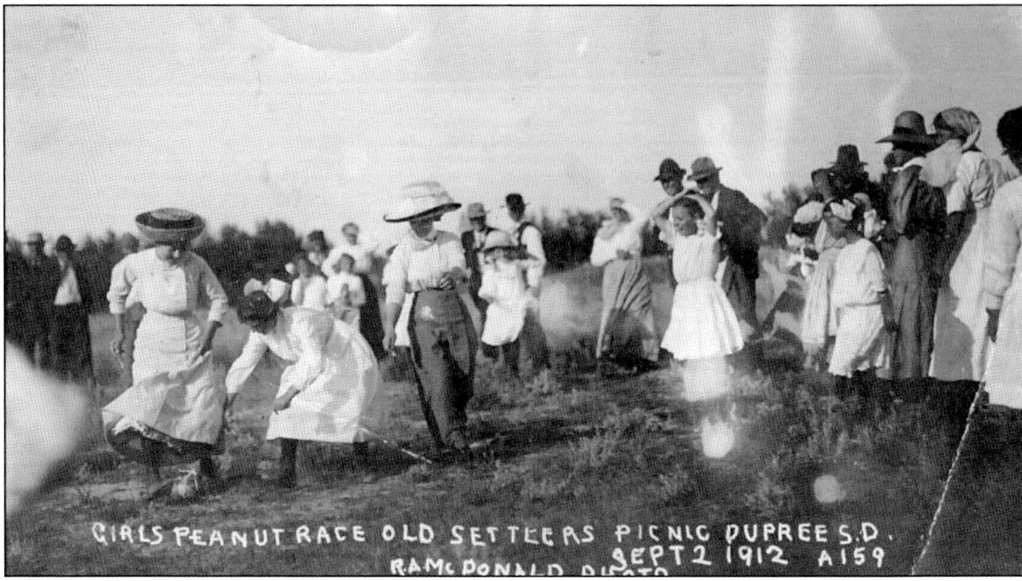

This photograph by R. A. McDonald shows the girls' peanut race at the Old Settlers Picnic in Dupree on September 2, 1912. (Courtesy of Thelma Frame.)

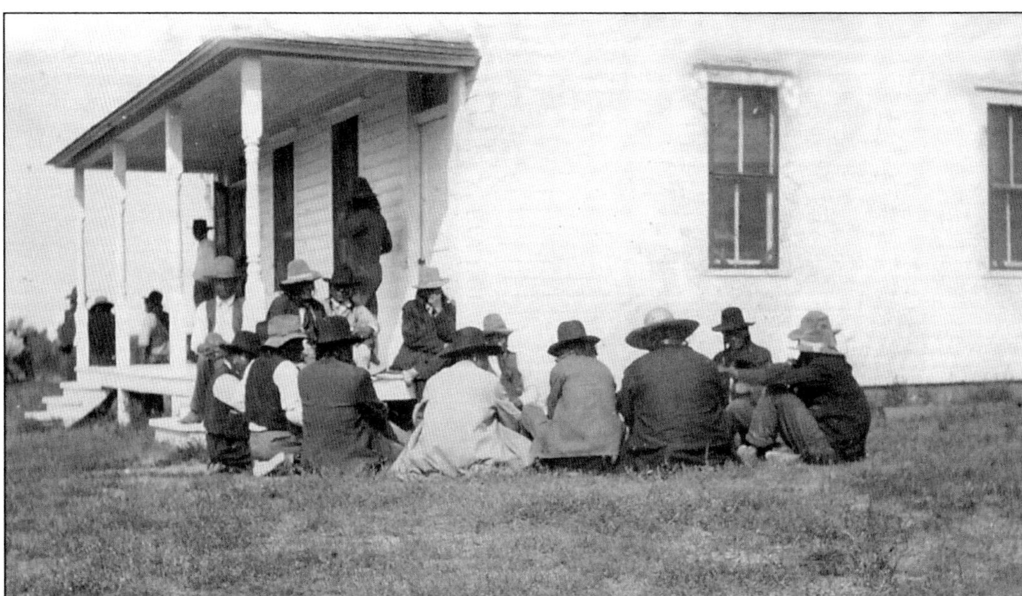
A group of Lakota men is gathered in a house that might be an Indian subagency office at Red Elm or Thunder Butte. For a while the Lakota leader Iron Lightning lived in Red Elm. The government sometimes built special houses for tribal leaders. (Courtesy of ZCHS/Harold and Joan Ross.)

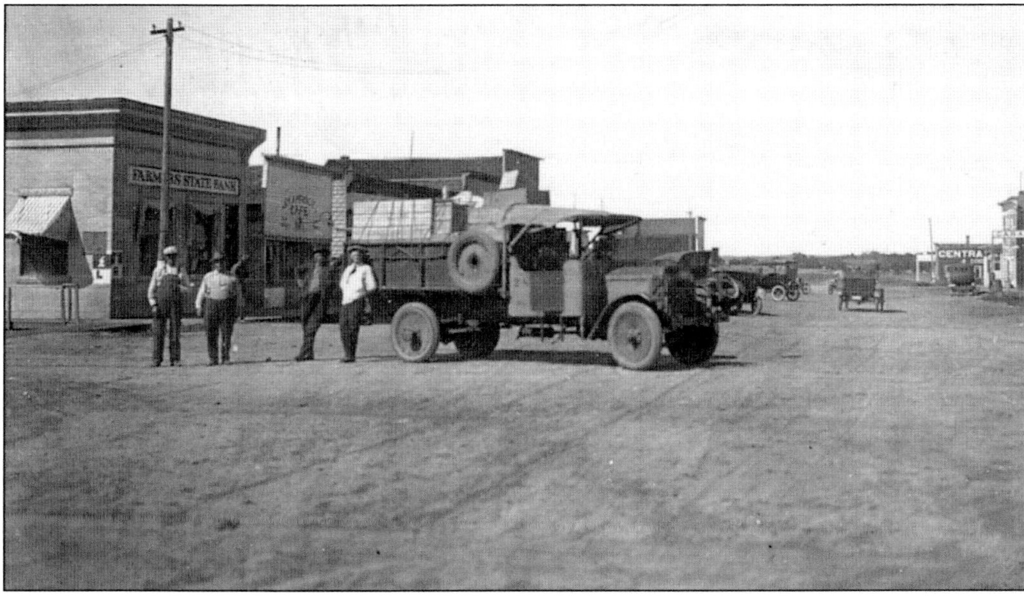

Four men pose next to this truck in 1925, which has South Dakota State Fair exhibits loaded and ready to go. Farmers State Bank and a café are in the background at left, and on the opposite side of the street is a business sign for a garage. (Courtesy of ZCHS.)

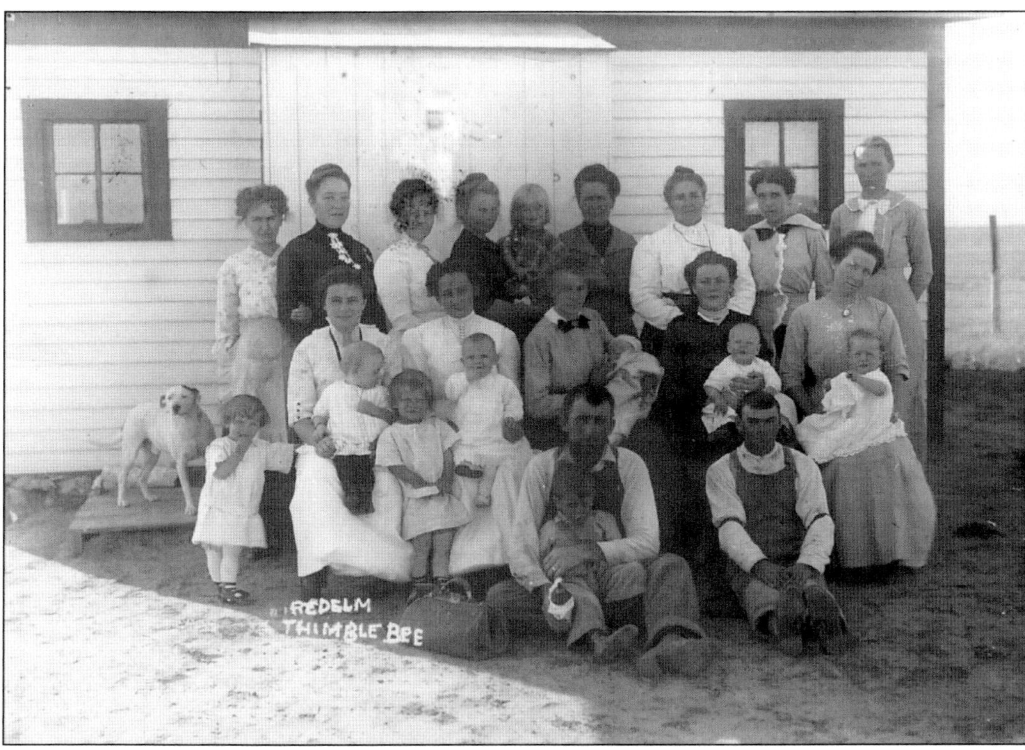

This photograph is labeled "Red Elm Thimble Bee." This club formed during World War I, along with the Women's Missionary Circle, Prairie Home Extension Club, and a Red Cross unit. The Good Will Club organized in 1934. (Courtesy of Thelma Frame.)

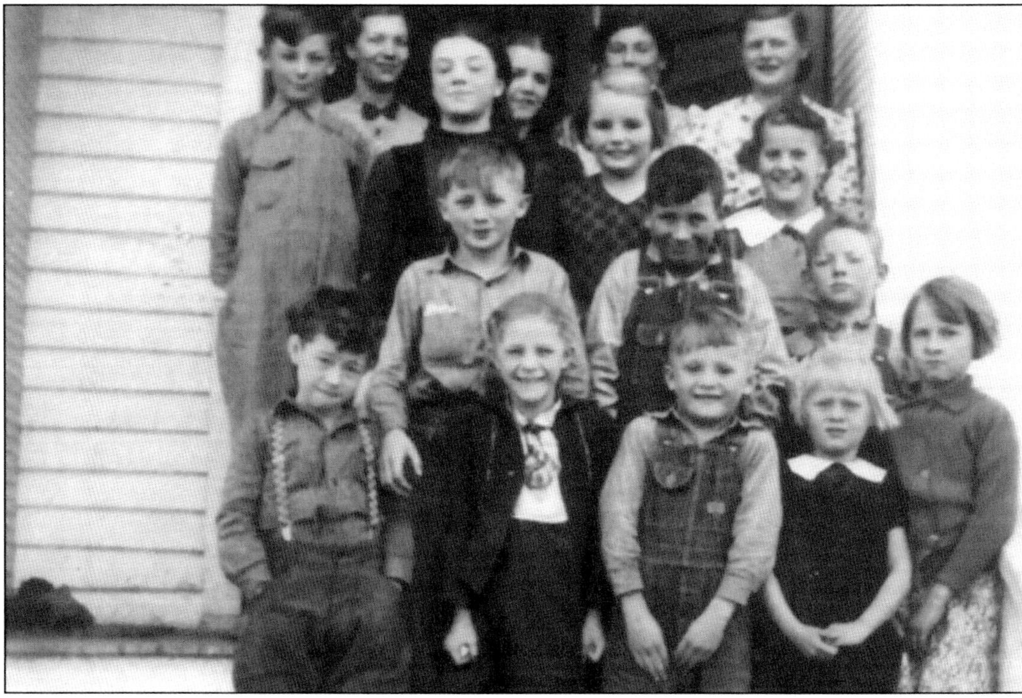

Students at the Red Elm School in 1938–1939 were (first row) Gary Reynolds, Joan Tibke, Raymond Ross, Lois Arvidson, and Alvina Bieber; (second row) Harold Ross, Lester Lammers, and Robert Eaton; (third row) Wesley Eaton, Jean Tibke, Dorothy Eaton, and Ruth Ross; (fourth row) Flora Menzel (teacher), Joyce Tibke, Eldora Lammers, and Hazel Ringsby. (Courtesy of Jean Tibke Vane.)

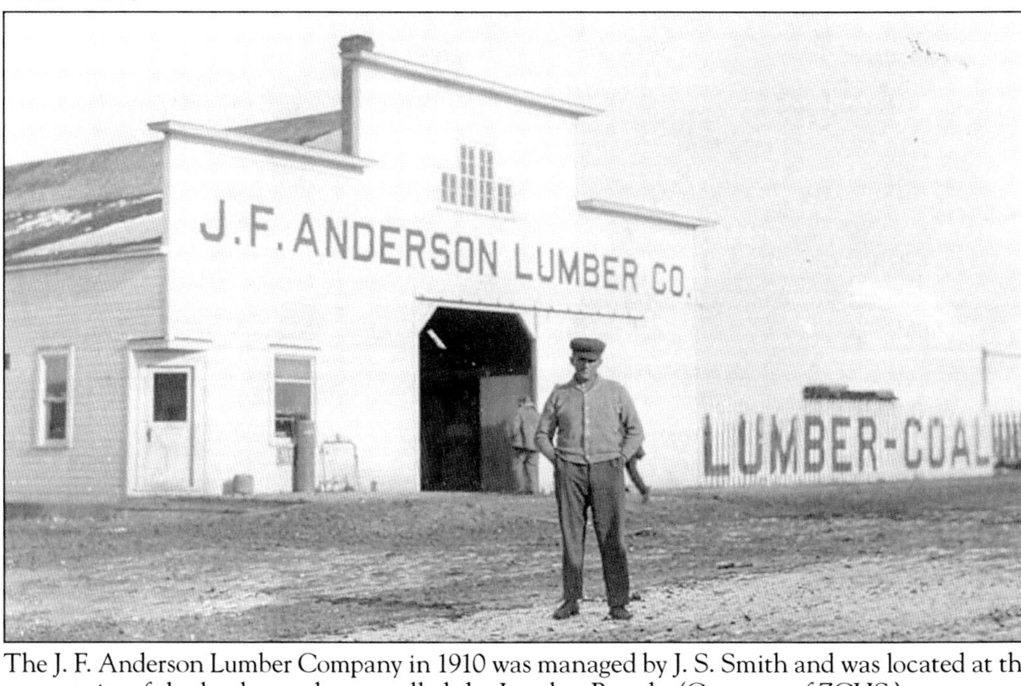

The J. F. Anderson Lumber Company in 1910 was managed by J. S. Smith and was located at the present site of the lumberyard, now called the Lumber Ranch. (Courtesy of ZCHS.)

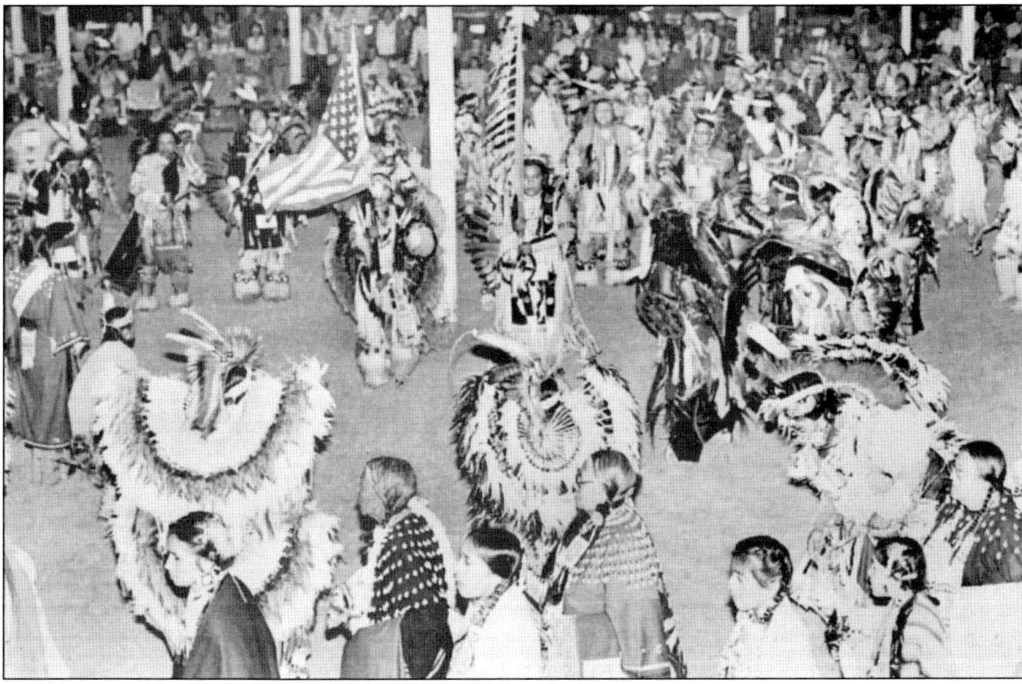

Prior to the creation of Ziebach County, Minnicoujou Lakota settled in the areas of Red Scaffold, Cherry Creek, and Bridger. Many of the families had earlier been at the Battle of the Little Bighorn and in Canada. Red Scaffold, South Dakota, was named by the Indian Department for nearby Red Scaffold Creek. The name comes from a burial scaffold, which was painted red. This picture is a Red Scaffold powwow. (Courtesy of Thelma Frame.)

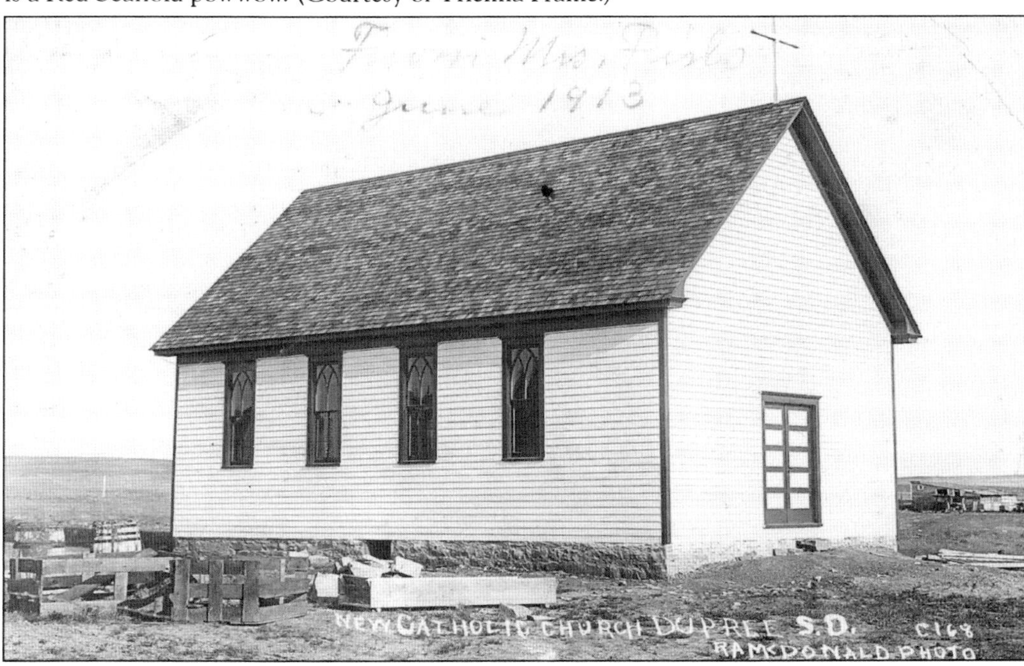

This June 1913 R. A. McDonald photograph is labeled as the new Catholic church in Dupree. The A. W. Robertson homestead can be seen in the background. (Courtesy of ZCSH.)

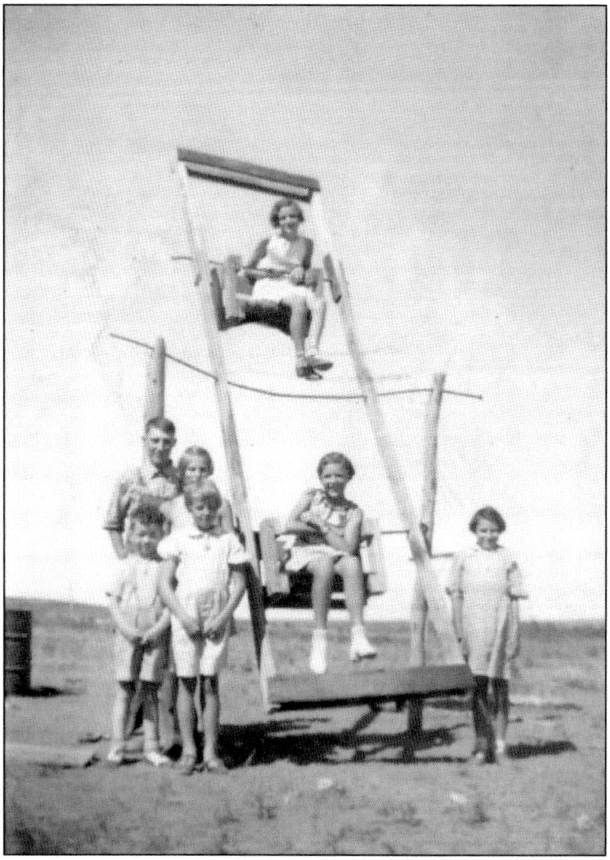

Pictured here is a Ferris wheel made by children in Red Elm in the mid-1930s. Red Elm also once had an outdoor drive-in movie theater for entertainment. (Courtesy of Jean Tibke Vane.)

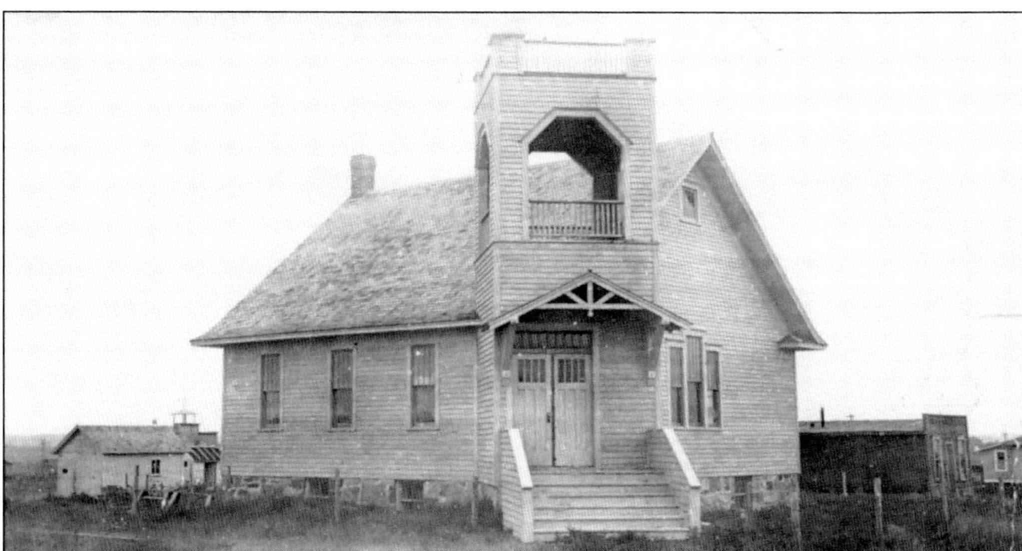

The First Congregational Church held services at the old Dupree town site, east of town. When the town moved to its current location, the first services were held in Berglin Hall, which was later the movie theater. A church was built in 1913, and a larger one was needed and built in 1917. Renovations have been made since then. (Courtesy of ZCHS.)

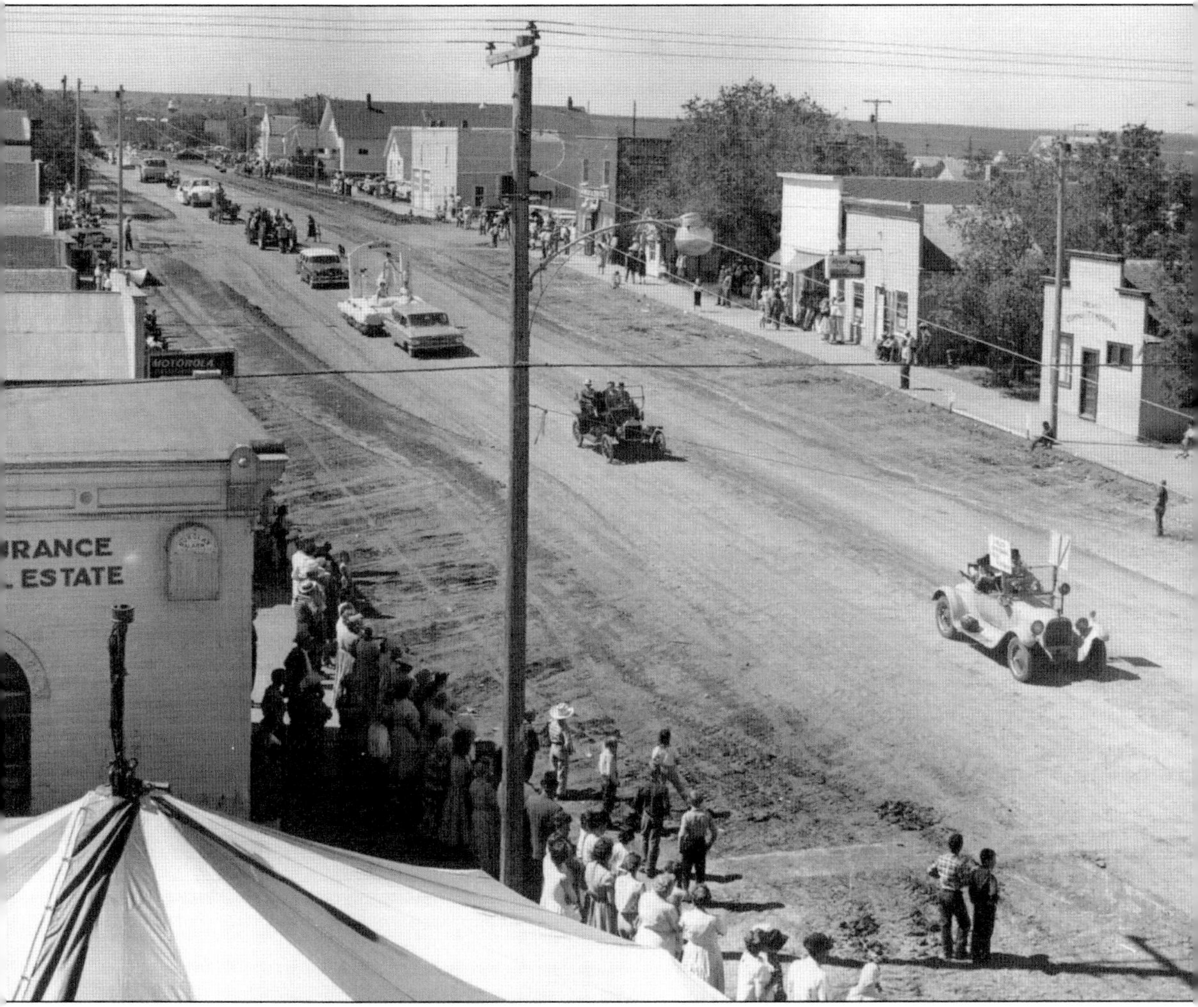

A view of the parade from the balcony of the Deis grocery store building is seen here. On the right side of the street the businesses were, from right to left, a hospital, city bar, post office (and later law office), barbershop (small building), Milan "Butch" Salisbury's Red and White Grocery Store, fire department, Masonic Lodge, Legion Hall, and Episcopal Church. The large building at the left side of the photograph is the bank. The carnival often set up on that street. (Courtesy of ZCHS.)

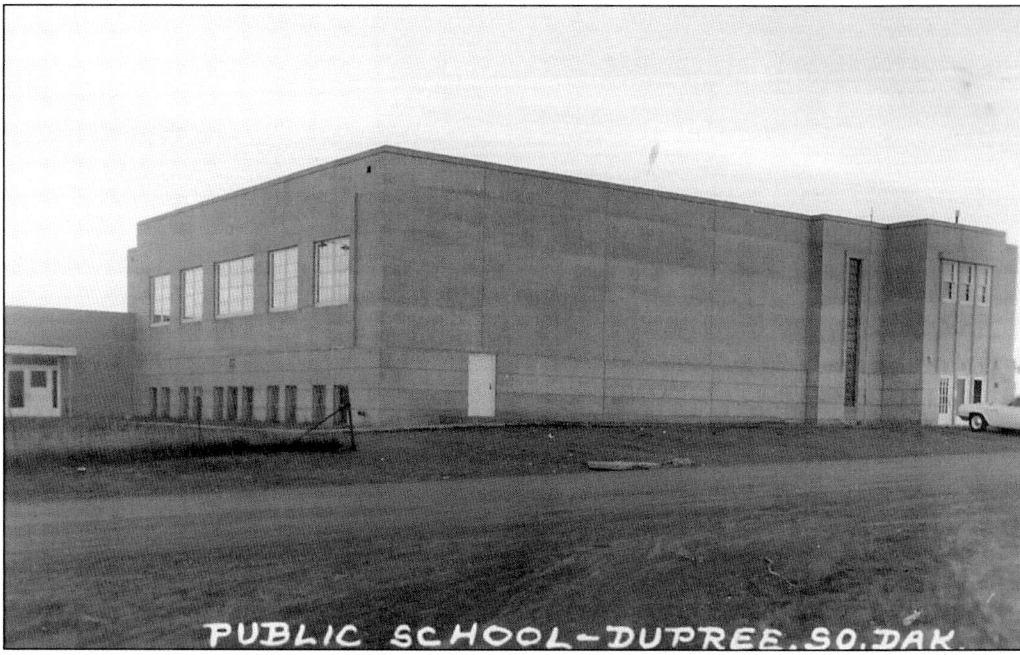

The Dupree Public School has the largest enrollment in Ziebach County. It continues to serve the community of Dupree, as well as a large surrounding rural area with busing. The current enrollment is approximately 350 students. (Courtesy of Shirley Menzel.)

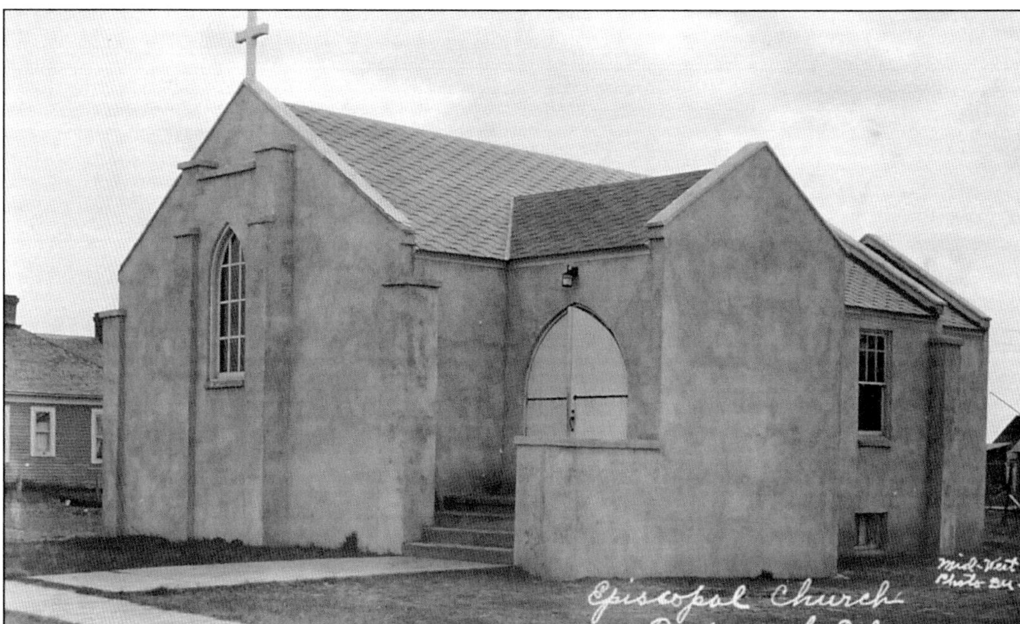

The Episcopal Church in Dupree was located across the street from the courthouse, on the west side of Main Street. A fire in the mid-1960s destroyed the organ, most of the furnishings, and building. There was also a separate rectory building behind the church. This church was replaced by a new building following a fund-raising effort. (Courtesy of Shirley Menzel.)

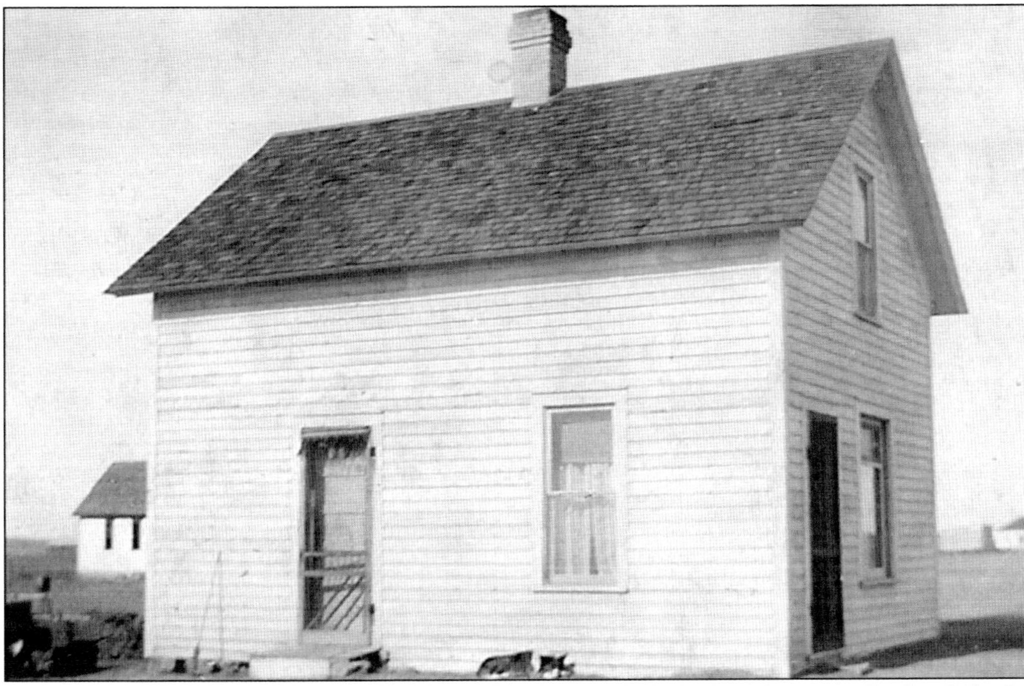

This is the A. W. Robertson homestead building, which was constructed in 1912. Fred and Shirley (Robertson's granddaughter) Menzel and Bob (Robertson's great-grandson) and Dondra Menzel have also lived in this house. Albert W. and Emma Robertson came to Ziebach County in April 1911 by railroad immigrant car and settled on their homestead just adjoining the town site of Dupree. (Courtesy of Shirley Menzel.)

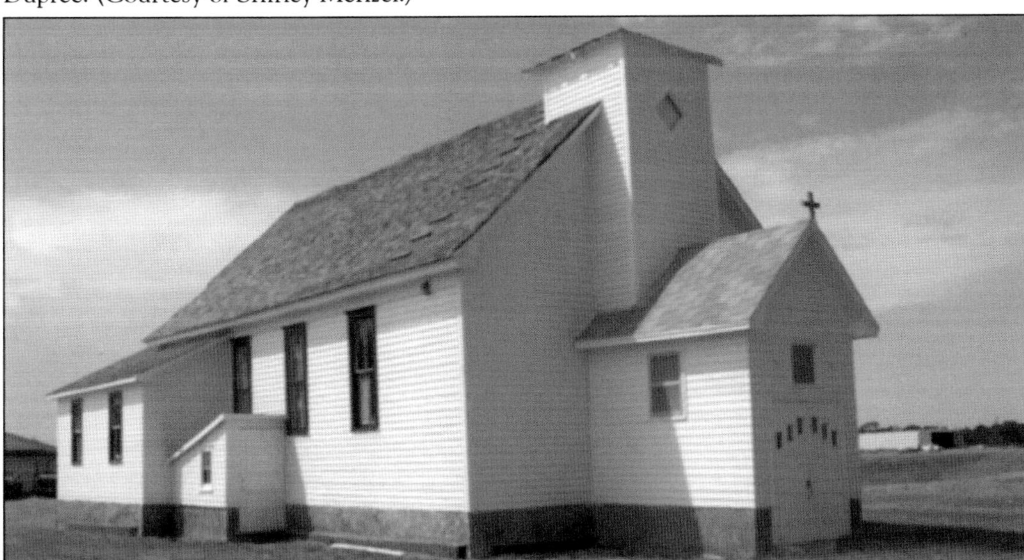

The Catholic church moved from the south end of Dupree to the north end. Plans are to use the 1913 church, which is being restored by the Ziebach County Historical Society, as a combined museum and visitor center. The ZCHS originated in 1979 and published *South Dakota's Ziebach County History of the Prairie* in 1982. The ZCHS was revived in 2003 with an objective to save the church, one of the towns few original buildings. (Courtesy of ZCHS.)

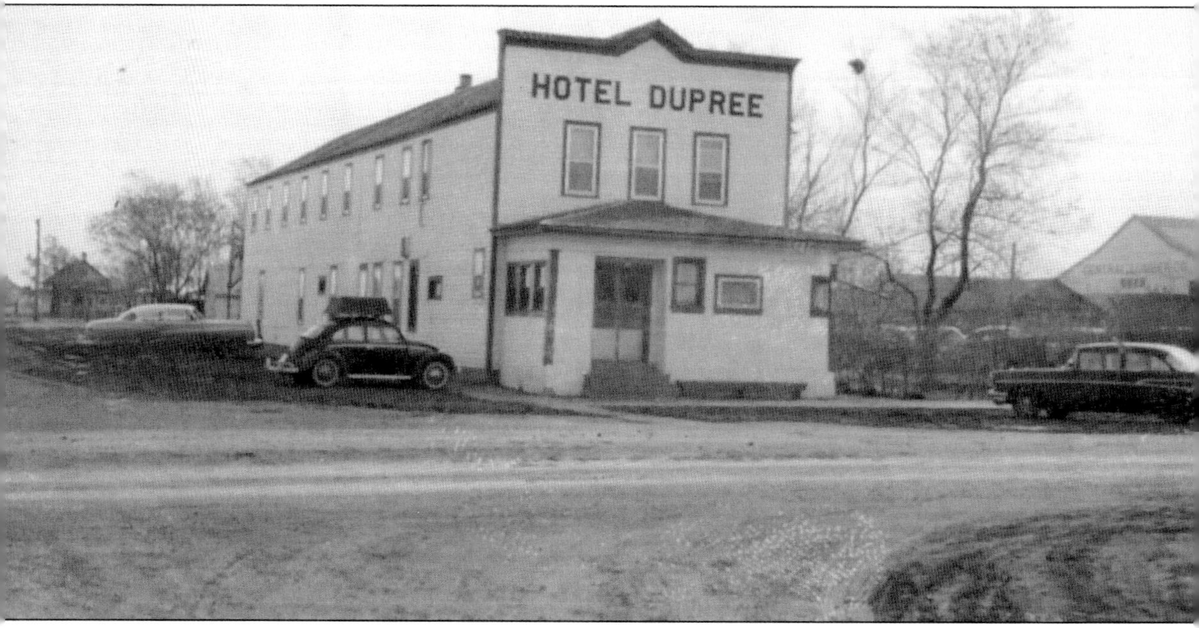

James Shelton purchased land in 1910 and built the Shelton Hotel. Matt Stephenson bought the hotel in 1931 and named it Hotel Dupree. Later owners included Ivan Fluharty, who purchased it in 1946; Bill Oschsner, who purchased it in 1950; and Jake Sprenger, who purchased it in 1959. Several people operated the hotel over the years, until it was torn down in 1980–1981 by Galen Denton Construction, having seen its better days. (Courtesy of ZCHS.)

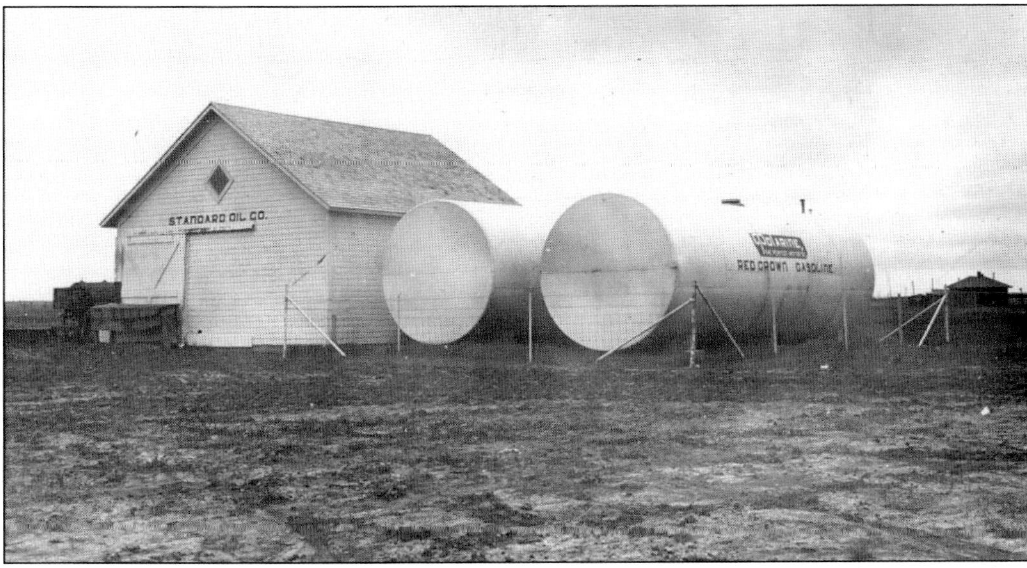

This was the Standard Oil Company's bulk station for Red Crown gasoline. This location is where the Ziebach County maintenance shop is, and Jim Frame later purchased the building for a shop. (Courtesy of ZCHS/Virginia Woodward.)

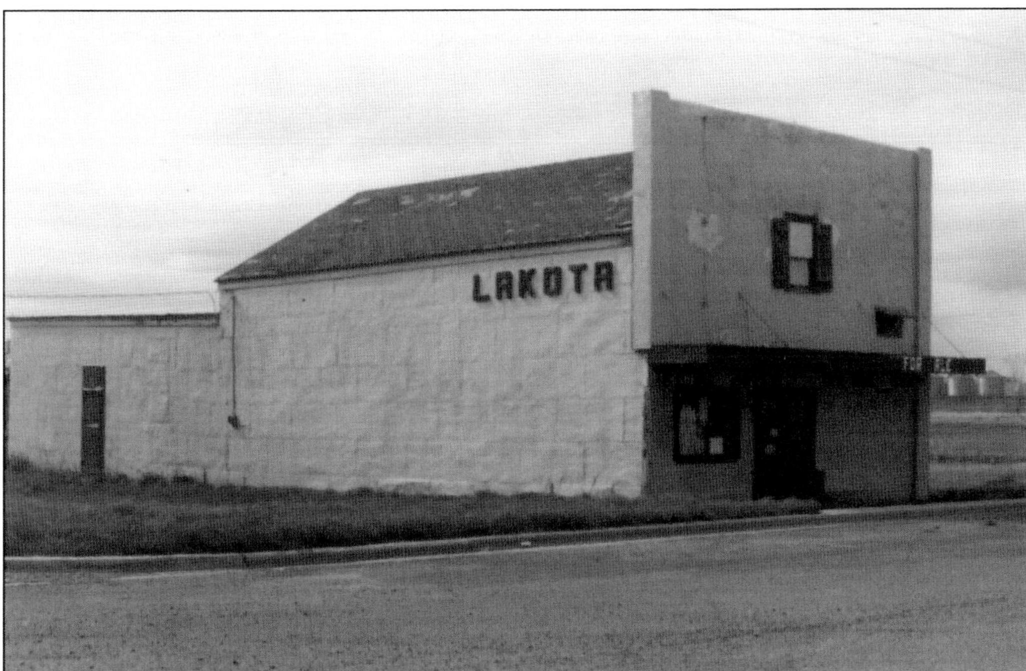

The Lakota Theatre was formerly the Lyceum Theatre and was built in 1910 for Andrew Beiglin. It was used as a community hall for a number of years. In 1919, it was made into a theater and the first silent pictures were shown. In 1955, the theater had modern developments and grew in popularity. This photograph was taken not long before it was torn down from the Main Street landscape. (Courtesy of Evelyn Anderson.)

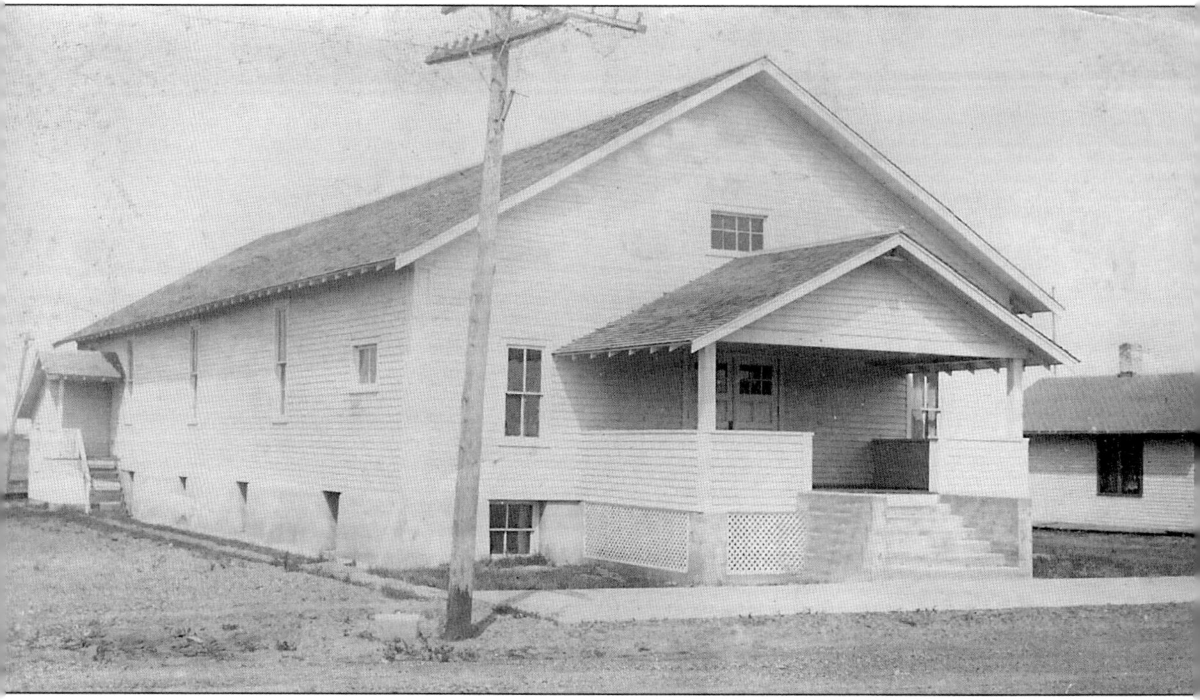

Edwin Hodgdon Post No. 124 is named for the first serviceman from the county to give his life for his country. Work began on the Dupree Legion Hall in 1921. The ground floor had a dance floor, a stage, and a balcony. The basement had a large dining room, kitchen, and clubroom. The deck area in front was added later. The building was known for community events, including public dances, concerts, basketball, roller skating, boxing, bingo, and displays. (Courtesy of Thelma Frame.)

This 1959 photograph of the Sprague family shows, from left to right, (first row) parents John and Edith; (second row) Darrel, Fern, and Hersil. Darrel and Hersil provided music at many community and country schoolhouse dances as the Sunshine Band. Darrel played guitar, Hersil played fiddle and guitar, and Jim Miller joined them, also on fiddle. Edith Sprague gave piano lessons to youngsters. John Sprague worked at the electric plant part-time and gave away peppermint candy to children. (Courtesy of Donovin Sprague.)

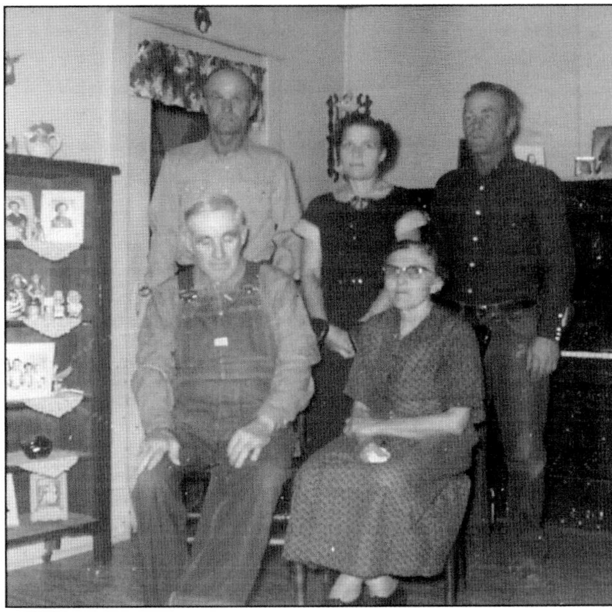

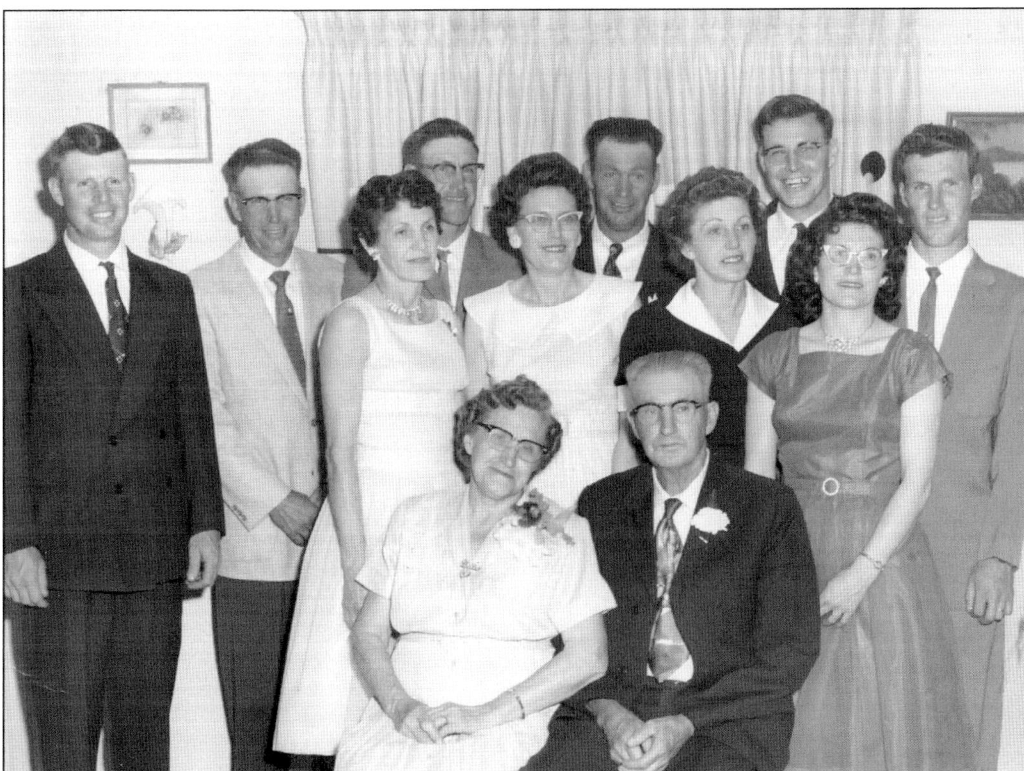

Shown here from left to right are members of the Pooley family: (first row) Maize McCartney Pooley and Will J.; (second row) Berneita, Loretta, Velda, and Geraldine; (third row) Delbert, Orval, Howard, William, Robert, and Donald. The photograph was taken at the 50th wedding anniversary of Will and Maize Pooley at Nampa, Idaho, on June 2, 1961. Will's parents were William and Sarah "Addie" Phillips. (Courtesy of Donovin Sprague.)

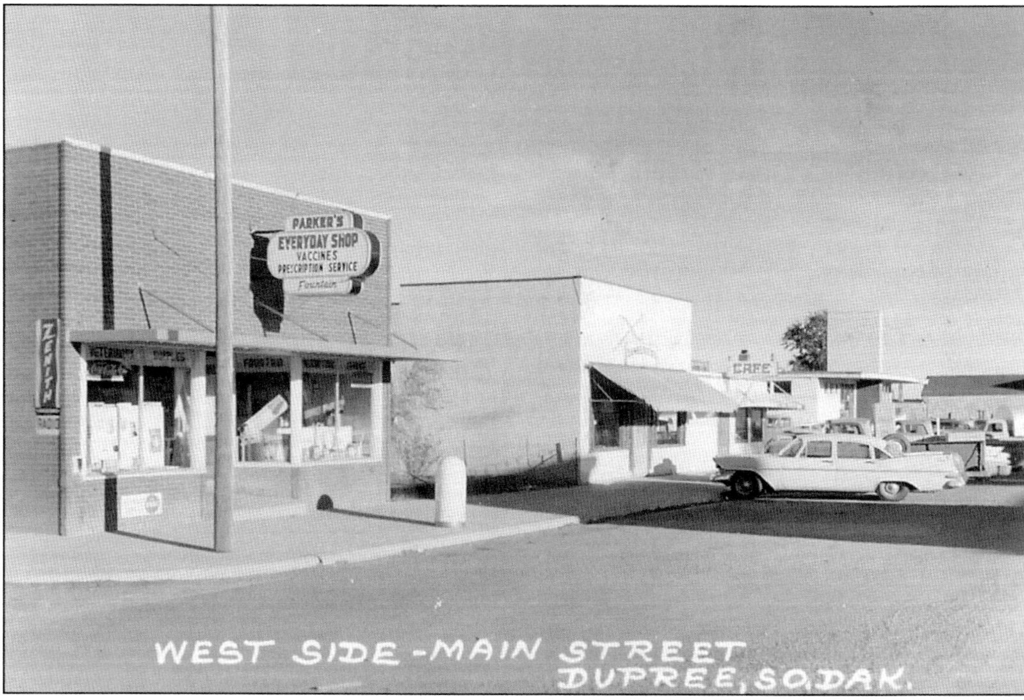

This photographs shows the west side of Main Street in Dupree. At left is the drugstore (Parker's Everyday Shop). The next building was the Damberger's Clothing Store, then the café, Silverman's Sales and Garage, and the last building at the right of the photograph may be the movie theater. Fred E. Mellow started the first drugstore in Dupree and ran it from 1910 to 1925. (Courtesy of ZCHS.)

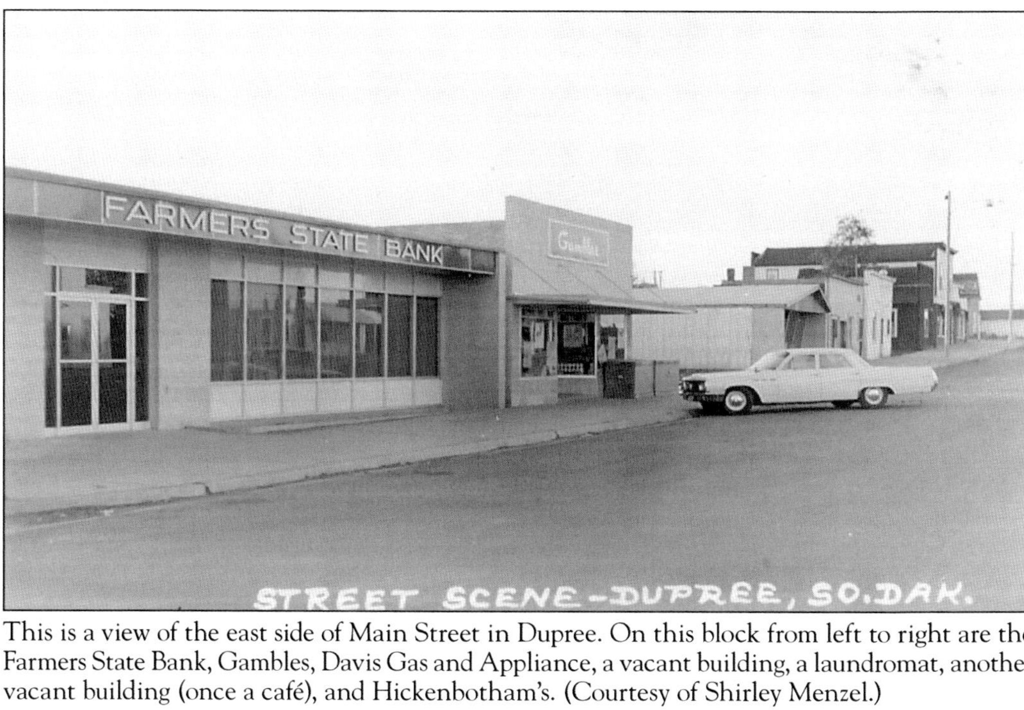

This is a view of the east side of Main Street in Dupree. On this block from left to right are the Farmers State Bank, Gambles, Davis Gas and Appliance, a vacant building, a laundromat, another vacant building (once a café), and Hickenbotham's. (Courtesy of Shirley Menzel.)

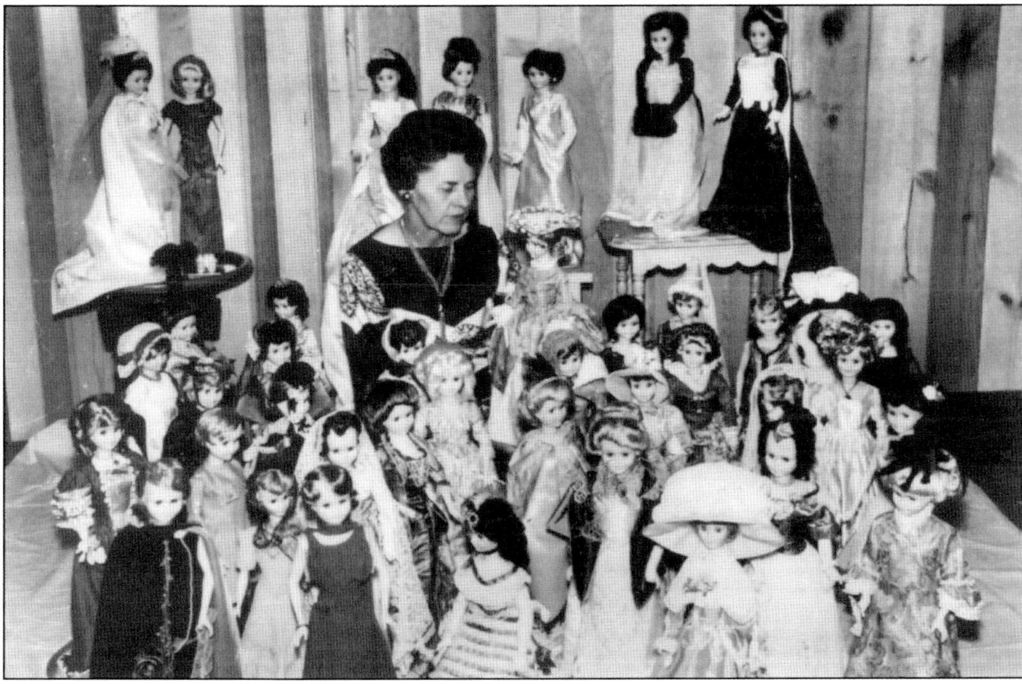

Lucille Silverman is pictured with her First Lady dolls, which featured a parade of women's fashion covering over 500 years. Lucille displayed the dolls throughout the country and the collection was also shown on the national television show "To Tell The Truth." Lucille and Adoph Silverman were longtime residents of Dupree. Adolph sold cars and operated a full-service garage. Their garage in Dupree was destroyed by fire in 1974. (Courtesy of Evelyn Anderson.)

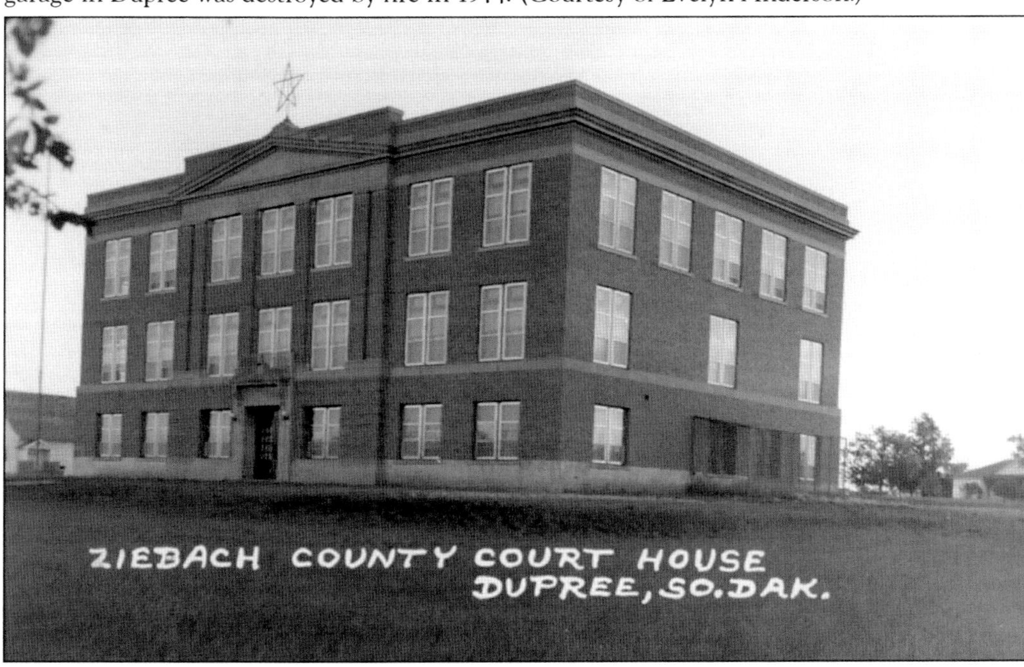

Pictured here is the Ziebach County Court House in Dupree, which is the largest town in Ziebach County and serves as the county seat. (Courtesy of ZCHS.)

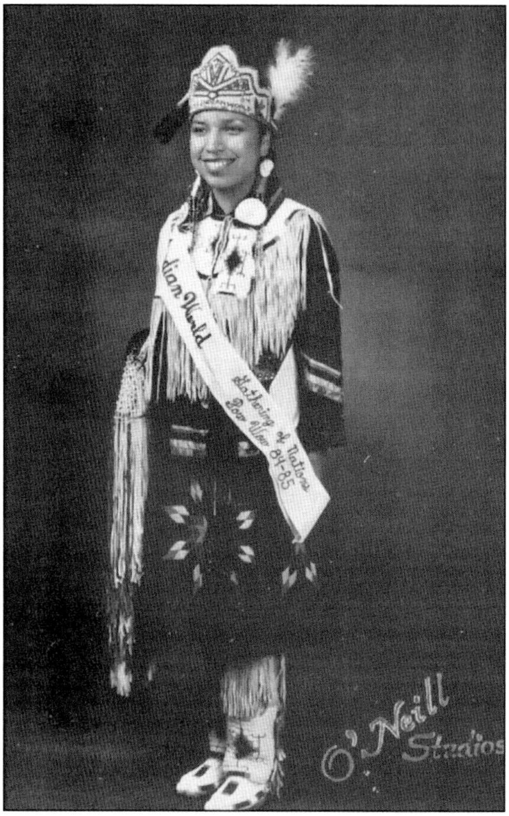

Codi High Elk won the title of Miss Indian World at the Gathering of Nations Powwow in Albuquerque, New Mexico, in 1984–1985. She is from Thunder Butte and is the daughter of Paul and Clara High Elk. (Courtesy of Thelma Frame.)

Stetson James Vrooman, the three-year-old son of Jace Vrooman and Korey Fischer, began his rodeo career riding a sheep in 2009. His roots in Ziebach County go back to Doug and Marcella (Dupris) Carlin. Other grandparents are Lawrence and Virginia Woodward, Harry and Marian Stambach, and Roy and Ella Vrooman. His maternal family includes Lee and Ruth Garrett, Andy and Joy Fischer, Delbert and Marietta Longbrake, and Fred and Ruth Dillabaugh. (Courtesy of Darla Vrooman.)

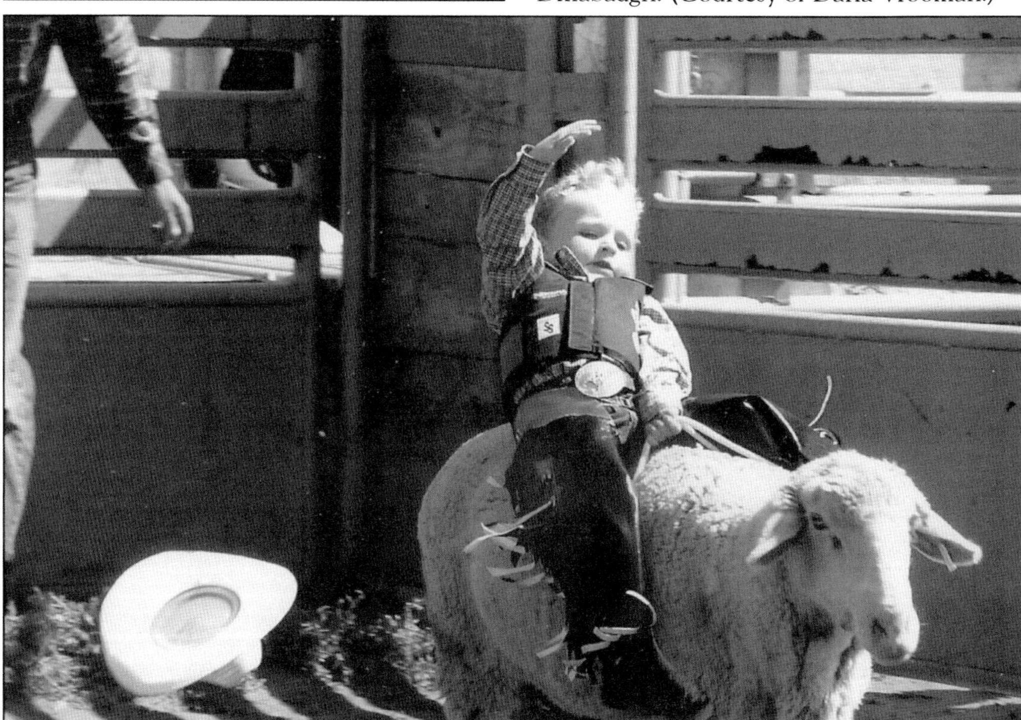

Bibliography

Blasingame, Ike. *Dakota Cowboy*. New York: G.P. Putnam's Sons, 1958.
Britain, Barbara. *Return To Shetek: The Courage of the Fool Soldiers*. DVD. Sioux Falls Community Foundation, 2007.
Dupree Golden Jubilee. "Call of the Prairie." 1960.
Cudmore, Ginny, and Jim Nelson. *Timber Lake and Area: 1910–1985*. Timber Lake, SD: Timber Lake and Area Historical Society, 1984.
Daczewitz, Dorothy, Thelma Frame, Jackie Birkeland, and Lucille Silverman. *Prairie Echoes*. 1961.
Fields, Trula. *A Baker's Dozen*. Sturgis, SD: Sand Creek Printing, 2009.
Flood, Renee Sansom. *Lost Bird of Wounded Knee*. New York: Scribner, 1995.
Frame, Thelma, and Beverly Lindblom. *Yesterday's News Vol. 1 and Vol. 2 1936–1941*. Rapid City, SD: Little Print Shop, 2001 and 2002.
Gilbert, Luke. *Brief History of the Cheyenne River Indian Reservation, Souvenir Program Commemorating 50th Anniversary of Cheyenne River Agency, 1891–1941*. 1941.
Graham, Col. W.A. *The Custer Myth: A Source Book of Custeriana*. New York: Bonanza Books, 1953.
Hassrick, Royal B. *The George Catlin Book of American Indians*. New York: Promontory Press, 1977.
Holden, Georgia Aydelotte. *Chief Hi Hawk: Thunder Butte Genesis*. Madison, WI: Fleetwood Art Studios, 1973.
Johnson, Carol. *The Way They Were: Ziebach County Rural Schools 1910–1978*. Rapid City, SD: Little Print Shop.
Johnson, Dirk. *Biting the Dust*. Lincoln, NE: University of Nebraska Press, 2005.
Johnson, Kate, and Chester Johnson. *The Trip: Trip by Car to the West Coast in 1934*. 1994.
Lee, Bob, and Dick Williams. *Last Grass Frontier: South Dakota Stock Grower Heritage*. Sturgis, SD: Black Hills Publishers, 1964.
Lee, Jamie. *Washaka—The Bear Dreamer*. Rapid City, SD: Many Kites Press, 2006.
Lewis, Mary, and Dale Lewis. *LeBeau: A Sputtering Flame*. Wasta, SD: Lewis Publishing, 2008.
Matson, William, and Mark Frethem. "Creation, Spirituality, and the Family Tree." Part 1. *Journey of the Heart*. DVD. Bill and Mark's Excellent Productions, 2004.
———. "The Authorized Biography of Crazy Horse and His Family." Part 2. *Journey of the Heart*. DVD. 2007.
O'Brien, Sharon. *American Indian Tribal Governments*. Norman, OK: University of Oklahoma Press, 1989.
Sprague, Donovin. "Saving Tatanka (Buffalo): The Story of Fred Dupree and Good Elk Woman." *Bison World*. July–September, 2009.
Sprague, Donovin Arleigh. *Cheyenne River Sioux*. Charleston, SC: Arcadia Publishing, 2003.
———. *Standing Rock Sioux*. Charleston, SC: Arcadia Publishing, 2004.
St. Pierre, Mark. *Madonna Swan: A Lakota Woman's Story*. Norman, OK: University of Oklahoma Press, 1991.
——— and Tilda Long Soldier. *Walking in the Sacred Manner*. New York: Touchstone, 1995.
Timber Lake and Area Historical Society. "Timber Lake and Area Centennial History, 1910–2010." Timber Lake and Area Historical Society, 2009.
Wyman, Walker D. *Nothing But Prairie and Sky: Life on the Dakota Range in the Early Days*. Norman, OK: University of Oklahoma Press, 1954.
Ziebach County Historical Society. *South Dakota's Ziebach County*. Pierre, SD: State Publishing Company, 1982.

INDEX

INDEX